WHEELS ACROSS AMERICA

WHEELS

ACROSS AMERICA

*A pictorial cavalcade illustrating
the early development of
vehicular transportation*

CLARENCE P. HORNUNG

A. S. BARNES & CO., NEW YORK

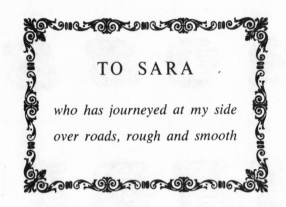

TO SARA

*who has journeyed at my side
over roads, rough and smooth*

Other books by the author:

TRADE-MARKS
HANDBOOK OF DESIGNS AND DEVICES
LETTERING FROM A TO Z
HANDBOOK OF EARLY ADVERTISING ART (2 VOLS.)

Print portfolios by the author:

PORTRAITS OF ANTIQUE AUTOMOBILES
EARLY AMERICAN AUTOMOBILES
EARLY AMERICAN LOCOMOTIVES
EARLY AMERICAN CARRIAGES
EARLY AMERICAN TROLLEY CARS
EARLY AMERICAN FIRE ENGINES

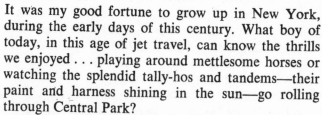
FOREWORD

It was my good fortune to grow up in New York, during the early days of this century. What boy of today, in this age of jet travel, can know the thrills we enjoyed . . . playing around mettlesome horses or watching the splendid tally-hos and tandems—their paint and harness shining in the sun—go rolling through Central Park?

The metropolis, I soon learned, was not only a mass of tall buildings hemmed in by tenements, but a world of never-ceasing activity. I early sensed that the city hummed with so much excitement because of *wheels*. *Wheels* . . . of drays and delivery carts, trolleys and El trains, coaches and carriages, bicycles and baby prams, roller skates and push carts, subways and freight trains . . . a vast, varied and restless panorama.

Among my first memories of the horse-and-buggy era are the impressive annual Horse Shows staged at Durland's Riding Academy, now the offices of the American Broadcasting Company. I was inordinately popular with the other boys, for my father was one of the riding masters and I was allowed free access to the stables after school and on Saturdays. We haunted the sweet-smelling stalls, developing great admiration for the animals while keeping a respectful distance from their rapier-sharp hooves . . . as we walked the aisles between the stalls. Younger boys, oblivious of danger, devised the game of running under the belly of a horse standing clear of his stall.

To me, every visit to Durland's was a heady thrill . . . the fancy equipages, the glistening harness belonging to the tally-hos and park drags held a matchless fascination. On special occasions I was allowed to ride in a stately coach or four-in-hand through Central Park. Those were the days when a fine carriage with a pair of four closely-matched horses was a symbol of social importance.

On Saturdays, I helped polish the carriages until my face was reflected in their dark satiny surfaces,

broken occasionally by creamy stripes or the ornate monogram of an opulent owner. My early love of a handsome vehicle has never rubbed off. I can still stand in almost-worshipful admiration before a fine carriage, in a museum or on parade.

My family moved often to new addresses. This meant getting adjusted to new schools and playmates, just when I had become interested in the little girl next door. But in those days, to attract new tenants, there was always the assurance of a month or two of free rent!

It was then the custom for boys to "snitch a hitch" on the trolley cars (they really were cable cars, I learned later) that rattled along on the principal avenues of the upper West Side. This had its dangers, but the compulsion to grab a free ride was strong and the fear of being branded a sissy by the neighborhood gang—if one did not conform—developed in most of us an indifference to danger. Not to be a member of a gang meant complete social ostracism. An outsider could not enjoy many cherished privileges: thrilling raids on Columbus Avenue fruit-venders' pushcarts; being permitted to collect wooden crates for the sky-high Election Night bonfire that invariably brought out the fire engines; community micky roasts; and a welcome aboard the raft in the Hudson . . . so cool and tempting on humid summer days in mid-Manhattan.

The Amsterdam Avenue trolleys had a particular attraction for us. A stolen ride on the back platform was another grand way to cool off, especially on the open cars used in warm weather. Timing was important but, after a few unhappy experiences, the juvenile offender learned how to judge the risks. We had to board the car while the conductor was busy up front collecting fares. Since it took time for him to work his way back, the hidden culprit had a chance of riding five or six blocks at the company's expense. Often cries of "Hitch behind!" from jealous kids on the street sent the irate conductor chasing

5

down the car to mete out justice, and the free rider went flying off into space.

Many times I remember flopping, face down, while the car sped along . . . for we had to jump or be grabbed and hauled aboard by the nape of the neck. After several such leaps, we acquired the knack of jumping clear of oncoming vehicles. But the street cobbles were rough and dirty and a sudden drop, while traveling at a good clip, usually meant bad scrapes and contusions of the knees. In those days we all wore long black stockings whether we liked them or not, and they were inevitably torn to shreds, revealing our bruised and bleeding legs. Such spills had unhappy repercussions at home. As I tried to slip through the door for a quick change of hose, Mother always seemed to sense that her Huck Finn was up to his knees in trouble again.

By the time I was ten or eleven, I had been introduced to the New York Central Railroad and its open tracks along the Hudson, below Riverside Drive. The long lines of freights were captivating . . . the red, brown and yellow cars with trademarks and symbols from all over the land beckoned as no class in geography or social science ever did. The cars had traveled thousands of miles before reaching New York. The least we kids could do was to welcome them.

"Hopping the freights" was another of the pastimes our parents knew nothing of, but we never tired of it. The greatest challenge came when a passing freight, going in the opposite direction, tempted the young trapeze artist to jump across five or six feet of thin air. We didn't always make it, and I remember a bloody incident when the ambulance carried Smitty off to the hospital where he had a close escape from a threatened amputation.

When I was barely twelve, we moved for a change, this time to 109th Street near Amsterdam Avenue, not far from a main thoroughfare. As we boys stood in the shadow of St. John's—then a raw, unfinished, puzzling mass of stone blocks with no resemblance to the great cathedral it is today—we watched the motor cars go by, spotting new names on brass radiators or whirling hub-caps.

"Whaddye know, here comes a Pope-Hartford! And there's a Panhard-Levassor . . . she's a beauty!" Then came a Matheson, an American Underslung, or an Apperson Jack-Rabbit. Occasionally our eyes hit upon something special like the princely Minerva or a Renault with the sloping radiator. The foreign makes carried particular merit as their numbers were thinning, by 1911 or 1912. The game of guessing car names was made more exciting by the hundreds of cigarette cards that all the kids saved and traded. These colorful treasures were the standard reference for settling disputes. On the reverse of each fine lithographed picture was a detailed description with such vital data as the number of cylinders, horsepower, wheelbase, price, and other facts of value when the arguments grew hot.

The interests of those early years still live and the memories of boyhood, sweet and precious, are still vivid after almost a half century. Many of these early incidents have been re-lived in my activities of recent years and the fond reminiscences have only served to freshen my viewpoint and add a special zest to the task of re-telling and re-drawing. Recollections culled from the dim past have been the basis of my series of drawings of vintage motor cars issued in various forms—from the limited, hand-colored editions of "Collectors' Prints" to the more popularly-priced "Autoprints" in smaller format. In these I have tried to preserve for this space ship era certain of the beauties of the early vehicles including not only motor cars, but locomotives, trolleys, carriages and fire engines.

If some recognition has come to me in other fields, it does not equal the delights of winning the gang's approval in riding free on the rear of a careening trolley car or the fascination of watching the wheels go 'round.

C. P. H.

New York, N. Y.
February 1959

CONTENTS

WHOA . . . GIDDAP!

FARES, PLEASE!

A - WHEELING WE'LL GO

WHOA.. ◦ ◦

THE WHIPLASH SPEAKS, *the cry of man commanding..."stop and go" signal to straining horses and wheels that spin.*

IN TOWN AND HAMLET *the "one-horse shay"...the village blacksmith, flying sparks, the clang of hammer and anvil...joy in a child's heart to see such stirring sights. On Main Street the passing parade...surreys, broughams, buggies, runabouts...coal carts, ice wagons, drays and dump trucks...the colorful cavalcade of man and beast, lending a warm humanity to transportation's history.*

16

GIDDAP

IN RUTTED MUD *on Pilgrim paths, fording the waters, fighting the wilderness trails...across desert wastes the hordes push forth, a people's will rolls on...in carriage, coach or Conestoga.*

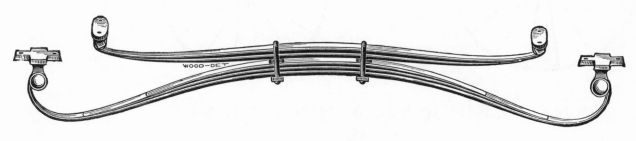

ALAS! IT DID NOT LAST *From hitching post to parking meter... from watering trough to service station...dobbin's quiet clop-clop is lost in the trillion-horsepowered motor cars sweeping down the highway....Sic transit gloria mundi.*

CARVED FOUR SEAT ROCKAWAY

C SPRING COACH

LIGHT COUPE ROCKAWAY

LIGHT BRETT

AMERICA...BEFORE WHEELS

Why the American Indians never evolved a wheeled vehicle has long been a puzzle to anthropologists. Other primitive peoples, early in history, had developed the wheel and adapted it to their various purposes. The Plains Indians had their travois, drawn by dogs or a small pony, a device of two poles crossed by a crude platform on which loads were carried. But the wheel was unknown in America before the arrival of the colonists. And, since nothing like the wheel exists in Nature, it is frequently referred to as man's greatest invention.

The American Indians, great hunters and skilled in many arts, apparently never considered the potentialities of the wheel. That they gradually lost their rich and beautiful continent to the invading and encroaching white men — Spanish, Dutch, English, French—is attributed primarily to the aborigines' failure to evolve and use the wheel.

The Wheel—by forms of which the early settlers wove their cloth, and would eventually roll along highways as yet unmarked and undreamed of, in the tiny hamlets on the shores of the Atlantic and its great bays and rivers!

Once wild beasts roamed the forest wilderness. Centuries later the Indians crept or sped along the animal trails, leaving a moccasin trace a foot or a foot and a half wide, through the primeval forests. These trails, from generations of use, had become marvels of the shortest distance between two points, usually leading from one lake or stream to another. Even today some of the turnpikes, east of the Mississippi, follow paths the Indians pioneered.

Foot travel along the dusky, vine-impeded trails was incredibly difficult for the white man who seldom managed more than a mile an hour on extended migrations, though the swift, bronze-skinned native runners were said, on occasion, to cover seventy-five or more miles from sun-up to sun-down.

So, while the white man's little settlements scattered from Maine to the Carolinas had at first almost no means of land communication, they possessed—from New England's shores, the Connecticut, Hudson, Delaware, Susquehanna and Potomac Rivers, and the Delaware and Chesapeake Bays—practically at their doors a ready means of water travel. Like the Indians, the settlers favored water transport. In the early years some of the settlers bought birch-bark canoes from the Indians but were often unable to navigate the light, capricious craft. Then they imitated the Indians in construction of another type of boat, hollowed from a solid log which, heavier and steadier, became more widely used.

Stage Coach, typical of those in use from about 1780 to 1800, succeeded the canvas-covered stage-wagon like the "Flying Machine," shown on the next page.

FROM WATER TRANSPORT...TO PLANKS AND CORDUROY ROADS

Colonies located on the shores of rivers, bays, and along the ocean had begun to construct small boats to be powered by sail . . . one of the first being the "Blessing of the Bay," launched at Mystic in 1631. Two years later she transported a number of settlers from Boston to the mouth of the Connecticut River. In the next 45 years, to 1676, the Massachusetts colonists had constructed about 730 vessels of some size, while others had been built in Maine, Rhode Island, Connecticut, New Amsterdam and Philadelphia.

But land routes were an imperative need and one, between Plymouth and Boston, was started in 1639. There were no coaches or carriages and very few horses. When settlers migrated, the men, women and children walked, driving their cattle and a few farm horses through the forests, sending their furnishings by boat. The establishment of inland towns, the avid desire of the colonists for news of one another, the need to send or to receive warnings of Indian attacks, led the New England colonies in 1638 to petition King Charles I, of England, to authorize a Colonial post service. The appeal was ignored.

The next year, the Massachusetts General Assembly designated Richard Fairbanks' house in Boston as the first official repository for Colonial mail. Language barriers soon ceased to exist, when the English gained possession of New Amsterdam in 1664, re-naming it New York. A closer link was forged between Boston and New York by the post rider who traveled between the two flourishing towns, at New York's English Governor Lovelace's orders. This service was initiated in 1673. A decade later, travel between Boston, New York and Philadelphia had become customary, though the roads were still the Indian trails widened into settlers' paths, supplemented by sail boats on waters along the routes.

Kier, in *The Pageant of America* says: "A beginning toward trunk-line roads was made in 1654, when the Common Road between Boston and Providence was opened, and later continued as the Shore Road to New York. Eventually another road, the Boston Post Road, connected Massachusetts Bay and the Hudson River. The King's Path was an early road joining New York and Philadelphia. . . . Travel over the colonial roads was largely limited to journeys of necessity. Post-riders toiled over them on horseback, and occasional pack trains carried goods. . . . Wagons and coaches were seldom to be seen." To prevent the post-riders from bogging down in quagmires, planks or logs were laid, usually by the local committees, and—across swamps—the logs were placed close together and covered lightly with earth. Such stretches . . . more general after 1700 than in earlier years . . . became known as corduroy roads. Though they served as bridges over mud, they were so incredibly rough that horses were lamed, and wheeled vehicles were jolted apart. From about 1700, when the traveler did not own a horse, he booked passage on one of the gaily-painted heavy "stage-waggons."

Two-wheeled Chaise, drawn by a single horse, representative of the private family vehicles built by local wheelwrights and blacksmiths, about 1687. Another two-wheeled type of private carriage, called the chair, lacked the leather top of the chaise. Such conveyances were considered, in Boston, a shameless luxury but their use spread.

Mail Carrier of the Mid-1700s, his road over rough logs was considered less hazardous than freshet-made swamps of Spring, and the choking dust of Summer. Post riders accepted commissions from residents of towns along their routes, and promised to execute errands with punctuality.

The "Flying Machine" of 1766, performed the journey from near New York to Philadelphia in a day and a half.

Corduroy Bridge on the road to Mount Mansfield, a 19th Century reminder of the 17th Century road construction that lamed horses and damaged vehicles. In isolated communities, such corduroy roads remain, in the 20th Century.

ARCHITECT OF THE NATION

The chaotic state of the young nation's roads was matched in its political chaos, by the time Washington had won the surrender of Cornwallis at Yorktown, in September 1781. Leaving the battlefield, Washington remained during the Winter of 1781-82 with the Continental Congress in Philadelphia, urging that the claims of the unpaid army be settled. He was in New York, when the American Army entered, as General Clinton evacuated the city, November 1783. On December 4, Washington took leave of his closest officers at Fraunces' Tavern and, by Christmas eve, was at his Mount Vernon home. For four years, he remained there, eager to end his life as a gentleman-farmer. But, much worried by the state of the nation, he declared: "Something must be done, or the fabric must fall, for it is certainly tottering." He wrote constantly to friends, and to the leading men of the country, urging steps

Washington's carriage was drawn by four horses with outriders and lackeys in rich livery.

The Morning of Washington's First Inaugural, 1789. The crowds are en route to Federal Hall, New York City.

toward an "indissoluble union," and had much influence in creating sentiment for a Constitutional Convention to be held in Philadelphia, in May 1787, to "render the Constitution of the Federal Government adequate to the exigencies of the Union."

Eager as he was to be excused, Washington was chosen one of Virginia's five delegates and arrived in Philadelphia May 13. The next day he was elected unanimously as president of the Convention. His strength of character is credited with doing more than any other single factor to bring the Convention to an agreement and to win ratification of the revised document. He sent copies to Patrick Henry and others, winning support in Virginia; and in a Boston newspaper declared: "It, or the Union is before us to chuse from," which made a powerful appeal in Massachusetts. Now, he believed, he could retire to private life. But the nation turned to him again, for its first president. No other name was considered, in any state, and Washington reluctantly accepted the honor. Receiving the notification April 16, he set out from his beloved Mount Vernon . . . over poor and rutted roads . . . and reached New York in time to be inaugurated on April 30, 1789.

"This ceremony," says the *Encyclopedia Britannica,* "was performed in Wall Street, near the spot now marked by Ward's statue of Washington, and in the presence of a great crowd which broke into cheers, as standing on the balcony of Federal Hall, he took the oath administered by Chancellor Livingston, and retired indoors to read Congress his inaugural. . . .

"He drove in a coach with four or six smart horses, and outriders and lackeys in rich livery. At receptions he came in a black velvet suit with gold buckles, yellow gloves, powdered hair, a cocked hat with an ostrich plume in one hand, and a sword in a white leather scabbard." Washington, early in his first term, rented in both New York and Philadelphia the best houses procurable, for he believed the head of the nation should be the guest of no man, and he declined proffered hospitality. He held a weekly levee, open to all.

Congress having decided against New York City as the permanent capital of the nation, the Federal Government was moved to Philadelphia in 1790, on condition that after ten years the seat of Government was to be on the banks of the Potomac River. The administration was moved in 1800 to the newly laid-out city of Washington, and John Adams took up his residence in what then was the uncompleted "President's House."

General Washington pays a formal call on Betsy Ross in Arch Street, Philadelphia, to thank her for the flag she had made to his and General Ross's suggestions.

The Liberty Bell was hastily moved, hidden later under a load of hay, and carried to interior Pennsylvania, as the British were marching on Philadelphia.

The Library in Fifth Street, Philadelphia. In 1731, Benjamin Franklin established the first circulating library in America.

STAGE-COACHES, POST ROADS AND TAVERNS

Before the private carriages had shocked staid Bostonians, there had been an elegant importation . . . the sedan chair . . . carried through the streets by servants. Such an effeminacy was frowned upon by many, though sturdy Benjamin Franklin traveled by sedan chair until late in the 18th Century. Country people had evolved crude barrows and carts, often with solid wood wheels; then came the locally built private carriages. Gradually, though the roads were little improved, and flat boats—fitted with sails —served as ferries until the beginning of the 1800's, passengers and freight were being regularly carried over certain established routes by stage-wagons.

By this time there were over 1900 miles of post-roads in the colonies, and the more elegant American mail-stage, with seats for nine passengers inside and two on the box, was making daily trips from New York to Boston, taking two days for the trip in Summer and, with bad weather in the Winter, often consuming a week. The driver of the stage had full charge of the mails. The best speed that could be made was eight miles an hour, and there were delays in crossing the rivers. Relays en route were frequent, while the heated horses were unhitched and fresh teams put in the traces.

In the taverns . . . which multiplied as stage coach travel increased . . . passengers found good cheer and, in Winter, blazing fires to offset the hardships of roads that still were generally more mud than solid earth. The taverns of the de luxe class were of the best old England type, renowned for deft service and chosen for their good repute by the proprietors of the better stage coach lines.

Fairview Inn, 1827, near Baltimore, on the Old National Road. Pioneers of the seacoast towns, already stifled by civilization, were setting forth over the Blue Ridge and the Alleghenies, for the Ohio and Mississippi valleys. Conestoga wagon trains arrived, half-a-mile in length.

26

A Relay on the Old Boston Post Road, 1815. Here is an Inn of the de luxe class, the landlord a source of good cheer, and good gossip. Other roadside stops, called wagon-taverns, catered to the wagoners, drivers of freight, and immigrants who, however gently bred, had to choose the cheapest accommodations. Tap-room or dining-room by day served as their common sleeping quarters. They brought their own bedding. The freight drivers and wagoners were often a rough and roistering lot, and the luxury of private sleeping quarters was not for them.

General **Andrew Jackson**, who defeated the British at New Orleans in 1815, on the way to Washington to become the country's 7th President, in 1829.

FAST MAIL AND SLOW PROGRESS

There was almost as much romance to the newspaper advertisements for the stage-coach lines, during the mid-1700's, as there was to the dashing horses as a coach came rolling into town. One John Butler, proprietor of a line making scheduled trips between Philadelphia and New York, informed the public, around 1750, "John Butler, with his waggon, sets out on Mondays from his house at the Sign of the Death of the Fox, in Strawberry ally, and drives the same day to Trenton Ferry, where Francis Hilman meets him, and proceeds on Tuesday to Brunswick, and the passengers and goods being shifted into the waggon of Isaac Fitzrandolph, he takes them to the New Blazing Star to Jacob Fitzrandolph's the same day, where Rubin Fitzrandolph with a boat well suited, will receive them, and take them to New York that night." John Butler's return itinerary to Philadelphia was detailed with equal care.

The "New and Extraordinary Travelling Accommodations," announced in 1812 on the poster (left), supply definite information as to departure and arrival hours, "and costs," but the romance of John Butler's "Sign of the Death of the Fox, in Strawberry ally" has vanished.

Few bridges had yet been built, and no provision was made for ferrying wheeled vehicles. Rates were set by Pennsylvania and New Jersey ferry acts for carrying pack-horses, farm animals, single persons, and for a horse and man. In 1723, the Pennsylvania colony created a ferry across the Schuylkill River, which led to many changes. It was possible to travel by land from New York to Savannah, by way of Philadelphia and Baltimore, but the only "long distance" road . . . on which commercial coaches and wagons were regularly operated before the Revolutionary War . . . was that between New York and Philadelphia. After the British defeat at Yorktown, interest in travel became so great that private capital was joined to public funds, to construct roads.

In 1792, Pennsylvania granted a charter to a private company to construct a road between Philadelphia and Lancaster, which was opened two years later. Baltimore, also commercially alert, built thoroughfares at great cost towards the West, to Reiterstown, and to Frederick. These roads were called turnpikes, and the volume of travel over them quickly proved their need.

Josiah Quincy, President of Harvard College, wrote his impressions of a stage-coach journey from Boston to New York: "We reached our resting place for the night, if no accident intervened, at 10 o'clock and, after a frugal supper, went to bed with a notice that we would be called at three which generally proved to be half-past two, and then, whether it snowed or rained, the traveler must rise and make ready, by the help of a horn lantern and a farthing candle, and proceed on his way over bad roads, sometimes getting out to help the coachman lift the coach out of a quagmire or rut." Dr. Quincy's journey, about 1774, occupied a week.

The Fast Mail, en route to New York, makes a gay spectacle at a relay tavern outside Philadelphia.

Luxurious equipage, before the famous old stone Church of Sleepy Hollow, on the Albany Post Road.

Changing the horses for the Fast Mail attracted the ancestors of those who later went to meet all trains.

THE TURNPIKE TAKES ITS TOLL

When a private company was chartered by a state to build better roads, authority was granted to collect tolls from those who used such roads. One of the first, chartered in 1792 by Pennsylvania, ran from Philadelphia almost directly west to Lancaster. Kier, in *The Pageant of America,* says: "At intervals long poles armed with sharp pikes were thrown across the road to stop traffic. At these poles the wayfarer had to stop to pay a fee for the use of the road: and the piked poles were then turned out of the way so that his conveyance could pass. The road was nick-named the Lancaster Turnpike, and all such roads took the name 'turnpike' from it."

Just as, when one of the great watercourses cut across a highway, a family living nearby would maintain the ferry house, so a household on or near the turnpike usually maintained the toll gate. Rates of toll varied. For "every score of sheep, or every Dearborn, Sulky, Chair or Chaise with one horse," the toll rate was six cents, while "every Chariot, Coach, Coachee, Stage, Phaeton or Chaise with two horses and four wheels" was required to pay twelve cents, on the Cumberland Road in Pennsylvania. The tolls also varied, according to the breadth of the vehicle's wheels. "Every cart or wagon, whose wheels do not exceed three inches by breadth, drawn by one horse or two oxen" paid four cents, while "all carts or wagons whose wheels exceed eight inches in breadth" traveled free. But, "just as today the rapid transit lines are apt to find spurious coins or slugs in their token boxes," writes Allan Forbes in *Taverns* *and Stage Coaches of New England,* "so in the old days there were some folks who tried to avoid the payment of tolls. They were called 'shun-pikers.' It seems likely that the word 'piker'. . . came down from the turnpike days."

The late 1790's became known as the Turnpike Era, and opened to farmers and settlers in the interior money-making market opportunities in long-established cities. Stock in turnpike and bridge companies was the first investment venture offered the early Americans, and found ready buyers. The need was so great, the success of the Lancaster Pike was

Spread Eagle Tavern, celebrated stop on the Lancaster Turnpike, 14 miles west of Philadelphia, 1795. Deerskin-clad hunter.

so pronounced, that these roads were soon being built in other areas. The turnpikes represented the first improvements in roads for over a century, and vastly accelerated travel. By 1827, the National Road was a crowded highway with farmers driving cattle and hogs the long way from Indiana to Baltimore. Over it, passed trains of pack horses and mules, freight-laden; and immigrants . . . on foot, on horses, in Conestoga wagons and in stage coaches. A few of the early toll houses, wayside taverns, and worn milestones may still be glimpsed today, but most of the old signs are rapidly being effaced.

Toll Rates, as posted for the Cumberland Road on painted signs at every toll gate. "Any person refusing or neglecting to pay toll, a fine of . . ." The penalty was left blank or has worn off this typical sign.

Mail stage, horn blowing, passes the slow freight. From the painting of Stanley M. Arthurs.

Old stage coach and six-horse wagon meet at a typical inn on an early turnpike.

BEYOND THE ALLEGHENIES

About the middle of the eighteenth century the celebrated Conestoga wagon made its appearance on colonial roads and trails of the back-country. It was designed in the Conestoga Valley of Lancaster County, Pennsylvania and first came to general notice in 1755. Basically, the Conestoga was a gigantic, lumbering affair, sturdily built with both ends higher than the middle of the wagon bed. These ends tapered in sharply making the carriage chassis much shorter than the roof-top. Its chief trade-mark characteristic was the white canvas covering, stretching from end to end, thus making the wagon visible for miles. The ingeniously contrived curved wagon-bed served to prevent its cargo from rolling and spilling as it went up or down hill in the rugged mountainous terrain of the Alleghenies. Another distinguishing feature was its gay color—underbody usually a dark blue and the upper woodwork always a gaudy red. The huge, broad-tired wheels and its lurking motion soon became a familiar sight along the national roads of the east and through the Mississippi valley.

This peculiar type of pioneer vehicle became the standard for overland transport during the westward expansion, not only of the Allegheny regions but for much travel to the mid-west. Drawn by four, six or even ten horses harnessed tandem, these cumbersome arks trundled their immense cargoes from Maine to Georgia, west to St. Louis and beyond, wherever people moved to pick up a new life. These wagons were not unlike seagoing boats rolling on wheels. They could traverse rough ground, ford streams, and had an amazing capacity for carrying all manner of household effects.

As generation upon generation of emigrants pushed inexorably westward, the Conestoga became the symbol of the frontier settler seeking a new home in the vast, uncharted reaches of America's heartland. Forever in the vanguard of travel, the Conestoga was decades ahead of the stage-coach, the riverboat and railroad. It sometimes traveled singly but more often found itself part of an enormous, picturesque caravan of scores, even hundreds of wagons stretching as far as the eye could see. An almost barbaric fascination hovered over the endless line of

Conestogas rumbling over Philadelphia's cobble street, in front of famed London Coffee House, a stock exchange before the Revolutionary War.

Philadelphia to Pittsburgh
in twenty days by Conestoga
wagon . . . a re-enactment
in more recent days.

march, as the wagons' ponderous wheels lurched onward, the bodies creaked and white Osnaburg tops swayed rhythmically. Little wonder that these frigates of the land, slightly altered for the prairie crossing, were later called "prairie schooners." The discovery of gold in California brought these wagons by the thousands from all parts of the east, putting the giant wagon factories to the test to meet heavy production schedules.

The Conestoga wagon weighed about 3000 pounds and had a carrying capacity of from three to four tons. It carried brakes and skids for rough going downhill, and a complement of tools for making repairs. In good weather a horse-drawn wagon train could cover from twenty to twenty-five miles a day, always at a walk. Oxen teams moved at a slightly slower gait.

Drivers generally walked alongside the team, seldom riding above on the seat. The family, especially women and children, rode inside the wagon, but when the going was particularly rough, all but invalids were obliged to step outside and walk, or even take a hand to help extricate the horse teams and wagons from becoming engulfed in a bad mudhole. There was no room on the wagon train for a slacker.

When not engaged on a westward trek, the Conestoga was employed to transport freight between places locally, where water transport was not available. The shrewd, hardy drivers of these freighters were a combination of merchant and teamster, always ready to sell, trade or haggle in anything from farm to kitchen utensils, from horseshoe nails to produce or fresh eggs.

Winter was not the time for moving families and household goods over frozen terrain, but the Conestoga wagon was not idle in winter. When the first snows fell and the roads froze over, wheels were removed and runners substituted. More weight per horse could be transported by sled, and two horses pulling the sled could account for as much as four horses, with wheels. The Conestogas proved their worth the year round.

Red, white and blue coloring
Conestoga wagons antedated the Revolution.
Top was of white Osnaburg, side
boards bright red and under-
carriage a bright blue.

High bows supporting cloth top
provided a spaciousness
to this covered wagon of
18th century origin.

The Accommodation, built by John Stephenson, carried 30 passengers in its three compartments and ran on rails.

The Sociable, built in 1829 by Wade & Leverich, was the first public conveyance with facing seats and rear entrance.

THE "ACCOMMODATION" AND THE "SOCIABLE"

By 1825 local transportation in the growing cities of the young republic had become a real problem. New York City had a population of 200,000, while Brooklyn, connected only by ferry across the East River, was a thriving village of some 15,000 inhabitants. Citizens of New York, at that time confined to what is now lower Manhattan, traveled to Greenwich Village or distant Yorkville and Harlem by stagecoach, operating on regular scheduled trips throughout the day. The wealthy rode in private carriage or coach . . . everyone else walked.

An enterprising New Yorker named Abraham Brower saw the need for a system of public conveyance, and in 1829 launched a vehicle called the *Accommodation*. It resembled a stagecoach and was built especially for Brower by the firm of Wade & Leverich. There were four rows of seats, each wide enough for three passengers who were seated in vis-a-vis compartments with entrance from the side. The body of this carriage hung on leather thorough-braces, after the manner of the post-coaches of the period. The line ran from Wall Street along Broadway to Bleecker Street, then considered "way uptown," the fare was a shilling a passenger for any part of the journey. In the same year, Brower followed with the *Sociable,* a new improved stage with rear entrance, steps and handrail. Here was a radical arrangement that had two rows of seats facing across a center aisle. The *Sociable* provided smooth riding, from a contemporary description, but there was insufficient headroom for standees.

Brower's innovation proved practicable and profitable, and soon rivals entered the field. By 1835 there were about a hundred public omnibuses operating in various sections of New York City. At first, fares were collected by a lad who stood on the rear steps, but soon afterwards the fare box made its appearance. The driver lowered it through an aperture in the ceiling, the fare was deposited and then drawn up. Change-making was a hazardous process, since the driver was perched on top and beyond the range of voice. This inconvenience caused much grumbling,

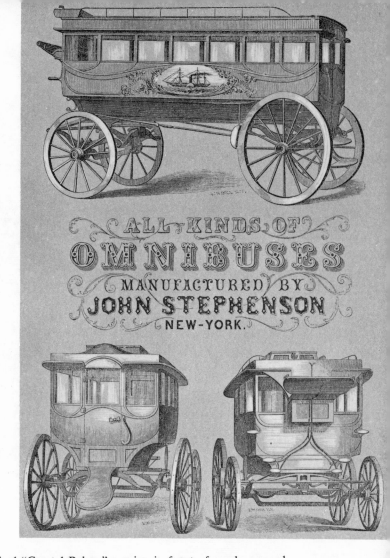

Advertisement of John Stephenson, 1853, announced "all kinds of omnibuses," pictured a typical side view with elaborate decorated panels, front and rear showing driver's seat and entrance step and rear door.

as passengers did not always have the exact fare ready. To stop the bus, a passenger had to signal by means of a cord or strap attached to the leg of the driver. A tug at the rope and the driver brought his omnibus to a sudden halt, often to the dismay of the passengers who were severely jolted by the rough tactics of ruthless drivers.

The New York *Journal of Commerce* for May 6, 1835, tells us that "the character of the omnibus drivers has become brutal and dangerous in the highest degree. They race up and down Broadway with the utmost fury, committing scenes of outrage, in which the lives of citizens riding in light vehicles are put in imminent hazard. Not content with running upon everything which comes in their way, they turn out of their course to break down other carriages. Yesterday, a gentleman driving down Broadway, and keeping near the west side, was run down by an omnibus going up, the street being perfectly clear at the time. A ferocious spirit appears to have taken possession of the drivers, which defies law and delights in destruction. It is indispensable that a decisive police action should be held on those men, or the consequences of their conduct will result in acts which will some day shock the whole city." Such lawlessness remained unchecked for decades.

Broadway buses marked "Crystal Palace" passing in front of newly opened St. Nicholas Hotel, in 1853. These buses continued uptown to the site of the great exhibition at 42nd Street, an hour's journey by slow stages.

Old Broadway stages in 1831, from a print in Valentine's Manual, show a variety of public omnibuses passing in front of St. Paul's Church and Barnum's Museum. Rear and side entrance buses, drawn by two and four-horse teams.

WAGONS TO THE WEST

About 1830, Americans east of the Mississippi, hearing tales of the rich lands that lay to the west, began to exhibit a restlessness that led to mass migrations. The panic of 1837 had created a degree of want and suffering never known before in peacetime. Good farms were hard to buy and earning a living in the few factories had become extremely difficult. Under the stress of hard times, the distant Oregon land beckoned with a peculiar fascination. By 1842 the westward trek, beginning as a mere trickle, became an unleashed flood with thousands of families selling all they owned in order to equip themselves for the great adventure.

The wagon trains plowed on in increasing numbers, generally drawn by oxen, sometimes by mules. The heavy wagons used were similar to the Conestogas of the Alleghenies, though sleeker and more compact, with less curve in the bed and freight boxes added at ends and sides. Once christened the "prairie schooner", this name stuck. Each wagon carried up to three tons of cargo, hauled by ten oxen. At the slow pace of bullocks a wagon train, consisting of twenty to thirty teams, traveled only about seventeen miles per day.

It was indeed a motley horde that made its way across the prairies and through the mountainous wilderness. At first came the explorers, hunters and trappers seeking a share of the fur trade opened up under the impetus of John Jacob Astor. Then came the gold seekers and fortune hunters, some from faraway European lands, looking for a part of Californian prosperity. Then followed U. S. troops, cattlemen, gunmen, sheriffs, stagecoach drivers and rivermen—a cavalcade of mankind bent on various missions, yet all hoping for a share of what the golden West had to offer.

There were two main trails for crossing the plains. In the north the Oregon Trail from Missouri or Iowa followed the Platte River and then across to Ft. Laramie, branching north and on to Oregon, or south to California. The southern route, known as the Santa Fe Trail, went from St. Louis to Independence, across Kansas to Santa Fe. It was the trade route that sprang into existence after Mexico revolted from Spain. Cotton cloth and other manufactured goods were carried to the Indians and furs brought back in return. Although unbridled competition sprang up among the traders they banded together in caravans while crossing the Indian-infested country.

An Army train crossing the plains in 1858. A mile long procession of wagons drawn by bullocks, hauling supplies, guns and personnel for western military posts, as illustrated in *Harper's Weekly*.

Crossing the plains with a hand-cart, many pioneers accompanied the wagon trains, pushing their worldly goods in carts or wheel barrows. Records indicate that a few hardy men crossed alone. From *Marvels of the New West*.

Old Oregon Trail shows well-worn ruts made by heavy cargo wagons. Armed guards flank wagons, widely separated.

Colony of Swiss emigrants passing through the small Georgia town of Mount Airey, heading for the southwest territory.

"Emigrant Train Attacked by Hostile Indians on the Prairie," painted by Champney and engraved by Nichols. This illustration was a double-spread feature in *Ballou's Pictorial Drawing-Room Companion* for August 15, 1857.

PERILS OF THE PLAINS

The pioneers who braved the plains crossing faced dangers and difficulties every step of the way. In many areas the terrain was treacherous, the weather always uncertain and the season often too short for the slow trek to the Pacific. Bands of settlers gathered in Missouri and Iowa in April hoping for an early Spring thaw so that the wagon trains could reach Oregon before snowfall. Heavy rains would render the deeply rutted trails impassable and the rivers too swollen for safe fording. Food and fresh water were constant problems, and while the buffalo herds offered an unlimited meat supply, at times they were not to be found.

The westward journey was marked with sad reminders of hardship and tragedy encountered enroute. Here and there hastily erected cairns told the grim story of family grief, adding their gruesome note to the scattered carcasses and skeletal remains that dotted the landscape at frequent intervals.

But none of the privations endured by the pioneers could compare with the cruelties inflicted by the fierce Indian attacks, an ever-present menace that decimated bands of travelers or wiped them out completely. Naturally, the redskins resented the white men, who were intruders on the Indian hunting grounds, killing the game and driving the great bison herds away from the region of the Oregon Trail. The valuable horses and cattle accompanying the emigrant trains were eyed with envy by the Indians. Thievery, formerly directed against enemy tribes, now was turned toward the unwelcome white pioneers. After many terrifying raids against the caravans, which continued to roll on in ever greater size, the Indians began to demand tribute for safe passage. It became the established custom of the Dakotas to visit the camp of every party arriving at Ft. Laramie and demand a feast. At first, the emigrants dared not refuse this request, but the growing insolence of the Indians mounted, resulting in open warfare.

In spite of dangerous attacks the wagon trains continued to pour into the northwest. The U. S. Army sent along military escorts for the larger trains but this was no assurance of safety. Savage Indian raids persisted, the infuriated natives often outnumbering the soldiers and emigrants.

"Pilgrims on the Plains" as sketched by staff artist Theodore R. Davis of *Harper's Weekly*, June 12, 1869. Keen reporter Davis gives us a glimpse of exciting stampede in corral, and family pathos caused by infant's illness.

"The Old Bone Man of the Plains" drawn by R. F. Zogbaum for *Harper's Weekly*, in 1885. Many a lone traveler and hermit of the west preferred the company of his animals to the social life of a seething community on the move.

"The Emigrants" painted by Frederic Remington, one of America's favorite artists who devoted his life to recording scenes and episodes of western life in all phases.

THE COACH THAT MADE CONCORD FAMOUS

A few of America's blacksmiths and wheelwrights, as early as 1687, were proving their ability in building carriages and coaches. The styles were reminiscent of those most used in England and in France, adapted to the rougher roads of the colonies. Just as the Conestoga wagon was later to become famous as the "freight car of the turnpike," and for the great westward migrations, the Concord coach became the favorite for fast travel on post roads, carrying the mails and passengers. Though many of the early coaches were elliptical, shaped much like a football, the Concord coach . . . named for the New Hampshire town where it was built . . . had its roof level to provide space on top to stow luggage and later, to seat passengers. These coaches had no springs, but were suspended on layers of steerhide called thoroughbraces. The best obtainable materials were used —high grade ash seasoned for at least two years— for the bodies, with selected oak, hickory, and elm for the other parts of the coach. Their curved panels, made by a process inspired by the French, were fashioned by clamping a board, usually of linden wood, to a form and keeping one side moistened before a hot fire until the wood was shaped like the form.

It was in 1813 when Louis Downing, aged 21, advertised in the *New Hampshire Patriot* that he had commenced the wheelwright business in Concord. His capital . . . the training received in his father's shop, $60, and a few tools. Twelve years later, he started to make coaches, being joined by J. Stephen Abbot of Salem. Soon John Borgum, an Englishman, expert in painting landscapes and other subjects, was also employed.

Very soon Abbot and Downing formed a partnership which endured twenty years, and was resumed by their sons in 1865. Of the many thousands of these Concord coaches, those used on the Western routes penetrated perilous country thick with Indians made hostile by the white man's constant encroachment on hunting lands. Where there were no Indians, the coaches were likely to be attacked by outlaws and desperadoes.

During the gold rush, Concord coaches rumbled West a hundred miles a day, changing their six-horse teams every twelve or fifteen miles. In 1868, thirty Concord coaches ordered by Wells Fargo and Company were shipped on flat cars in a single train, to Salt Lake City, for service over the Sierra Nevada mountains, by way of Placerville and Virginia City. These Concord coaches were gems of beauty, each door with a handsome panel, no two of which were alike. The scrollwork decorations, by Charles Knowl-

Sleek-bodied Concord coaches soon became known, on Eastern roads as the *travelers' conveyance de luxe.*

First to achieve the ascent to Mt. Washington, in 1861, Concord coaches were owned by the fashionable hostelries and boys' schools of New England. The coach for Crawford House was built about 1880, for Abel Crawford whose name is perpetuated in Crawford Notch.

ton, were also varied on each coach. The shipment, with sixty harnesses and spare parts, was valued at about $45,000.

The durably built Abbot-Downing coaches and carriages were shipped from Concord to every part of the United States, and to Canada, Mexico, South America, England, Australia and South Africa. Many of America's leading hotels . . . the Brevoort and the Astor in New York, the Tremont and Vendome in Boston, the Palmer House in Chicago . . . owned a number of Concord coaches. Orders were filled for special panels on the coach doors. Potter Palmer ordered four coaches of canary yellow, "on each door . . . a painting of the hotel done in John Borgum's best manner." The little town of Concord became world-famous.

Tough and sturdy, from its seasoned white ash spokes to its oxhide boot, the Concord coach served as the public conveyance and dray of the West.

Crawford House stage coach was typical of those used in the tourist regions. Earlier stages, being elliptical and curved at top and bottom, were cramped for headroom.

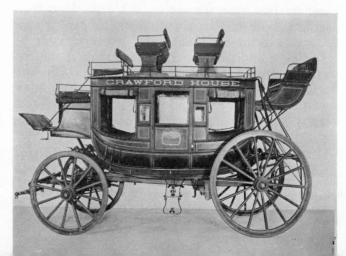

"NEITHER SNOW, NOR RAIN, NOR HEAT . . ."

Butterfield's Overland Mail-coach starting out from Atchison, Kansas, January, 1866. Each arrival was greeted by cheering crowds as mail and baggage were always welcome.

Prior to the discovery of gold in California there was no regular line of communication between the eastern United States and its Pacific territory. The steamers that sailed around the Horn constituted a very slow and intermittent contact. As a result of being cut off from the centers of trade and government Californians stirred up a great deal of agitation during the 40's and 50's. The governor and legislature pushed a vigorous program, not only for the building of railroads but for the regular schedule of an overland mail service to supplement the semi-monthly mails that arrived by slow boat. A monster petition bearing 75,000 signatures was sent to Washington in 1856, resulting in Congress' appropriation of $550,000 for three wagon roads. Finally, in 1857 a bill was passed authorizing a line "from such point on the Mississippi River as the contractors may select, to San Francisco in the State of California, for six years—cost not to exceed $300,000 per annum for a semi-monthly service, $450,000 for weekly and $600,000 for a semi-weekly service."

The Post Office advertised for bids as prescribed and received nine, the successful bidders John Butterfield, William Fargo and others, all experienced in the express business. Postmaster Brown, from Tennessee, insisted upon a southerly route in spite of angry protests from many sections of the north. The final route formed a roundabout semi-circle from St. Louis, via El Paso and Fort Yuma, a distance of 2800 miles, favored over the northerly route via Salt Lake City.

On September 16, 1857, service was inaugurated on both east and western terminals, after a year of

energetic preparations during which hundreds of way stations were built, wells sunk for water, teams procured and drivers trained. The first trips carrying only mail and papers, arrived ahead of the 25 day schedule. Both in St. Louis and San Francisco, the opening of the line was the occasion of much rejoicing—long parades, brass bands, salutes and unbridled jubilation were the order of the day. The famous Concord coaches, sturdily built spring wagons, stood up remarkably well under the continuous strain of the long journey. At first they carried few passengers but later on they were enlarged to accommodate up to nine inside and as many who dared cling to the outside seats were carried on top. Teams of four to six mustangs—"wild as deer"—sped the coaches over the usual 10 to 15 miles between stations. The fare from St. Louis was $100 to the east, $200 for the western trip, and meals were extra.

Wells Fargo stage coach, one of an order shipped from builder in Concord, N. H. to Salt Lake City. It saw much service through the Sierra Nevada mountains to Sacramento, starting in 1868.

From San Francisco, this heavily laden overland mail carries its full complement of passengers headed east, in 1858. No women in evidence though occasionally one braved the tiresome journey.

Main Street, Denver, Colorado, outside offices C. A. Cook Co., banking house and agent for the overland despatch. Ox-drawn prairie schooners appear in greater numbers than horses and buggies.

Supply wagons waiting to board ferry boats for crossing the Rappahannock River, at Port Royal, Virginia, in 1862.

Battery wagon containing military telegraphic equipment, just behind the front lines.

THE WAGONS GO TO WAR

The differences between the North and South were great and numerous but there was one point of agreement—without wagons to transport supplies and military equipment the troops would have gone hungry and empty-handed. The Union forces enjoyed a distinct advantage in this regard, because the main carriage manufacturing centers were located in their territory, mainly in Massachusetts, Connecticut, New York and New Jersey. Further west at South Bend, Indiana, the giant plant of Studebaker Brothers turned out supply wagons by the thousands.

Early in the War between the States, the Union Quartermaster Corps established a number of wagon

Supply train getting ready to move, at Culpepper, Virginia, 1862.

"What-is-it" wagon of Matthew Brady, Civil War photographer, at Petersburg, Va.

Mule-drawn wagon train at Chickamauga, where troops were quartered during the Spanish-American War, 1898.

parks, huge encampments where vehicles and their mules were quartered. Brady Station, Virginia, attached to the Army of the Potomac, was typical of many such depots where wagons were repaired, mules were shod, equipment made and readied for the task of battle. The larger supply wagons made contact with important railroad centers, bringing material closer to the front lines, hauling supplies along with soldiers as the scene of battle shifted.

Wagons were, for the most part, sturdily built of seasoned ash and hickory, as the wheels had to withstand great strain over poor roads and rough terrain. Canvas tops were regulation, seldom removed in the hottest weather. Such wagons served to haul all manner of things badly needed in the conduct of the war with but one exception—soldiers almost never rode the wagons—they walked alongside.

Many ambulances like this were built during World War I for U. S. Army, by Studebaker.

Heavy construction similar to Conestoga wagons, is evident in this baggage wagon.

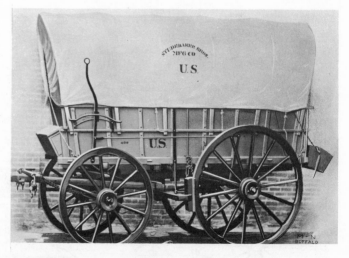

Built in volume by Studebaker, this Army wagon is one of 100 sent on peace mission to Utah Indian territory in 1857.

Washington coachee, the only existing type of light family carriage used in mid-Atlantic states, still intact.

CELEBRITIES AND CARRIAGES

Just as people of means, today, prefer to drive about in swank limousines, in a former day the great and near-great drove impressive looking coaches and broughams. The latter were among the most sought-after of elegant vehicles. American carriage builders borrowed the brougham from England, where Lord Brougham, its originator, gave it his name and blessings. The finest skill, craftsmanship and materials went into the brougham, made by firms like Hooper, Cook and Brewster.

For parades and occasions of state, our presidents and elder statesmen selected the barouche, a real mark of distinction. As many as six people, seated vis-a-vis, could ride comfortably in the barouche. Traveling down flag-draped avenues, our presidents and visiting dignitaries waved to enthusiastic admirers along the line of march while their gleaming black coach was pulled by high-prancing steeds on display. The handsome and delicate barouche came from France where it was known as the *caleche,* still so called in French-speaking parts of Canada.

The master carriage makers of this country took great pride in the vehicles ordered by presidents and people of note. Washington's coach was built for him in Philadelphia, while special open barouches for Presidents Lincoln and Grant were built by Studebaker, great carriage builder of that day.

LaFayette's barouche, used during his triumphal tour of the United States in 1824-1825. It was built by John Ourlet, a Baltimore coachmaker, by order of the Government.

Daniel Webster's carriage presented to him by the citizens of the State of New York, in recognition of his statesmanship. Manufactured by Wood, Tomlinson & Co., New York, at a cost of $2500 including a span of horses and harness equipment.

General Grant's administration witnessed a
continuous procession of politicians and office seekers,
most of whom drove in elegant carriages, such as these.

Mrs. Millard Fillmore, when she was the first lady of the land, was presented
with this magnificent wine-colored carriage by the generous citizens of New York.
With silver trim and blue silken seat coverings, its appearance created a stir
on all occasions. Built in1851 by Wood Tomlinson & Co., New York.

Streams of traffic poured up and down busy Broadway endangering the lives of all who attempted the crossing. Genin offered to erect this bridge at his expense. From *Gleason's* in 1852.

Loew Bridge across Broadway at Fulton Street was built in 1866, only to be torn down two years later. The stages, coaches and commercial vehicles made this a most dangerous thoroughfare.

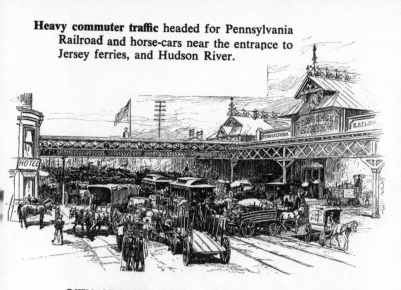

Heavy commuter traffic headed for Pennsylvania Railroad and horse-cars near the entrance to Jersey ferries, and Hudson River.

Overhead trestle designed to avoid vehicular traffic and horse-cars near the entrance to Jersey ferries, at the Hudson River.

CITY CROWDS AND A BRIDGE FOR PEDESTRIANS

Traffic congestion—vehicular confusion—pedestrians in danger—these age-old problems plagued our founding fathers, especially in crowded New York City streets. The areas of greatest difficulty were downtown Broadway and the waterfront thoroughfares leading to ferry-slips. Countless plans and proposals for the relief of transit jams and the protection of travelers were advanced, as early as 1840.

Genin, an enterprising merchant-hatter occupying a busy spot on Broadway, across the street from Saint Paul's, offered to erect a bridge structure at this point. In 1852, *Gleason's Pictorial Drawing Room Companion* heartily endorsed this plan, as well as the generosity of the "merchant prince whose charity bids fair to supersede all others. At present, this most dangerous crossing . . . in the highest degree hazardous for the ladies and children. By means of this ornamental structure they might pass over pleasantly and safely. The cost would be about $5000 and Mr. Genin is willing to incur the whole expense of erecting the bridge and keeping it in repair." Genin's Bridge, as planned and illustrated herewith, was never built, but another structure called the Loew Bridge, less ornate in design, was erected on the spot in 1866. Two years later, this was completely demolished after a storm of protest by influential merchants on the opposite side of Broadway who convinced the City Council that the bridge was a folly.

Elevated sidewalks and bridges above crowded streets continued to intrigue the populace and be the subject of heated debates, as the need to solve traffic congestion grew more urgent. Alfred Speer obtained a patent and widespread publicity for his novel plan for an endless traveling sidewalk overhead. The elevated railway structure was to have small carriage seats moving along on a continuous chain, and sidewalks on both sides of the track were to be provided with benches for pedestrians. Stairways at frequent intervals were to give access to the sidewalk. But, after much fanfare, the plan was dropped.

Bridging overcrowded streets leading to ferry approaches where the stream of commuter traffic encounters the hundreds of wagons and horse-cars along West Street. From *Scientific American*, Feb. 8, 1890.

Endless traveling railway sidewalk proposed by Speer for downtown New York's busy streets. Slow-moving carriage seats could be boarded without difficulty, one of many plans to solve congested traffic problem, in 1872.

49

HEIGH HO! COME TO THE FAIR

The country fair, with its excitement, fanfare and side-shows is a peculiarly American institution developing somewhat differently from the established shows of the Old World. The earliest appears to have been the Berkshire Cattle Show of Elkanah Watson's Berkshire Agricultural Society, in western Massachusetts, 1810. The news of its success spread and before long the fair became an accepted habit with the American people.

In 1841, the first state fairs were held at Syracuse, New York and at Newark, New Jersey. Participation by the local farmer did not take place, at first, because of the difficulty of transporting his livestock. But the farmer attended with his family, enjoying immensely the stimulating experience of contact with the outside world. His farm wagon or carriage got him there though many of the roads of that day were forbidding.

The first truly national exposition was the Crystal Palace Exhibition at New York, in 1853, following the Crystal Palace Show in London, 1851. Then came a succession of regional fairs throughout the nation, at Buffalo, 1869, Louisville, Kentucky, 1870 and the Cincinnati fair extending from 1870 to 1872. Proof of the growing interest was recorded in attendance figures for the Cincinnati fair: 300,000 the first year and almost double in the third year it ran. Without question, America was becoming fair-minded,

pointing the way towards success for the Centennial of 1876.

On March 3, 1871, an act was passed by Congress creating a United States Centennial Commission to promote "an International Exhibition of Arts, Manufactures and Products of the Soil and Mine in the City of Philadelphia" in 1876. Preparations for this great event were carried on energetically, and by the spring there were erected on the 450 acres assigned in Fairmount Park five main buildings, including a Carriage Exhibition Building. Every state, as well as a great many foreign nations, was represented.

The hundreds of exhibits ranged the whole gamut of human endeavor, with special emphasis on industry and manufactured goods. Agricultural exhibits were numerous, and transportation in all phases was stressed. Coach and carriage makers, both from here and abroad, showed "The World on Wheels," including a great variety of barouches, phaetons, broughams, cabriolets, sulkies, omnibuses, stanhopes, landaus, britzkas, victorias, buggies, hansoms, and all manner of commercial vehicles.

The visitors attending the fair arrived by train or carriage. For those who traveled in horse-drawn conveyances, many made the comparison between the carriages exhibited and their own, and placed orders for immediate delivery.

The crush on Opening Day at the Centennial, Elm and Belmont Avenues, Philadelphia. Traffic was snarled as thousands of vehicles endangered milling crowds on streets.

Main Building at the Philadelphia Centennial, 1876. All types of vehicles and horse-drawn surface cars were on hand.

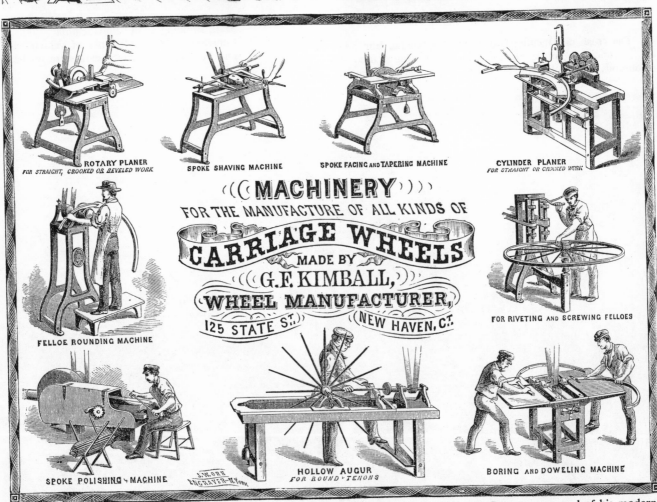

ROTARY PLANER
FOR STRAIGHT, CROOKED OR BEVELED WORK.

SPOKE SHAVING MACHINE

SPOKE FACING AND TAPERING MACHINE

CYLINDER PLANER
FOR STRAIGHT OR CROOKED WORK

(((MACHINERY)))
FOR THE MANUFACTURE OF ALL KINDS OF
CARRIAGE WHEELS
MADE BY
G. F. KIMBALL,
WHEEL MANUFACTURER,
125 STATE ST. NEW HAVEN, C.T.

FELLOE ROUNDING MACHINE

FOR RIVETING AND SCREWING FELLOES

SPOKE POLISHING MACHINE

HOLLOW AUGUR
FOR ROUND TENONS

BORING AND DOWELING MACHINE

Wheelwright Kimball, of New Haven, Conn., was proud of his modern mechanical equipment, featured in one of his advertisements.

Top left: **Blacksmith shop** and testing section of the carriage building plant of Brewster & Co., New York, 1879.

Left Center: **Body making** and varnishing rooms of the Brewster plant. Carriages were always supported on "horses" and had to be lifted off by several workmen.

WHEELWRIGHTS AND FINE FELLOES

Describing the growing carriage industry at the time when it was making great strides the *Scientific American,* in its Feb. 8, 1879, issue says: "The special features of American pleasure carriages, in comparison with those of Europe, are to be found in their fine lines, extreme lightness, and beauty of finish—peculiarities which, however paradoxical . . . are entirely consistent with superior strength and durability." To overcome European bulkiness called "solidity," the American wainwright set up manufacturing techniques unheard of to the foreign coachmaker. His English counterpart, however, when he had need of a stick of peculiar shape, set about whittling it down from a block "letting bulk atone for the loss of tenacity incident to cutting across the grain. The American invented a method of steaming and bending a straight-grained stick to the shape desired."

Because of the tremendous number of wheels needed for all types of vehicles, a huge wheel industry developed with machinery for performing special operations. These included spoke shavers, rotary planers, tapering machines, felloe rounders, boring, doweling and riveting machines, polishers and hollow augurs for drilling tenons in wheel hubs. As new designs for carriages were planned on the drawing board, new machines had to be perfected to meet the demands for new shapes. These new forms were invented in the designing rooms, drawn to exact size on a large blackboard where they were studied meticulously. The wheelwright understood from long experience, whether to use ash, hickory, elm, oak or whitewood according to the service each part was expected to perform. The powerful bending machines accomplished the required curvature without breaking the grain. The complete assembly of a wheel was a series of separate operations topped off with the placing of the iron rim or tire around the felloe. This final phase was the work of the skilled blacksmith who knew how to apply the heated rim without scorching the delicate felloe. As the rim cooled off, it contracted and pulled all segments of the felloe into position securely.

Carriage building required extensive establishments because practically all parts of the vehicle with the exception of lamps and special hardware were manufactured on the premises.

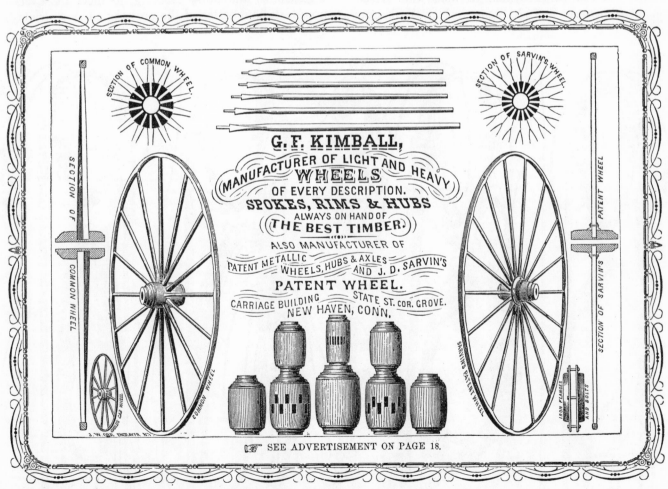

SEE ADVERTISEMENT ON PAGE 18.

Advertisement of wheel maker, appearing in catalogue of C. & D. Cook & Co., 1859. This catalogue of hundreds of pages is well illustrated with numerous engravings and advertisements of merchants and makers.

The various carriage, coach and wagon pictures, shown on the following five pages, are of actual vehicles at the Carriage House of the Suffolk Museum, Stony Brook, New York—one of the finest collections of its kind in the United States.

STYLED FOR THE CARRIAGE TRADE

The horse and buggy age, gone and all but forgotten, will always be recalled with fondness and nostalgia as the era just before the coming of the automobile. It ended about 1910 but just when it began is a matter of conjecture. One might arbitrarily say about 1850, its vintage years spanning the time of Lincoln to McKinley in the White House. The era of the carriage in its heyday is shorter than one may think.

The golden day of the horse in America fostered a flourishing industry which produced all manner of equine accoutrement. Broadly speaking, the carriage trade, particularly in its earliest days, centered around New England. There, its many factories produced carriages, harness and other horse furnishings that were shipped to all parts of North and South America. At the turn of the century there were more than 4500 vehicle concerns in this country that employed about 126,000 men and paid yearly wages of $70,000,000.

There were some celebrated names in the carriage business, none of greater esteem than Brewster. James, a descendent of William Brewster who arrived on the *Mayflower* in 1620, came to New York from Northampton, Mass. He set up shop in 1810, after being employed in New Haven with the firm of Cook, one of the finest coach-makers. By 1830, the name Brewster on a carriage was like sterling on silver— a mark of distinction for which the more affluent citizenry was willing to pay a higher price. Brewster strongly influenced the design of America's most popular 19th century road-wagon or buggy, as it came to be known. He also greatly improved the lines of the coach, phaeton, and the rockaway, which was the first completely American carriage affording the coachman protection in bad weather.

About the time when Brewster had become established in New York, and Lewis Downing had opened his carriage shop in Concord, the town of Amesbury, Mass., prospered with as many as 25 shops busily turning out carriages and sleighs. Westfield, too, in the same state, was already known as the "Whip City"; while in Connecticut, at Hartford, George J. Capewell was making a fortune as the "horse nail king." All over the East and the Northeast, hundreds of factories flourished, making bridles and bits, saddles and saddle-blankets, harness and whips, carriage trunks and horse clothing, to meet the ever-more-fastidious tastes of the growing carriage trade.

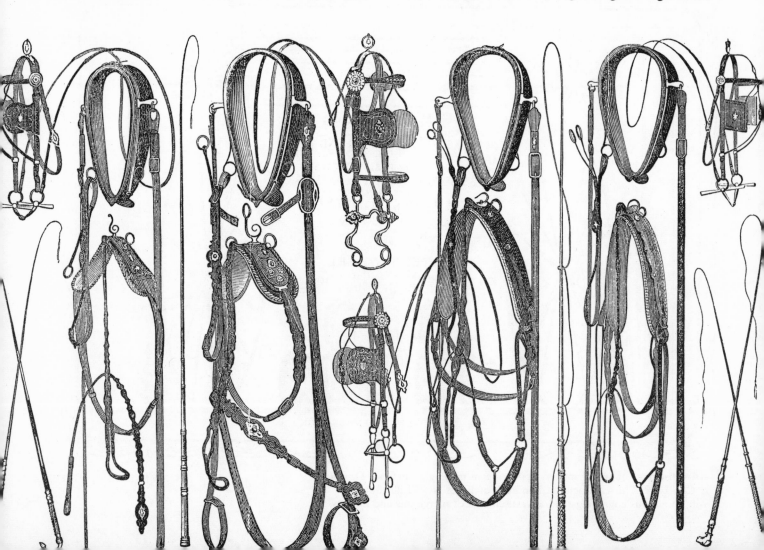

Buckboard surrey, with fringe on canopy, made of natural wood. Built about 1900.

Rockaway, an original American creation, gave protection to the driver. This is a three-seat curtain type, c. 1855.

Lady's phaeton, built around 1860. This type of body was imitated in many of the early automobile prototypes.

Runabout with side-bar springs, c. 1890. Extremely narrow box body, with step directly behind front wheel.

Phaeton with fringed canopy, c. 1895. This is a generic body type with frame under seat built higher than the floor.

Harness equipment, whips and saddlery formed an important part of every stable. From an advertisement, c. 1859.

Country wagon, two-seat canopy-top, c. 1860. Simple, box-like shape with rear and side curtains.

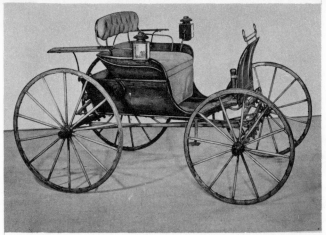

Runabout, pony size, of natural finely polished wood. c. 1900.

Basket phaeton, pony size, made in Ohio, c. 1910.

Open stage, side panels decorated. Made in Concord, N. H., c. 1850.

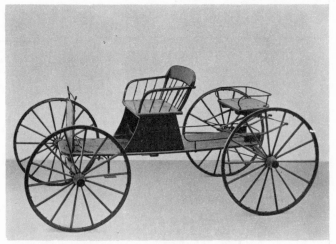

Buckboard, rumble seat, pony size. Its springiness enabled it to ride smoothly and "buck" rough roads. c. 1890.

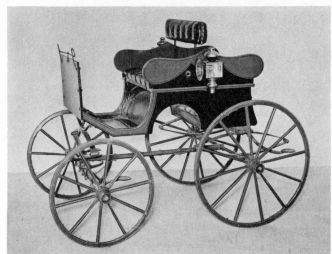

Trap, pony size, seating four. Similar to dog cart. c. 1900.

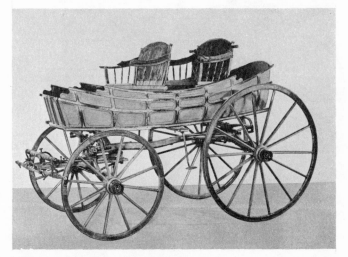

Pleasure wagon, two-seater, with boat-shaped body. Side panels are curved and stencil decorated. c. 1820.

Governess cart, spindle-panel. Children sat facing each other, driver in rear. c. 1900.

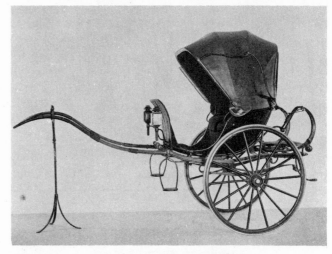

Whitechapel cart, built in 1867 in London. The first car used in America for tandem driving, a leader in the annual parade.

Breaking cart, pony size. Long shaft to accommodate kicking colt. c. 1895.

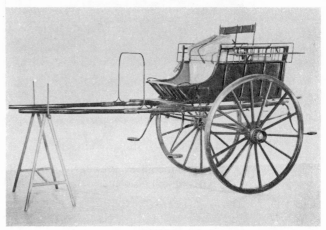

Cabriolet, of French design, for the man-about-town. Combined grace, luxury and correctness, for formal driving. c. 1900.

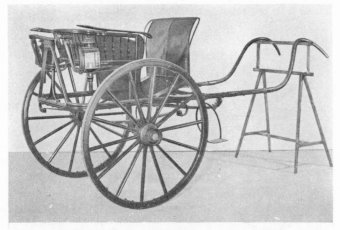

Tilbury gig, invented by English coach-maker. Owner-driven, groom sat to his left, awaiting orders, arms crossed at chest. c. 1900.

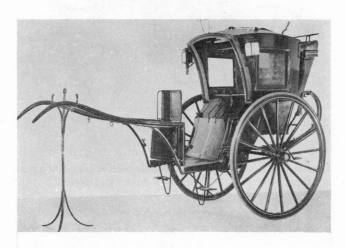

Hansom cab invented by English architect, J. A. Hansom, in 1834. Proved popular for privacy in town driving. c. 1900.

Vis-a-vis, natural wood, curtain quarter.
Made by Brewster & Co., N. Y. c. 1890.

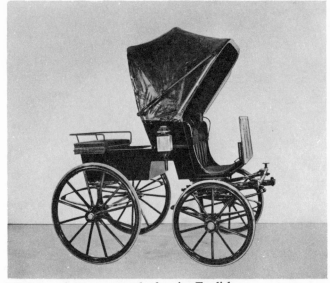

Stanhope phaeton, named after its English
designer. Made by Brewster & Co., c. 1900.

Brougham, built by Brewster & Co., 1890.
Groom and coachman sat at same level.

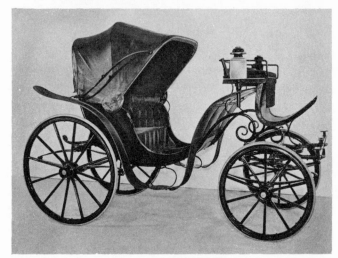

Victoria, named after Queen Victoria who
chose it as her favorite carriage. c. 1880.

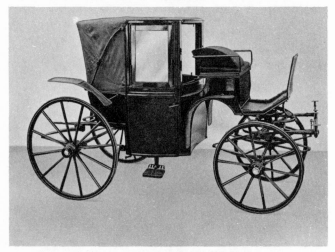

Landaulet, with top up and closed.
Seated two inside, and driver, c. 1885.

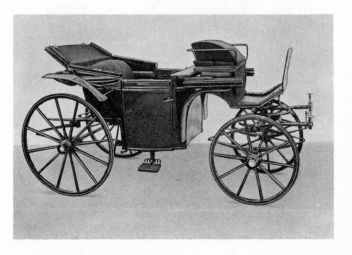

Landaulet, with top folded back and open.

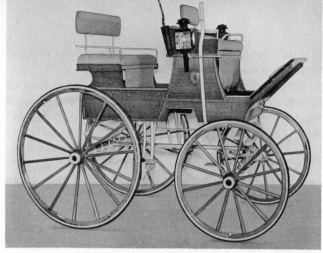

Game wagon built of natural wood. Used as a hunting or sporting carriage. c. 1910.

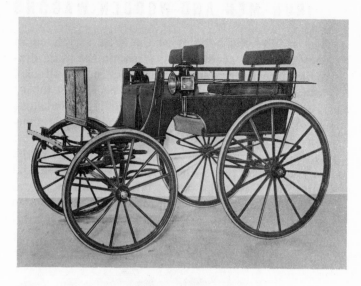

Trap, a four passenger phaeton. Built in Brooklyn, N. Y. in 1885.

Mail phaeton, built in 1867 in London. A massive carriage, fashionable for park driving. Two servants sat on rear seat.

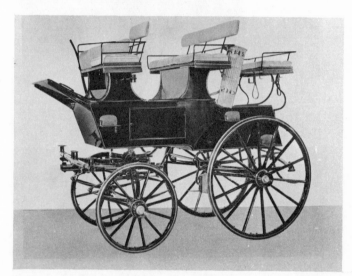

Roof-seat break, a four-in-hand vehicle for exercising and breaking in horses. A pleasure carriage for country picnics and hunt-races.

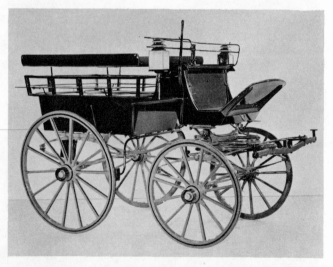

Wagonette built in England about 1890. Also favored by Queen Victoria. Sometimes driven four-in-hand.

Omnibus built by Brewster & Co., c. 1890. Called station bus in England, opera bus in America. Passengers face each other.

IRON MEN AND WOODEN WAGONS

The saga of the building of the West as related in most historical accounts lays stress on the more dramatic aspects of wagon trains and Indian attacks, with little, if any, reference to the pedestrian job of keeping supplies and shipments rolling. The stout waggoners who drove and manned the heavy lumbering wagons that penetrated into the mountainous, mining country, the dredging teams that paved the way with new roads, the woodsmen who felled and carted logs from the deep wilderness—these courageous teamsters and their sturdy wagons are as much a part of the great westward movement as their romantic counterparts whose stories have been oft-told in word, song and cinema.

Remington, Russell, Rogers, Poore and a host of artists and painters who endured the hardships of western life were impressed by deeds of strength and daring of the wagon teams, both man and beast, and have left us pictorial records of what they saw. Popular magazines like *Harper's* and *Leslie's* realized how eagerly the public awaited news of the goings-on in mining territory and dispatched their top-flight artists to cover this activity. Reporting on the transportation of ore diggings *Harper's* said: "In many mountain regions the grades are steep, and the roads of necessity narrow, being cut in the side of the canyon, with precipitous drops on all sides. In these descents where team follows team in quick succession, there is danger as well as excitement, and although great precautions are taken, serious accidents do frequently occur. Each wagon is furnished with a

"**Army Mail Ambulance**—a 'busted' brake and a 'downgrade'" as painted by Frederic Remington for *Harper's Weekly*, Sept. 20, 1890.

"**On the way** to new diggings—halt in a rough pass of the Rocky Mountains," drawn at the scene for *Harper's Weekly* of May 1, 1875 by artists, Frenzeny and Tavernier. Long

powerful brake, capable of stopping and holding it in the deepest places of the road, even when loaded. Upon this, the driver relies for safety, as the sailor does upon his anchor, and from the beginning of the downgrade he keeps it in active service. Our illustration (upper right) shows one of these huge wagons whirling past a wayfarer who has sought refuge by the side of the narrow road. Sometimes a wagon train passes in a long file. Another wagon bursts into sight, screeches past and vanishes . . . until, one passes with a bell behind it. This is the last wagon and the traveler may now pass in safety."

The ascent into high regions required stamina and strength on the part of all. Long teams of mules were needed, and as they wound around treacherous curves this presented extra difficulties, keeping the harness in line. All hands pitched in when the going got very rough, the men straining as much as the overworked mules.

"From mine to mill," drawn for *Harper's Weekly*, Sept. 14, 1878 by Henry R. Poore. The gold and silver ore was often dug out of deep veins in the mountainous regions, taken downhill in heavy wagons, built for rough going. The waggoner used all his strength, hoping his brake would hold.

mule teams were needed to haul up the steep grades, as motley gang of workers followed on foot, and on horseback.

Road-building used large gangs of men and equipment, especially two-wheeled carts and scoops. As cities grew, new streets had to be cut and widened, like the scene in the suburbs of St. Paul Minn. Drawn by W. A. Rogers for *Harper's Weekly*, Oct. 15, 1890.

MAIN STREET

Going to town, by carriage or buggy, was a deeply ingrained American custom throughout the past century. In thousands of villages and towns, the highlight of the week was the family shopping trip on Saturday. Often the farmer, on such a visit, would trade his produce like eggs, fruit or vegetables for dry goods or household items needed at the general store . . . calico or cottons for the missus, flour, sugar or coffee for the kitchen larder.

There were those who predicted the disappearance of the horse with the coming of the railroad but, on the contrary, there were more horses and finer breeds as the nation prospered and grew. With the exception of the Civil War years and the Reconstruction era that followed, barns and carriage-houses boasted better quality horseflesh for faster and more stylish driving. The prominent merchant or country squire bought a better buggy, with case-hardened axles, steel springs, and a top for inclement weather. If money was no object, even a rockaway, coach or brougham and, of course, a new spanking team to match his finer vehicles.

Many retail businesses on Main Street were conducted on the sidewalk nearest the establishment, while Old Dobbin or the team of dapple-grays was

In the late seventies Broad Street, Chattanooga, looked like this.

The ubiquitous cotton bale wagons pulled by mule-team, in Ardmore, Oklahoma.

Farm wagons crowd the streets in Court-House Square, Lexington, Kentucky.

hitched to the water-trough or hitchingpost. The farmer from the sticks engaged in busy transactions while his family trudged the streets, eyeing or buying commodities for the week.

On Main Street, U. S. A., the grain dealer's was a very important stop on the visiting farmer's busy schedule. His store was generally built around a wide driveway to allow hand-trucking of bags, barrels and bales. To one side of the entrance was usually a crudely improvised office, with a window for the display of grain samples. The simple placards told their story: "No. 1 Yellow corn"; "No. 2 White oats"; or "Fancy white middlings." His walls were often decorated with colorful lithos of famous race horses, agricultural calendars, black and white broadsides of a coming Fair, plus a sprinkling of patent feed posters. Over the owner's cluttered rolltop desk, there hung, more than likely, *The Horse Fair* . . . certainly a few *Currier and Ives* featuring the latest in horse-drawn carriages.

The town livery stable was a scene of hectic activity. Here, while Farmer Jones did his trading, he also parked his horse and buggy, where for the sum of twenty-five cents his horse would be fed and watered. In the more progressive towns public tie-racks with feed troughs were provided, especially for those who arrived early.

Elm Street, Dallas, Texas, resembled a western town, except for cotton wagons.

At the turn of the century, main streets in leading cities were the scenes of vehicular confusion with wagons, carriages and horse-drawn street cars milling about.

R. F. D., U. S. A.

City dwellers have always had the benefit of mail delivery, whereas their country cousins had been obliged to come to the town post office to pick up their mail. Toward the end of the nineteenth century, this inequality led to serious protest, and many political leaders in Congressional districts sensed that a real opportunity existed to gain favor with their back-home constitutents. Farm journals picked up the issue, and the general movement gained such momentum that, under the recommendation of Postmaster-General Wanamaker, "village delivery" was inaugurated in 1890. This included towns with a population under 10,000 or with gross postal receipts less than $10,000.

The National Grange promoted the issue, after this feeble and inadequate start had been made. By 1892 Congress had before it a bill asking for an appropriation of six million dollars for the creation of a true rural free delivery service, patterned after many model systems functioning in Europe. The bill died in the House, partly because of the current depression. But the various state granges kept up a drumfire of agitation for passage of the bill, assisted by representatives from the rural districts. Finally, in 1896, Congress had made sufficient funds available for an honest-to-goodness test of rural services,

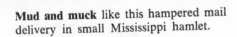

Mud and muck like this hampered mail delivery in small Mississippi hamlet.

"Red Man's Parcel Post" painted by Frederic Remington from *Harper's*, in 1895. The western mail coach had to cover much ground to make delivery.

The little white box wagon and white horse brought happiness to out-of-the-way places in the deep south.

carried out in widely scattered sections of the country. Some routes covered the Allegheny foothills, the Arizona fruit belt, the grazing lands of southern Washington and the backroads of New England. First reports of the test were discouraging due, for the most part, to the terrible road conditions encountered in most regions.

By the closing days of the nineteenth century enough interest, experiment and pressure had been brought to bear upon the Postal Department to appoint special agents for a nationwide rural delivery service. In 1897 routes totaled only 82 miles, by 1900 there were over 1200 miles and by 1907 this had been increased to 37,000 miles served. The greatest deterrent had been the poor roads which made it difficult for delivery wagons to get through in bad weather. Many wagons sunk to dangerous levels when rainfall converted the dirt roads into impassable quagmires. Many vehicles had to be abandoned under the circumstances and the animals rescued with difficulty. The farmers, aided by the growing numbers of motorists now using the roads, agitated for improvements so that rural free delivery could reach all.

Early mail wagons, especially built to order, were simple, boxlike affairs. They were often painted white and had a single door for quick closure in inclement weather.

Mishaps from bad roads plagued many a mailman, as late as 1913, when post road projects were under way.

Great expectations with daily mail delivery at the crossroads, in 1896.

Mud and mire, a foot deep on Hunting Park Avenue, just four miles from Philadelphia City Hall . . . mid-winter, 1891.

Ice and snow and hardened mud . . . a formidable obstacle to smooth travel, New Rochelle, N. Y.

American mud on country roads was the Public Enemy No. 1. Abandoned vehicle tells story of the horse's defeat.

In the ditch wrecked buggy gives mute testimony to strain on light wheels.

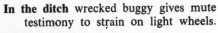

THROUGH MUD RUTS AND MIRE

The time: 1900. The nation accustomed to the clatter of hoof-beats was beginning to hear strange chugging noises sputtering from an occasional "horseless carriage" as it bounced along, hesitatingly, over roads deep in ruts. A stoneboat dragged by a team of horses or yoke of oxen, whipped by a farmer bent on working off his road taxes, smoothed down the rough spots and filled in the chuckholes.

For three centuries transportation had fanned out slowly, first along the Indian trails, rivers and canals, then railroads. In the West, settlers had been induced to take up farms by grants of land, and farmhouses were a mile or more apart. Towns were often separated by ten or twenty miles and crude dirt roads, often impassable in winter, threaded their way through sparsely settled countryside. The greatest obstacle to travel occurred during periods of heavy rain or spring thaws which transformed dirt and gravel roadbeds into deep slough, dotted here and there with ponds of water and ice.

In the opening years of this century American farmers paid almost one billion dollars to have their produce hauled to market, and this exorbitant charge was due in the main to bad roads that made hauling

Farmers' slough on main road between Cleveland and Warrenville, Ohio, two miles from city limits, in the spring of 1891.

New Rochelle side street in winter, 1892, a deserted village unfit for vehicular traffic.

over long distances hazardous. But oddly enough, it was not the farmers who agitated for better roads —but more restless members of a free-moving society —Americans on the go, starting with the cycle groups and followed by the early motorists, indignant at the condition of the country's roads.

In the year 1900 seven states inaugurated highway departments. The United States Office of Road Inquiry, which had been in existence, though inactive, commenced to prod the states to provide better roads. Information on road building was widely disseminated. Agricultural colleges, influential with the farmers, did their share in awakening the farmers to the need for improved roads. In 1904 the Office of Road Inquiry was reorganized, and published a highway census showing some two million miles of roads. Of this total mileage, all but 150,000 miles were unimproved. Of the small fraction in better condition, most roads were surfaced with gravel and only 250 miles, apart from city streets, were paved.

The cost of macadam roads (fine broken stone, rolled and smoothed with oil) ranged from three to five thousand dollars for a 15 foot ribbon of roadway. Most highway engineers of this period could not foresee the coming of the motor and therefore maintained that a twelve foot road was sufficient for two vehicles to pass.

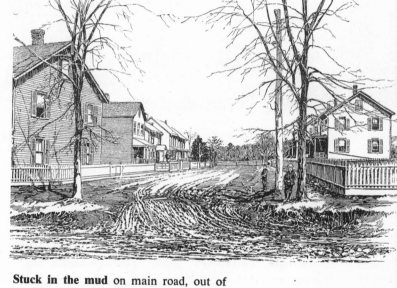

Stuck in the mud on main road, out of Cleveland, these beasts of burden find the going too rough.

Team of horses rest awhile before renewing the struggle against knee-high mud.

Harlem Lane, Sunday afternoon, as sketched by Stanley Fox in 1868. The celebrated trotting course was the scene of animated races between rival horse-fanciers in uptown New York.

HORSES AND HOOF-BEATS

Nowhere was there such a massed concentration of horses as could be found in certain sections of New York City, particularly along Third Avenue near Twenty-fourth Street. The area developed into "the greatest horse-market on the world", to quote *Scribner's Monthly* of January, 1879, a center where dealers, stables and exchanges lined the streets for blocks around. The locality seethed with animals and wheeled conveyances, milling about and charging the air with an aroma of horsy smells unmistakable at any time of the day or season. It was always an exciting experience to watch the sharp-eyed horse trader who could tell from a cursory examination the animal's character and capabilities. Here, one saw a team of heavy percheron stallions being considered for hauling a huge brewery truck—a smartly clad gentleman studying a pair of thoroughbreds as a possible acquisition to his racing stable—a Shetland pony to draw a handsome wagonette for some lucky children. There were dapple-grays, chestnut fillies, roan Clydesdales, sorrel geldings, mares, mules, trotters and pacers—any type of horse the eager trader might be angling for. Grooms were busy with curry combs, while others looped or braided tails or straightened manes to set their ani-

mal off to best advantage. The scene was an unforgettable one, belonging to an era of equine supremacy. This was the day of the horse—who could doubt that his dominion would last forever?

Up in Central Park, designed for pleasure and recreation, the smart set and plebian met on common ground. In fine weather the park became a vast parade ground where the wealthy strutted the pride of their stables and the spectator looked on with awe and envy. Central Park, two and a half miles long, boasted ten miles of perfect carriage roads and five miles of bridal paths. The carriage parade, a notable sight of the city and a "must" for out-of-towners, took place between four and five in the afternoon. The procession of fancy equipages brought out everyone including the aristocracy, the parvenus, celebrities of the stage and those who came to see how the other half of the world lived.

Further to the north another exhibition of horseflesh could be witnessed on Harlem Lane, where trotting races were held in good season. Trotting, a universal mania of the day, held a peculiar fascination for most New Yorkers. Wealthy horse-fanciers drove their curricles and sulkies, drawn by long, lanky, gawky-looking horses, their pride and joy, not at all like the sleek, showy, caparisoned animals that figured so prominently in the carriage parade.

The Horse Market, Bull's Head, New York, as drawn by
A. R. Waud for *Harper's Weekly,* in 1869. Traders and
buyers from all over the country made this the
largest horse center in the world.

This 1870 lithograph by Currier and Ives depicts Harlem Lane
in upper Manhattan. In the foreground Commodore
Vanderbilt with his team races publisher Bonner with "Dexter."

Along West Street, New York, the open delivery wagons brought produce from nearby farms to commission merchants located at or near the marketplace.

WAGONS AND WHARVES

Nowhere in the great sprawling metropolis that called itself New York was there a busier, more hectic area of endless excitement and traffic confusion than on the long streets bordering the waterfront. Along the East River from Pike Street on the south to Fourteenth Street on the north, the river was alive with "express lines" of clipper ships sailing for all parts of the world. Many graceful vessels were bound for the California coast by way of Cape Horn—a long voyage done in the record time of ninety-six days. New Yorkers spoke with pride and romantic emotion about the adventurous trip to the west, in ships controlled by Manhattan's merchant princes whose lines reached ports of India, Java and Sumatra. Along West Street facing the Hudson, the many wharves docked boats bound for Boston, Providence, Baltimore and Savannah. Interspersed, were the numerous ferry slips to accommodate commuter traffic between New York and Jersey points.

Dead axle drays were in common use to haul crates and bales in the city. Could be built to any length and had load capacity up to four tons, if drawn by a team.

South Street, riverside thoroughfare facing the East River, where bowsprits of picturesque clipper ships pointed threateningly over the heads of horses and drivers, delivering crates to ship chandler shops and wharves. Scene in 1878 prompted Walt Whitman to refer to this as "mast-hemmed Manhattan."

Gansevoort Market, near West 12th Street and Washington Street, New York, in 1890. Since earlier times this had been known as the "Farmer's Market," specializing in produce.

Trucking traffic under the Brooklyn Bridge, New York, paralyzed by snow-covered streets in mid-winter. Barrels and casks are carried in drays with chain-linked stakes along sides, transfer and merchandise drays carry heavier crates, while canvas-topped express wagons transport assorted boxes and smaller parcels.

"The countless masts, the white shore-steamers,
    the lighters, the ferry-boats, the
    black sea-steamers, well modl'd,
The down-town streets, the jobbers' houses
    of business, the houses of business of the
    ship-merchants and money-brokers,
    the river streets,
Immigrants arriving, fifteen or twenty
    thousand a week,
The carts hauling goods, the manly race of
    drivers of horses, the brown-faced sailors . . ."
                        Walt Whitman

71

"TO MARKET, TO MARKET..."

The markets of a great metropolis like New York City have a romantic history as old as Manhattan itself. As far back as 1635 the stout Dutch burghers under Governor Wouter Van Twiller ceased to be mere Indian traders living on the fruits of barter. The West India Company, who owned New Amsterdam and managed it as a closed corporation, opened a general provision store with prices listed. The leading citizens were cattle dealers and market gardeners, and from such humble beginnings the intricate market system developed.

Washington and Fulton, New York's largest markets, are household words throughout the nation. Fulton Market opened in 1821, the successor of the Old Vley or Fly Market, extended along the East River on either side of Maiden Lane. It was convenient for the fishing boats which docked nearby, as well as ferries that connected with Brooklyn and Long Island where much of the farm produce was grown. Washington Market, successor to the Old Bear Market originally built in 1772, moved to its present site in 1813. As the city grew, it was enlarged to accommodate the increased business. The New West Washington Market was overhauled and modernized in 1888, its plan including lanes of stalls where meats, fish, fruits, vegetables, groceries and specialties were sold in sections apart from one another.

During the dark hours of early morning, as hundreds of wagons of all descriptions converge upon the market regions, pandemonium reigns as traffic chokes the thoroughfares for blocks around. *Harper's Weekly,* in its December 29, 1888 issue, reported

Quincy Market, Boston, as with other large metropolitan centers, re-enacts the same scene . . . confusion of wagons and pedestrians headed in any direction . . . accidents and affrays were frequent. *From Harper's 1882.*

"the downtown streets were taken possession of, from this rustic invasion, which was as relentless as the grip of an octopus. The mayor's office was for years bombarded with complaints and reproaches that such important avenues of traffic should be choked up by the huge produce vans, even for a limited period in the morning."

Life in the marketplace begins to seethe shortly after midnight as the wagons approach. Each driver is anxious for the pick of the best place, the best prices and the desire to unload and be gone, and in this aspect rivalry often results in bloody noses. Many of the vans are bulky, measuring twenty-five

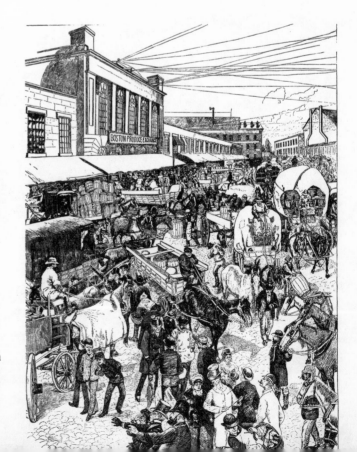

feet long and ten feet high. Such a load is drawn by four horses, with several farm hirelings on hand to unload in jig time. "The business of the Clerk of the Market," continues *Harper's,* "to collect the twenty-five cent fee from each waggoner, is no sinecure. The tax is often exacted at the expense of ugly language freely spilt by the elusive brutes who man the trucks. They have to be pursued in many cases into the lowest dives before the reluctant quarter satisfies the toll. When the waggoner cheats the city it costs his employer nothing and means drink-money." A more picturesque, more thrilling chapter of early city history is difficult to find.

Newly built market called the New West Washington Market replaced old sheds with stone and brick stalls, separated by arches and leading to avenues of shops. Produce wagons outside have wide, overhanging bodies to carry bigger loads, Dec. 1888.

Upper left: **Washington Market,** New York, as sketched by Stanley Fox, in 1866, a group "of low, straggling sheds, divided into irregular lanes and stalls, where order is impossible and cleanliness nearly so."

New Fulton Market, New York, opened in 1882. Located in lower Manhattan on the East River, it became the principal center for fresh fish delivered by the Atlantic fleet, with wharves nearby.

BROADWAY TO TWENTY-THIRD STREET

The transit needs of the growing metropolis resulted in a network of stage lines criss-crossing the city in a crazy-quilt pattern. The important north and south thoroughfares were, naturally, the first to receive service, followed by crosstown streets like Grand, Fourteenth and Twenty-third Streets. The most-traveled of all the lines was the all-important Broadway line starting at South Ferry, proceeding northward through busy Wall Street, thence over to Broadway and up along a portion of Ninth Avenue eventually reaching Twenty-third Street, which at about the mid-century mark represented the northern extremity of the populated area of Manhattan.

The Broadway buses, besides being the busiest, were the cause of much protest because of the recklessness of their drivers. Rivals would race to a corner at which stood a single fare, as buses swayed with wild abandon. Shouts of anger and strong language would follow, as the successful driver took off with the lone passenger. Such a race always

John Stephenson built hundreds of omnibuses like this, and afterwards became the world's largest builder of horsecars and trolleys.

Broadway at Maiden Lane, to the right, shows the many signs plastered on commercial buildings and overhead telephone and telegraph lines. From a lithograph by J. J. Fogarty, 1880.

aroused the ire of passengers, though the onlooking spectators on the sidewalks found much occasion to watch with interest and glee. Small boys, with a special fondness for sitting alongside the driver and a secret yearning for the day when they might also graduate into this favored position, would occasionally find an affable driver who happily would grant their heart's desire.

As the Broadway omnibus passed along its familiar route it encountered conditions of traffic congestion, the worst that New York had to offer. Wall Street was always in a turmoil as so much of its exchange business was conducted from the street. Turning into Broadway near Trinity Church, the bus found its going slow indeed. The clutter of many buses, the number of vehicles of all types and the hordes of pedestrians trying to cross at important street intersections made travel a constant adventure of narrow escapes and near-accidents. From Fulton north, into the plaza opening up into what is now City Hall Park, was a danger zone of the worst kind. The opening of the new Post Office, in the '80's, only added to the wild confusion.

Broadway and Park Row, in front of the newly built Post Office, shows streams of omnibuses and vehicles flowing in all directions.

Looking down Maiden Lane from Broadway, the omnibuses and mail trucks vie for the right-of-way at busy cross streets. Jewelry firms solidly occupied this district for almost a century.

Wall Street in front of Sub-Treasury Building during a financial panic, May 14, 1884, shows frantic crowds and snarled traffic, with Broadway buses brought to a standstill.

Sunday morning on a Fifth Avenue omnibus in 1895, as painted by G. W. Joy. Car card advertisements made their appearance at an early date.

UP FIFTH AVENUE TO EIGHTY-SECOND STREET

Street railway interests, riding the crest of a popular wave in the 1880's, made a strong bid for laying tracks on New York's most fashionable thoroughfare. Fortunately for the residents and property owners, such a "street grabbing scheme" as reported in *Harper's Weekly,* was blocked and the "obnoxious street cars were banned in favor of the Fifth Avenue Transportation Company, Ltd. The company proposes to operate an omnibus line over Fifth Avenue from Bleecker Street station of the elevated road, on South Fifth Avenue to Eighty-second Street." The new bus line followed the northward expansion of the city, and the movement of leading mercantile establishments into the Fifth Avenue section. From this point on, an address on this smart shopping street became a mark of distinction and envy.

European visitors to Gotham were shocked by the manners of bus-riding New Yorkers. One irate Frenchman, giving his impressions in *Revue des Deux Mondes* related strange tales, some grossly exaggerated: "It was the practice of ladies, on entering a crowded Fifth Avenue omnibus to seat themselves on the knees of the gentlemen already placed. There were well-dressed, well-bred New Yorkers clinging to straps, jaded, jammed, jostled, panting in the aisle of these hearselike equipages, to reach their goal. The average man spent an hour or more going to and from business, thereby losing an immense amount of time. And wasn't time money?"

The new fleet of buses was to number fifty at the start, to run at block and a half intervals, and to charge five cents for the trip. The upper seats on the buses proved favorites with both young and old.

New Fifth Avenue omnibus as approved and put into operation in 1885. Color scheme: black body, blue panels, running-gear red—it was designed to resemble private conveyance.

Looking north on Fifth Avenue and Thirty-fourth Street. At the left, the Waldorf-Astoria. Interspersed with buses may be seen hansom cabs, electric cabs and an occasional auto, in 1904.

Fifth Avenue and Thirty-fifth Street, looking south, in the 1880's. Within a decade the Waldorf-Astoria was to rise near this point.

Private cabs and hacks also made their appearance on the avenue. Many a smart New Yorker with his private stable, preferred the cab to the crowded omnibus.

This chariot street car, a patented bus with double doors opening at the rear with speedier entrance and exit facilities, made a bid for the avenue passengers.

COACHING DAYS AND COACHING WAYS

The Start with a Fresh Team, as drawn by Max F. Klepper for *Harper's*, August 24, 1895. Many fine four-in-hands were driven by the ladies—with escort and footmen always in attendance.

For those who could afford the luxury of coaching, there was nothing to compare with the thrill of holding the reins and snapping the whip at a pair of high-stepping prancers or a team in tandem. For those who could not, there was the sound of the distant bugle-note, the approaching cloud of dust as the bright red coach and its merry passengers came whirling by.

The drag or tally-ho was very different from the stage-coach. It was built to provide each passenger with a comfortable seat on top, affording an unobstructed view. The interior was reserved for servants, champagne and luncheon baskets. Twelve people including driver could be accommodated on top. The guard, with long brass bugle, sat in the rear to one side. A few notes on the bugle was the signal for the start or finish of a trip. Gentlemen of the Coaching Club wore bottle-green cutaway coats with brass buttons and high white hats. As the coach stopped to pick up a fair passenger, a little iron ladder was suspended from the side, and the footman, in shining livery, stood guard as many hands escorted the new arrival to her elevated seat above.

Maintaining a coach and four involved not only the costly coach but a quartette of handsome animals, carefully selected. Two footmen were needed to keep everything in running order — in fact, on bad stretches of road they did almost as much running as the horses.

Opening of the Coaching Season at Hyde Park, London, set the pace for American standards. Coaches, costumes, grooms, harnessing were identical on both sides of the Atlantic. From a drawing by John Charlton, 1892.

A Drive through Central Park, drawn by Schell and Hogan for *Harper's Weekly,* June 12, 1880. Mounted policeman keeps crowds in hand, as parade of celebrities passes by.

DRIVING FOR PLEASURE AND PRESTIGE

At the conclusion of the Reconstruction Era following the Civil War, the industrial revolution in America was beginning to show handsome profits. A growing moneyed class reaped the biggest benefits, spawning a society in which the amenities of better living included larger homes and domestic staffs, liveried grooms and pleasure vehicles. The emergence of this group became the nucleus of a new "carriage trade", a term loosely applied, with some measure of opprobrium, to those who could afford the best.

Throughout the land, especially noticeable in the leading cities, coteries of wealthy enthusiasts supported a number of coaching clubs and societies. The principal delight of the select membership was to sponsor driving meets and get-togethers, and show off their fine conveyances to best advantage. Gold cups and blue ribbon prizes played their part, along with the prestige of belonging. From this higher echelon of society down, the pleasurable sport of driving touched many middle-class families who could afford a carriage or two. It was mainly this group in their surreys, runabouts and buggies whose carriages dotted the thoroughfares of the city and countryside, from the closing years of the last century well into the first decade of the present. The urge to drive and be seen in a fine carriage, was a burning ambition in thousands of homes. It fostered an ever prosperous carriage industry and led to the opening of fine boulevards for drives.

A Spring Day on Riverside Drive, New York, from a lithograph by Thulstrup, 1900. Fashionable phaeton is followed by electric Locomobile near Grant's Tomb.

Victoria carriage was very popular for park driving, especially in the 1890's. Carriage built by Studebaker. Drawing by Gray-Parker.

80

The Coney Island Concourse, as drawn by Schell and Hogan for *Harper's Weekly, August 4, 1877.* With the widespread popularity of carriage driving the Park Com-missioners extended the King's Highway road from the Fair Grounds to Coney Island, thus affording a "delightful carriage-way to the sea."

In fashionable Brooklyn, victorias with footman were numerous. Long drives through parks and down to Coney Island afforded much pleasure.

This Spider Surrey with fringed top, used for family groups of four or five, was in popular demand from about 1880 to 1910.

TANDEM AND TALLY-HO!

At Jerome Park, Westchester, on racing day, 1886. Built by Leonard Jerome for the American Jockey Club in 1866, this park was modeled after the British pattern and became the scene for exhibitions of the finest in horseflesh.

The Coaching Club was organized by prominent New Yorkers of wealth and leisure led by Colonel William Jay, Leonard Jerome, De Lancey Kane and others who wished to establish four-in-hand driving as a fashionable sport. To these gentlemen and their host of enthusiastic followers "form" was as important as "family"—the observance of fine points of decorum became an obsession: a driver's apron, when not in use, was to be folded outside out; artificial flowers must be affixed to the throat-latch of every horse.

The cult of coaching, as it had been practiced in England for centuries, became one of the most ele-gant diversions of the elite—if a man aspired to any position of social leadership he must first achieve mastery as an amateur whip. Kane, an ambitious sportsman, introduced an astonishing new practice by driving his coach and four from Madison Square to a Westchester country club where he and his guests lunched, afterward driving to the city. He called his equipage the "Tally-ho" thus providing a generic name that soon became the adopted reference for the huge, handsome display coaches.

Many of these scenes of bustling activity centered around Madison Square. Here, and in nearby areas,

Park coach or drag, at left, built about 1890. Box on the roof called an "imperial" used when going to races, carried an outing luncheon. Sketch, above, by Gray-Parker.

Roof-seat break, c. 1890, was the popular alternative to the heavier park drag. In the lower body it stored bottle racks, cane basket, folding ladder and luncheon baskets.

Opening of the coaching season, starting out at Madison Square, New York, in 1883, as sketched by H. A. Ogden for *Harper's Weekly*. Many park drags and tally-hos in the parade, while at the right center may be seen one of the new Fifth Avenue omnibuses.

Parade of the New York Coaching Club, passing up Fifth Avenue, May 23, 1885. Fine quartette of prancing horses, trained for capers, puts on a magnificent show as the lead coach, headed for Central Park, sets the pace.

were located the Hotel Brunswick, the Holland House, the Hoffman House, the old Union Club at Twenty-first Street and, later on, the Waldorf-Astoria at Thirty-fourth Street and Fifth Avenue. From these clubs and hotels of approved station, members of the coaching fraternity gathered to proceed up the Avenue to Central Park, entering at Fifty-ninth Street. With the passing years, the city became accustomed to this exhibition of finery and ostentation, as the art of coaching flourished and its vogue was accepted by the large crowds of gaping sidewalk spectators always on hand.

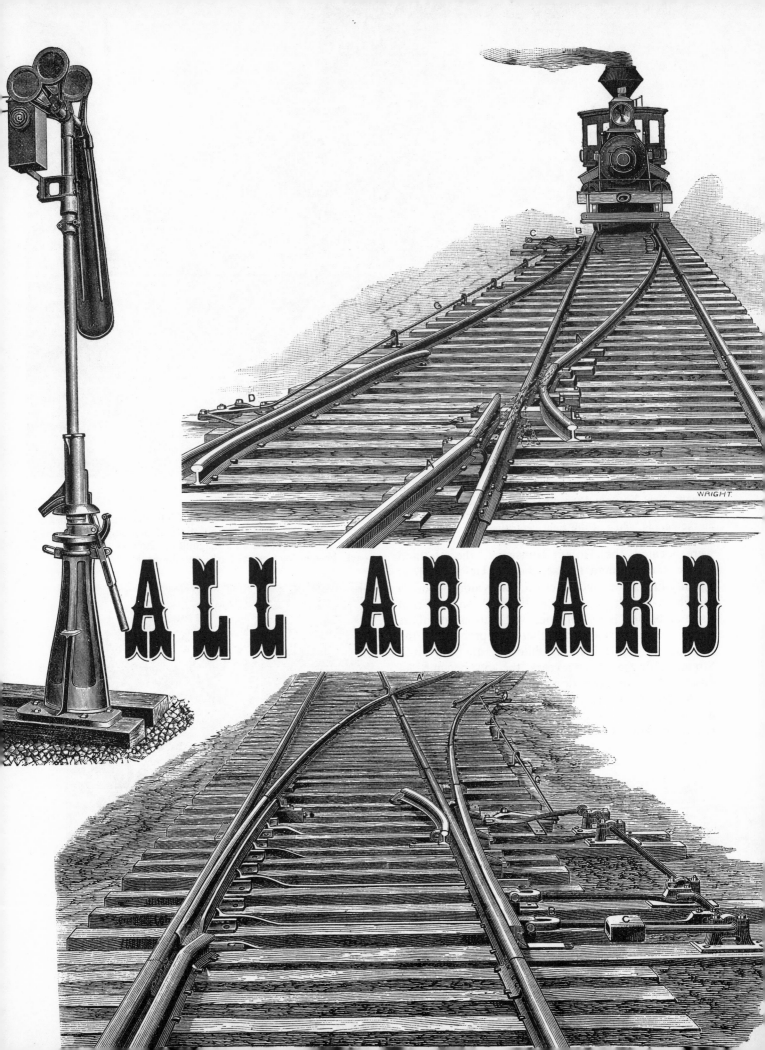

ALL ABOARD

THE WHISTLE SHRIEKS . . . the slow grind of wheels, the groan and grunt of steam, and off she goes. The dream of Watt and Newcomen, Stephenson and Stevens, Baldwin and Pullman . . . the heartbreak of some, the death of others, the prize of full measure for patient seekers and toilers.

THE IRON HORSE belching fierce clouds of black smoke . . . buffalo herds thundering in its wake. Emblem of beauty and power, symphony in steel . . . Camel-back, Mogul, Consolidation . . . huge driver-wheels relentless in pursuit of time and space.

ONWARD ACROSS THE PLAINS, the workers sweating and swearing to span a continent . . . bridging the angry gorge, tunneling through stone and granite to link East and West, one nation indivisible, interlaced with iron . . . composite, cohesive, united . . . many in one.

SWIFT CARRIER OF MAN and merchandise, conveyor-belt to the marketplace . . . speeding the mails, parcels and packages, produce of soil and product of mine, fresh fruits from sunny lands . . . in welcome abundance. Its multi-powered magic builds hamlets into cities, settlements into commonwealths, small enterprises into vast industrial empires.

FAREWELL TO STEAM and fiery steed . . . their sounds and smells, whooo-whooo's and friendly bells fast disappearing down the corridor of the ages . . . time-honored . . . long-remembered. *Requiescat in pace.*

THE "GENERAL" · 1862

EIGHT WHEEL PASSENGER LOCOMOTIVE · 1876

THE "DE WITT CLINTON" · 1831

TEN WHEEL DOUBLE=ENDER LOCOMOTIVE · 1883

Experimental railway and locomotive, built by Colonel John Stevens in 1825, operated on circular track on his Hoboken estate.

The Rack Rail, Stevens' engine, had cogged wheels and rails. The wheels were ordinary wagon wheels. Used for demonstration.

"Railways are strips of oak plank, the wheels made to fit the rails. In this way one horse can haul nearly three times the weight that he could manage on a common road." (Editorial in the *Philadelphia Aurora,* January, 1801)

THE FIRST PRACTICAL INVENTORS

Many exceptional men—Thomas Savery, Newcomen, and James Watt in England; Oliver Evans and others in America—had evolved more or less crude versions of steam engines, and some of these had been tested by use in coal mines, grain mills, river dredging, as well as on the land, before 1800.

Colonel John Stevens—scion of an outstandingly wealthy New York family, graduate of King's College in 1768, and an ornament to Colonial society —became an ardent believer in the value of steam as a motive force. He had seen various trial demonstrations where the equipment was crude and the construction had been done by self-taught men with slim, or no financial resources, and he started to make experiments of his own. In 1783—a year after his marriage, and the end of the Revolutionary War —he bought a great estate in a place called Hoboken, across the Hudson from New York City. Impatient with the ferry service, he purchased the line and, in the 1790's, had put his improved steam engines into boats and scows which kept afloat and attained four miles an hour. In 1825, when he was well past 70, he had built a steam locomotive which he operated on a circular track constructed on his Hoboken estate. In 1830, John Stevens still busied himself promoting the use of steam locomotives. New Jersey, in 1815, had granted him the first charter for a steam railroad; before 1820 he had obtained several other such licenses, and had started the Camden and Amboy Rail Road and Transportation Company. But his was not the first such line in America. A few years earlier several men, influenced by his ideas, had built four steam engine roads: the South Carolina Canal and Railroad Company; the Mohawk and Hudson; the Baltimore and Ohio; and the Delaware and Hudson.

George Stephenson, the English inventor, was born in 1781—more than 30 years after Stevens, and with a totally different background. The son of a fireman of a colliery engine at Wylam, near New-

The first "trains" on the Baltimore and Ohio Railroad were horse-drawn, operating on 13 miles of road between Baltimore and Ellicott Mills, Maryland. The trains started in 1829.

castle, he had worked first as a cowherd, then drove a colliery "gin-horse." At 14, he earned a shilling a day as assistant fireman to his father; at 17, he was the "plugman," attending a pumping engine. He had not yet learned to read but, eager to study the inventions of James Watt, he attended night school and made rapid progress. An engineman at Willington Quay at 21, he was engine-wright of the High Pit two years later, at a salary of £100 a year. When Stephenson was authorized in 1813 to build a "traveling engine" for use on the tramroads between the colliery and the port, nine miles off, his engine the "Blucher" made a successful trial in July, 1814. Eight years later, he urged the directors of the Stockton and Darlington railway, then being built, to use steam instead of animal traction. When the road was opened, September 1825, the first public passenger train in the world was drawn by Stephenson's locomotive "Active," afterward renamed "Locomotion."

Later, Stephenson was employed on the Liverpool and Manchester railway and here again he persuaded its directors to give the steam locomotive a trial. They offered a prize of £500 for a suitable machine and, in the Rainhill trials, October 1829, Stephenson's engine, "The Rocket," was chosen. Two years later, when the road was formally opened, it employed eight engines built by Stephenson at his Newcastle works which he and two associates had started in 1823.

John Stevens had never doubted that the steam engine rail road was the one means by which America's unsettled frontier could be profitably opened for development. In 1813, when the New York Canal Commission was planning the great canal across New York State, Stevens wrote that a steam-powered rail road could be built at much less cost. However, the canal was constructed and had already played its powerful part in making New York America's greatest harbor, before the steam locomotive, a score of years later, threatened water-borne transportation with competition.

The Delaware and Hudson Canal Company sent Horatio Allen to England in 1828, to explore the possible use of a steam engine to replace horses on its Carbondale mine tram line. Allen was present at the Rainhill trials, saw Stephenson's "Rocket" demonstrate its pulling power, and purchased another English locomotive, the *Stourbridge Lion*. This passed all tests successfully, but proved too heavy for the American tracks.

Stephenson's engine "America," ordered for the Delaware and Hudson Canal Company, 1828: "first practical locomotive in U.S."

The Stourbridge Lion, purchased in England by Horatio Allen, for the Delaware and Hudson Canal Company. A huge lion's head was emblazoned on the front of the boiler.

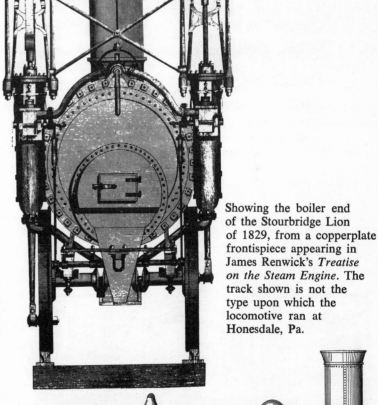

Showing the boiler end of the Stourbridge Lion of 1829, from a copperplate frontispiece appearing in James Renwick's *Treatise on the Steam Engine*. The track shown is not the type upon which the locomotive ran at Honesdale, Pa.

Thrilling trial between Mr. Peter Cooper's locomotive *"Tom Thumb,"* and one of Stockton and Stoke's horse-cars, on the Baltimore and Ohio Railroad, August 28, 1830. As the train passed the horse-car, there was wild excitement.

The spirited race between the "Tom Thumb" and the galloping horse occurred between Baltimore and Relay, Maryland. One of a series of historical paintings by H. D. Stitt.

Peter Cooper's little locomotive weighed less than one ton and had a boiler about the size of a flour-barrel.

AMERICA'S FIRST TRAINS ON TRACKS

When "rail road" was mentioned, around 1825, most Americans thought of a carriage on wheels, drawn on rails by one or more horses. In 1830, engineers were busy constructing such roads with wooden rails, often overlaying these with iron plates to increase their serviceability. The rails, it was said, would enable the horses to pull greater loads, and would reduce the jolts and jars suffered by the passengers.

About 1837, a school text book: Peter Parley's *First Book of History,* said in its chapter on Maryland: "The most curious thing at Baltimore is the railroad. I must tell you that there is a great trade between Baltimore and the states west of the Allegheny Mountains. The western people buy a great many goods at Baltimore, and send in return a great deal of western produce. There is, therefore, a vast deal of travel back and forth, and hundreds of teams are constantly occupied in transporting goods and produce to and from market." The illustration accompanying this intelligence showed a Conestoga wagon drawn by six horses. The history continued: "Now, in order to carry on all this business more easily, the people are building what is called a rail road. This consists of iron bars laid along the ground, and made fast, so that carriages with small wheels may run along them with facility. In this way, one horse will be able to draw as much as ten horses on a common road. A part of this rail road is already done, and if you choose to take a ride upon it, you can do so. You will mount a car, something like a stage, and then you will be drawn along by two horses, at the rate of twelve miles an hour." This was the early Baltimore and Ohio, which had started laying its rails in 1829 . . . as described six years later.

When the Delaware and Hudson Canal Company first operated the rail road from its canal at Honesdale, Penna., to its coal mines at Carbondale, both horses and stationary engines were being used. It was for this road that Horatio Allen had been sent

The **"Best Friend"** of the South Carolina Railroad, first locomotive built in the United States for actual railroad service. Shown with military detail on its first excursion trip, January 1831.

to England, "the only place where a locomotive was then in daily operation." Mr. Allen, a civil engineer who had worked on the New York State Canal, ordered the "Lion" from a locomotive works at Stourbridge, and two more locomotives from Stephenson's works in Newcastle. Allen had personally demonstrated the "Stourbridge Lion" on the Delaware and Hudson's tram way, saying that there was "no need to risk the life of more than one." Since there was, as yet, no unanimous opinion as to the advantages of locomotives over horses, Allen also reported to the South Carolina Railway Company that he was influenced in favor of the locomotive "on the broad ground that in the future there was no reason to expect any material improvement in the breed of horses, while, in my judgment, the man was not living who knew what the breed of locomotives was to place at our command."

About 1830, Peter Cooper had experimented with a little locomotive on the Baltimore and Ohio Railroad. Gleefully, 45 years later, he related to a meeting of the Master Mechanics' Association of New York, how he had beaten another car, drawn by a horse!

Horse-power locomotive on treadmill invented by C. E. Detmole, captured first prize of $500 offered by the South Carolina Railroad.

The **"West Point,"** made its first gala excursion trip, March 1831, on the South Carolina Railroad. Cotton bales safeguard the musicians.

BOXES AND COACHES ON WHEELS

Much of the romance and glamor of the early stage-coaches could be seen in the early railroad coaches. The driver on his box, the side entrance door, the seats inside with passengers facing one another . . . all traced their lineage directly to the horse-drawn coaches that had for centuries raced and rumbled on the roads of England and the Continent, and along the post-roads of Colonial America. Horace Porter, in his chapter on Railway Passenger Travel, published in *The American Railway,* 1887, said: "The modern railway car has been evolved from the old-fashioned English stage-coach. England still retains the railway carriage divided into compartments that bear a close resemblance inside and out, to stage-coach bodies with the middle seat omitted. Old prints of the first railway carriages reveal them as substantially stage-coach bodies mounted on car wheels, such as appeared in 1831 on the Mohawk and Hudson cars, where two coach bodies were coupled together. After the double truck system was adopted, three coach-like bodies were constructed as one coach." The next step was the development of the rectangular car, pioneer in shape of the present day railway coaches. "The railroad was a decided step in advance," Horace Porter wrote, "compared with the stage-coach and canal-boat, but when we picture the surroundings of the traveler upon railways in the first ten or fifteen years of their existence, we find his journey was not to be envied. He was jammed into a narrow seat with a stiff back, the deck of the car was low and flat, and ventilation in winter was impossible. A stove at each end did little more than generate carbon oxide. The passenger roasted if he sat at the end of the car, and froze if he sat in the middle. Tallow candles furnished a 'dim religious light,' but the accompanying odor did not savor of cathedral incense. The dust was suffocating."

For the four-wheel car, the early American car-builders patterned after the English, employing

wheelwrights and carriage-makers. All, on both continents, labored under the fallacy that the equipment and rolling stock should be as light as possible, to save wear and tear on the rails. The early railway carriages either had no covering at all, or they had light tops of canvas or leather, like road-wagons and stage-coaches. But open carriages were not long used here.

The short curves of American roads compelled the abandonment of the four-wheeled car with rigid axles and, at an early date, the *bogie* or swivel truck was introduced, along with the lengthening of the car body.

Typical early railway carriages, here illustrated, are, counter clockwise: 1) *Passenger car* hauled by Peter Cooper's *Tom Thumb* in its victorious race on the Baltimore and Ohio; 2) *Sail car* designed by a mechanic. Tried out on the Baltimore and Ohio but, as it could not tack against the wind, it was soon discontinued. 3) *The Flying Dutchman,* horse treadmill geared to the axles. Winner of a $500 prize for the best horse-motor car, it was very successful . . . one horse could draw a carload of 20 passengers at 20 miles an hour. 4) *Two coach-like cars* hauled by the locomotive *De Witt Clinton,* on the formal opening of the Mohawk and Hudson road, July, 1831. 5) *English-built* small car for use on a mine road in Nova Scotia, 1838; it carried four passengers. 6) *Bogie car* with a center aisle, used on the Baltimore and Ohio, 1835. 7) *First carriage* in the world constructed exclusively for passenger traffic, Stephenson's design for the Stockton and Darlington Railway, England, 1825. 8) *Hoboken-built* car, used on the Camden and Amboy road, 1831, first drawn by horses at breakneck speed between Bordentown and South Amboy, a distance of 35 miles, with relays every 8 or 10 miles. 9) *Horse-drawn* passenger car *Ohio,* used on the Baltimore and Ohio Railroad, September 1830.

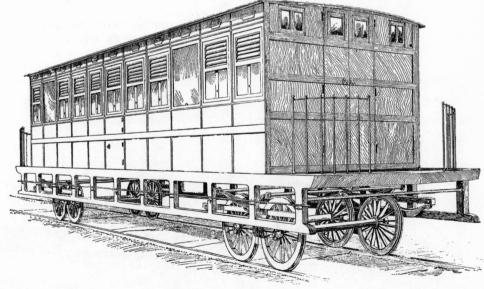

The John Bull was originally constructed in 1831 for the historic Camden & Amboy Railroad, now a part of the Pennsylvania Railroad. Now preserved in the Smithsonian Institution.

The De Witt Clinton, third locomotive engine built in America, and train of coaches. First trip of 14 miles from Albany to Schenectady was made on August 9, 1831.

THE "JOHN BULL"...1831

John Stevens' son, Robert, who was president and chief engineer of the Camden and Amboy road, went to England in the Fall of 1830, to buy rails, track equipment, and a locomotive. To pass the time on shipboard, he whittled several models of improved rails, including that known today as the T rail; he also designed a hook-headed spike. In England, he ordered from the Stephenson works a locomotive, called the *John Bull.* It was shipped by the packet *Allegheny* from Liverpool to Philadelphia, and taken by sloop to Bordentown, N. J. A young mechanic, Isaac Dripps—who is said never before to have seen an engine, and who lacked drawings to guide him—successfully assembled the parts in a shed near the Bordentown track. The *John Bull* had

been constructed with the usual square front-end of an English locomotive but, in America, where cattle and horses were likely to wander on the tracks, the engineers provided it with its much-talked-about "cow-catcher." This had been mounted on an extra axle to the front of the engine, to clear the way.

The *John Bull,* "with a construction car as a tender and an apple-whiskey barrel for a water tank," hauled a train of cars, exhibited to the New Jersey Legislature in November, 1831, as the kind of conveyance which Stevens proposed to use, if the authorities of the state should see fit to grant them the "exclusive privileges" of a railway across the state. These exclusive privileges were enjoyed for over 50 years. The *John Bull* was last under steam at the Chicago Exposition, 1883.

Cowcatcher on the John Bull engine was credited to Isaac Dripps. This device to clear the tracks of stray animals was a distinctly American invention.

THE "De WITT CLINTON"...1831

Built at the West Point Foundry Works for the Mohawk and Hudson Railroad, the *DeWitt Clinton* was the third successful locomotive constructed in America. It was put into experimental service in July, 1831, and made its first excursion trip, August 9, 1831, with a train of passenger coaches from Albany to Schenectady—a distance of about 15 miles in 46 minutes. Horse-drawn rail cars traveled the same distance in one and a quarter hours. One of the excursion passengers, William H. Brown, roughly sketched the "singular-looking affair and its equally singular-looking appendages" before boarding the train. He later presented to the Connecticut Historical Society a "profile or black outline". . . which silhouette was pronounced a truthful representation

of the train and correct likenesses of the engineer and passengers represented in the cars. The cars, or coaches as they were then called, were the old-fashioned stage-coach type, with a driver's seat on the outside at either end.

William H. Brown's "profile or black outline" of the proud *DeWitt Clinton* hauling its tender and two coaches was used forty-two years later as an illustration by the Chicago, Rock Island & Pacific Railroad as it proclaimed itself the best route to California and intervening cities. But, in 1831, it was being predicted that the railroads would kill the game, ruin the farmers, and that passengers would find it impossible to breathe in the rapidly-moving trains. The reproduction of a painting by E. L. Henry shows the opening run of the *DeWitt Clinton*.

Advertisement featuring silhouette of the De Witt Clinton train, as it appeared on handbill issued in 1873.

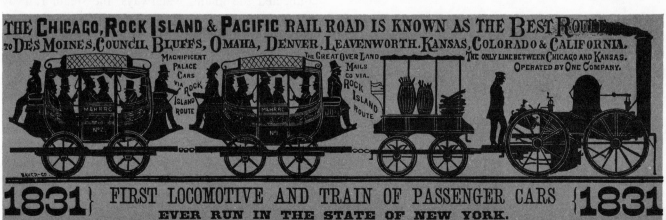

THE CHICAGO, ROCK ISLAND & PACIFIC RAIL ROAD IS KNOWN AS THE BEST ROUTE
TO DES MOINES, COUNCIL BLUFFS, OMAHA, DENVER, LEAVENWORTH, KANSAS, COLORADO & CALIFORNIA.

MAGNIFICENT PALACE CARS VIA ROCK ISLAND ROUTE

THE GREAT OVER LAND MAILS GO VIA ROCK ISLAND ROUTE

THE ONLY LINE BETWEEN CHICAGO AND KANSAS. OPERATED BY ONE COMPANY.

1831} FIRST LOCOMOTIVE AND TRAIN OF PASSENGER CARS {1831
EVER RUN IN THE STATE OF NEW YORK.

The first excursion trip with a train of passenger cars was made from Albany to Schenectady, on August 9th, 1831. Before the train started a sketch was made by an artist and original picture was presented by the artist to excursionists of that date are still alive and have stering of THE FINEST PALACE CARS IN

AS SEEN IN 1873.

cut out of black paper, as shown above. The the Connecticut Historical Society. Many of the pressed their broadcloth on the luxurious uphol-THE WORLD, which are built and run by the

Chicago, Rock Island & Pacific R.R. Co. bet.

Chicago, Omaha, Leavenworth & Atchison.

Old Ironsides, the first Baldwin locomotive, 1832, built for the Philadelphia, Germantown and Norristown Railway.

THE RAILROADS MEET THE PACKETS

Before the early 1830's, travelers who journeyed by packets on the rivers and canals, connected with the horse-drawn stagecoaches where it was necessary to go by land. On the route from Philadelphia to New York, it was customary for passengers to take the steam-boat at the old Chestnut Street Wharf in Philadelphia, making the trip of 27 miles up the Delaware to Bordentown, in about three hours. Then came the 35-mile drive across New Jersey, consuming four hours more, including a few minutes' stop for a horn of "apple-jack" or a "peach and brandy" while the horses were being changed; then a trip up the North River from South Amboy to the Battery in New York City, taking two hours more. Ten hours from city to city was considered fast time. Now, in many stretches where the stagecoach had connected the inland waterways, the steam railway was moving in.

Contemporary handbills published the packets' schedules and that of the connecting trains, pointing out that "by this arrangement there is no delay, as the Packets will leave . . . immediately after the arrival of the cars." Simultaneously with the Baltimore and Ohio, the New Castle and Frenchtown road was being constructed. Capitalists found the outlook for railways so promising that, before the close of 1831, the Legislatures of many states had passed enactments legalizing the construction of the roads within their borders, "designed to form a link in the grand

The Mississippi, 1834, for the Illinois Central, was at home on the Natchez and Hamburg road from 1836 to 1838.

Baltimore & Ohio Railroad's famous Atlantic locomotive
and two Imlay passenger coaches, in 1830.

chain of inter-communication with neighboring commonwealths."

Typical of the early locomotives was *Old Ironsides,* the first of many famous locomotives to be built by Matthias Baldwin, a Philadelphia jeweler. Baldwin had journeyed up to Bordentown in 1831, when the *John Bull*—imported for the Camden and Amboy—was being assembled, and is said to have been influenced in his meticulous design by Stephenson's locomotive. He was commissioned by the Philadelphia, Germantown and Norristown Railroad to build a locomotive for use on that line and, despite the lack of trained mechanics and proper tools, met with a good measure of success. *Old Ironsides* ran its trial trip November 23, 1832 and, a day later, the *Chronicle* said: 'It gives us pleasure to state that the locomotive engine built by our townsman, M. W. Baldwin, has proved highly successful. In the presence of several gentlemen of science and information on such subjects, the engine was yesterday placed upon the road for the first time. . . . The engine (with her tender) moved from the depot in beautiful style, working with great ease and uniformity. She proceeded . . . a distance of six miles, at a speed of about 28 miles an hour, her speed having been slackened at all grade crossings. It is needless to say that the spectators were delighted."

Old Ironsides went into regular service three days after her trial run. The carriages used were stagecoach types.

The Atlantic, built by Phineas Davis, a York, Pa., watchmaker
won the B. & O. competition for a steam engine, 1831.

Early railroad train consisting of locomotive (The English *Novelty* renamed the *Daedalus*), car with freight, carriage for passengers and a private carriage or horse-equipage mounted on a flat car—first indication of private cars of the future. From an engraving by A. J. Mason, 1832.

HAZARDS OF AN EARLY TRAIN RIDE

When Phineas Davis's "Atlantic" locomotive made her gala early runs on the Baltimore and Ohio, in the summer of 1832, she hauled double-decked Imlay coaches. One wonders as to the state of those dainty costumes, the large hats, and the awnings after a few miles. This train was the first to enter Washington, D. C., leading a procession of trains on August 24, 1835.

One Judge Gillis, who took his first train ride behind the "DeWitt Clinton" between Albany and Schenectady has left behind this account of his experiences: "The train was composed of coach-bodies placed upon trucks. The trucks were coupled together with chains. . . . There being no smoke or spark-catcher for the smokestack, a volume of black smoke, strongly impregnated with sparks, coals, and cinders, came pouring back the whole length of the train. Each of the outside passengers, who had an

umbrella, used it as a protection against the smoke and fire. They were found to be but a momentary protection, for I think in the first mile the last one went overboard, all having their covers burnt off, when a general melee took place among the deck passengers, each whipping his neighbor to put out the fire." The passenger car "Ohio," propelled by horses on the Baltimore and Ohio, September 1830, had "three seats for 12 passengers inside, one seat for three behind, and three could sit in front with the driver. Passengers could also climb to the top by a light ladder and occupy two longitudinal sofas back to back along the center of the top, where they were protected from falling off by the wire railing."

In his review of the evolution of passenger cars since the early 1830's, J. E. Watkins wrote in *Harper's Weekly*, August 25, 1888, "The car immediately behind the locomotive was laden with wool, so that the sparks from the wood fire would do no

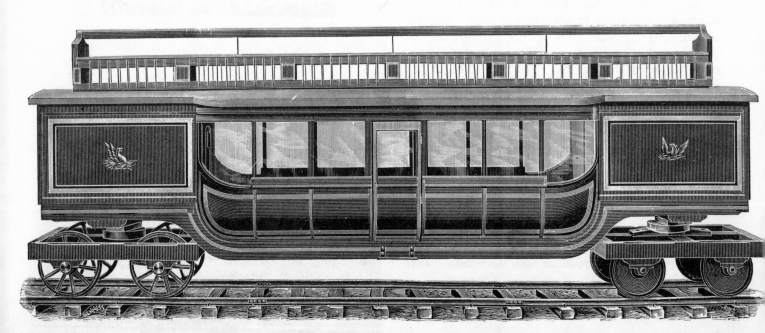

The Atlantic drawing two Imlay coaches with upper-deck accommodations under canopy, for 8 to 10 passengers. This train led a procession into Washington, D. C., in 1835.

damage. The three-bodied passenger car doubtless contains half a dozen politicians, discussing the question as to whether Clay, Jackson, or Wirt should be elected President in November. *'The rich who ride in chaises'* seem very comfortable as they glide along, occupying the family carriage, which in those days was much more comfortable than the passenger car, with its straight-backed seats.

"The 'horse-box,' with room for two horses, the groom, and one carriage, is quite an institution even in these days (1888), on English trains; and many of the American *bon-ton* take their horses and carriages on the same train with them from New York and Philadelphia to Long Branch and other fashionable resorts, the cost of putting 'a horse and carriage box' on an express train amounting to twenty or thirty single passenger fares." The Albany and Schenectady, and the Camden and Amboy had coaches with numbered seats, reserved in advance.

Forerunner of the modern passenger car, this is one of the earliest built in America, used on the Western Railroad of Massachusetts, later the Boston and Albany.

The first bogie passenger car with swiveling trucks at either end. Built for Pennsylvania Railroad, 1834.

Freight and passenger cars, in 1848. Jeffersonville, Madison and Indianapolis Railroad.

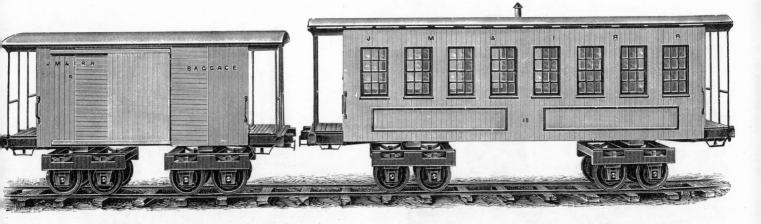

The **John Stevens,** 1825.

The first steam traction engine in the world was built by Oliver Evans, in 1804. Named the *Orukter Amphibolos,* it actually was amphibious—a thirty-foot scow mounted on wheels, the first vehicle in America that could move under its own power. Evans, apprentice at fourteen to a wagon-maker who discouraged his studies and forbade him the use of candles, persisted in educating himself nights by the uncertain light of wood shavings, saved from his day's work. He eventually invented a machine for carding wool, and other machines, including endless belts and a revolving rake, which reduced by half the human labor in his and his brothers' grain mill in Eastern Delaware.

Three years before the Colonies' Declaration of Independence, Evans was confident that he knew the way to build a small high-pressure steam engine. His own state showing little enthusiasm, he went to Philadelphia in 1800. Four years later the Philadelphia Board of Health gave him an order for a five-horsepower engine that could be used for dredging and dock cleaning. This was the *Orukter Amphibolos.* A number of years before his death in 1819, Evans wrote: "The time will come when people will travel in stages moved by steam engines, from one city to another, almost as fast as birds fly, fifteen to twenty miles an hour. . . A carriage (steam) will set out from Washington in the morning, the passengers will breakfast at Baltimore, dine at Philadelphia, and sup in New York on the same day."

The **Herald,** 1831; Baltimore and Pennsylvania Railroad.

The next steam locomotive in America was that of Colonel John Stevens; the first to run on track in America, built to prove the practicability of railroads, and demonstrated on his Hoboken estate. Of the other early locomotives on these pages, a number were displayed at the Columbian Exposition, 1893, showing the progressive stages in the development of American locomotives. According to some authorities, the *Herald* was built abroad and used in 1831

The **George Washington,** 1835.

The **James,** 1832.

The **Experiment,** 1832.

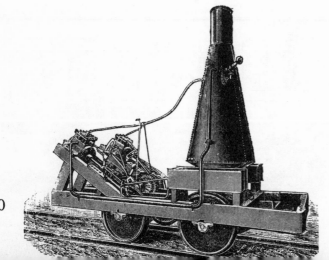

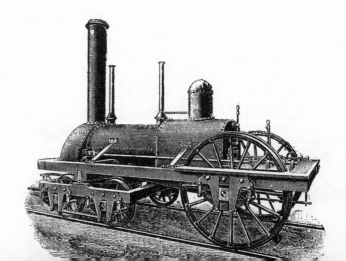

on the Baltimore and Susquehanna Railroad. Ross Winans later added a swiveling truck. The *James*—the second locomotive built by William T. James, in 1832—ran for several years on the Baltimore and Ohio, then on the Harlem, where it exploded. William Norris of Philadelphia built the *George Washington* in 1835. That it hauled a load of 19,200 pounds up the Belmont inclined plane at the Philadelphia end of the Philadelphia and Columbus Railroad, in 1836, was regarded as an amazing achievement. The *Experiment,* also known as *Brother Jonathan*—the first locomotive to use the bogie, or swiveling truck—was designed by John B. Jervis in 1832. By 1837, a great advance had been made in locomotive design. Norris had built the *Lafayette,* and Henry R. Campbell the *Campbell*—with coupled driving axles, one before and one behind the firebox, and a four-wheeled truck. The *Campbell* was called the first American-type locomotive.

Locomotives of unusual design, referred to as "crabs," were introduced in 1837, developed by Ross Winans. Winans was another of the remarkable Americans who, lacking training, managed to learn how to build locomotives. He had been a horse-trader, selling animal horse-power to the early Baltimore and Ohio; then—like several other engine-builders—he developed a swiveling truck. Eventually he ran the Baltimore and Ohio shops, and built a number of successful locomotives for that line. The *Mazeppa* engine, originally built as a "grasshopper" type, was converted to the "crab" type in 1837. The cylinders were changed from vertical to horizontal and were placed into position at the rear end of the frame, suggesting the motion of a crab. This engine had a record of over 50 years' service. The *Buffalo,* built in 1844, was a modified form of "crab," known also as a "mud-digger." This, designed by Ross Winans, was the first engine in the world having four coupled axles. In subsequent engines, the vertical boiler was replaced by one of the horizontal type.

The **Lafayette**, 1837.

The **Henry Campbell,** 1837.

The **Mazeppa** or Crab type, 1837.

Rack railroad locomotive, 1848; Madison and Indianapolis Railroad.

The **Buffalo** or Mud-Digger type, 1844.

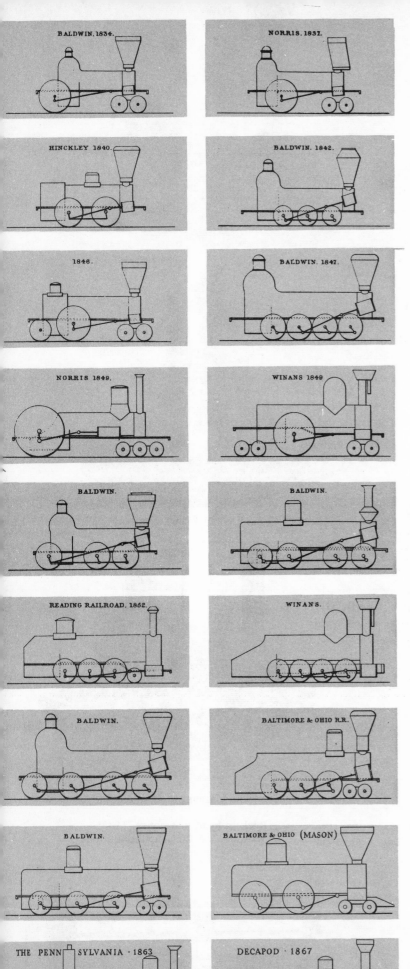

BALDWIN, 1834.

NORRIS, 1837.

HINCKLEY 1840.

BALDWIN, 1842.

1846.

BALDWIN, 1847.

NORRIS 1849.

WINANS 1849

BALDWIN.

BALDWIN.

READING RAILROAD, 1852.

WINANS.

BALDWIN.

BALTIMORE & OHIO R.R.

BALDWIN.

BALTIMORE & OHIO (MASON)

THE PENNSYLVANIA · 1863

DECAPOD · 1867

NATIVE TALENT AND INVENTIVE SKILL

Phineas Davis—the watchmaker of York, Penna.—had won the Baltimore and Ohio's competition for a steam engine in 1831 with his *"Atlantic,"* the first "grasshopper" type, with vertical boiler and cylinders. The piston rods were connected with the cranks by lever beams attached to the boiler, from which long connecting rods passed down to the cranks, resembling the hind legs of a grasshopper. The engines gave good service and one—exhibited at the Chicago Exposition of Railway Appliances, 1883—was said to be the only locomotive in the world which had been in actual service for nearly 50 years, having started in July 1834. The *"Atlantic,"* the first engine to burn anthracite coal, and the *"Traveler,"* completed in 1833, were built at the Davis shop in York. Later, six additional "grasshopper" engines were built in the Baltimore and Ohio's Baltimore shops,

At Left: Diagrammatic representations showing the evolution of the American-type locomotive. Note variations in wheel and driver arrangements.

Another of Jervis' inventions, in 1831, was the rotatable truck, essential to sharply curved tracks.

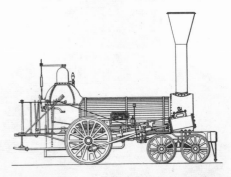

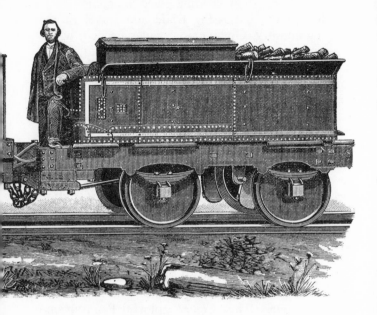

Famous "grasshopper" locomotive, exhibited at Chicago, 1883, invented by Davis; one of nine built for the Baltimore and Ohio road.

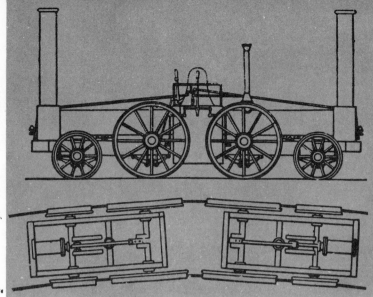

The "South Carolina," built in 1831, gained flexibility with double-ended swivel trucks.

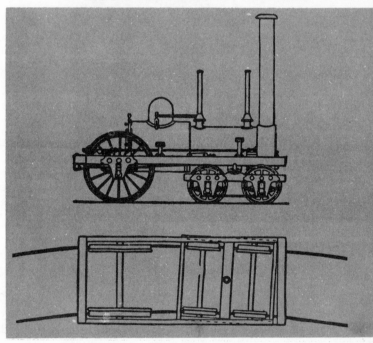

John B. Jervis was the first, in 1831, to use a swivel truck for sharply curved tracks.

under the direction of Mr. Davis. The policy of inviting native talent to compete in the design of an engine suited to the road—instead of importing a British locomotive and adapting it to the road—was much criticized, but the experiment worked well. The Baltimore and Susquehanna, a neighboring road, had imported an English engine which could not be used on the short curves of the line until the small front wheels were removed and a swiveling four-wheeled truck was substituted. The South Carolina Railroad, one of the earliest steam railways in America, also encouraged native talent, opening with an engine which had been designed by Horatio Allen.

Phineas Davis is also credited with the idea of using the wrought iron ring in the cast iron road wheel, by which the chill of the tread and flange was perfected, and danger of fracture reduced. The chilled cast iron wheel is a purely American invention.

The "Norris," 1843, had two pairs of driving wheels, but still afforded no protection for the engineer.

Leaf springs were soon fitted to locomotives on some of America's early steam railroads.

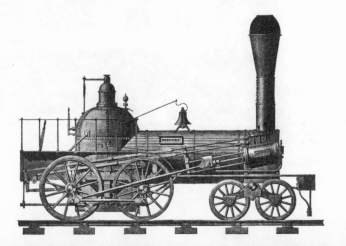

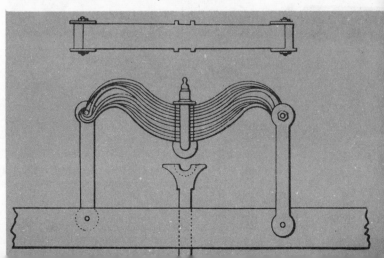

Camelback locomotive built by Ross Winans was placed in B & O service in June, 1848.

The relatively light locomotives which had been built up to 1837 were now yielding place to engines better adapted to the increasing trade and travel of the growing country. Greater power was needed, which could only be attained by greater weight; and greater speed was being demanded, which required a different type of locomotive. With all the functional modifications and changes being incorporated in the new locomotives—the Rogers Locomotive Works of Paterson, New Jersey, in 1837, had built the *"Sandusky,"* the first engine with a driving wheel counterbalance—there was also a tremendous interest in the decoration of engines and tenders. A 4-4-0 type locomotive built for the New York Central (Hudson River Railroad) by the American Locomotive Company in 1860, shows this elaborate ornamentation, as well as the early use of an eight-wheel tender.

It was not unusual for locomotive makers to recruit outside artists to paint scenic panels on cabs and headlights, and to apply ornate gold lettering to the new models. The *"Tiger,"* colorful Pennsylvania Railroad locomotive of 1856, is typical . . . its decorations in brilliant reds and greens, with a great display of polished brass, were considered the last word in locomotive décor. In keeping with its name, its panels revealed palm trees, desert sands and a crouching tiger. This was built by Matthias W. Baldwin, once a jeweler!

The *"Stevens,"* built in 1850 for the Camden and Amboy Railroad (later, a part of the Pennsylvania), had six truck wheels and two huge driving wheels. Its boiler, arranged to slope down in the rear, was fired through an opening in the sloped back which was below the driving axle. Most of the weight of this locomotive was carried by the truck. It was also known as the *"Crampton,"* a type patented in England in 1843 by Thomas Russell Crampton, an able

Crampton engine, a type first patented in England in 1843. Placed in service here in 1847 on Camden & Amboy Railroad.

The Pioneer, built for Utica & Schenectady Railroad in 1836. Later, sold to western railroad interests.

William Mason, often referred to as the "father of the American-type engine" built this in 1856 in Taunton, Mass.

engineer. He was not however the originator of the idea, as Baldwin had already built engines with the driving wheels behind the fire box, in 1833. The English Crampton engines had little success anywhere, except in France where they were popular.

The *"Pioneer,"* built for the Utica and Schenectady Railroad in 1836, was the 37th locomotive to be constructed by the Baldwin Locomotive Works. Sold to the Michigan Central, and named the *"Alert,"* then sold again in 1848, to the Galena and Chicago Union Railroad, she became known as the *"Pioneer"* of what has developed into the great Chicago and Northwestern Line.

The *"William Mason,"* constructed in 1856, was the first locomotive built by the noted New England engine maker, William Mason, for the Baltimore and Ohio road. Mason is often referred to as "the father of the American-type engine," incorporating beauty with utility.

Railway tracks were being laid without interruption and, by 1850, they criss-crossed many states, totalling about 9,000 miles of track. Throughout the 1840's only about 300 miles of track had been laid each year; during the 1850's the figure had increased to 2,000 miles annually. By 1860, there were 30,000 miles of railway tracks in use in the United States.

An article from the *Philadelphia Ledger,* reprinted in the *Railroad Gazette,* August 10, 1883, said: "It is estimated that there are ten million car wheels whirling over this country at the present moment, conveying millions of passengers and more millions of tons of freight . . . yet how many of the multitude who trust their lives on the rails pause to consider how many complex problems have been solved in the gradual evolution of the old-time stage-coach into the modern iron horse and his train?"

The Tiger, built for the Pennsylvania Railroad in 1856, made a colorful picture in brilliant red and green and polished brass.

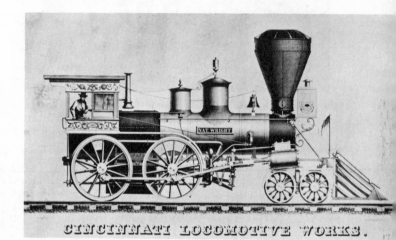

The Nat Wright, built for the Pennsylvania by the Cincinnati Locomotive Works in 1854.

The Pioneer made railroad history when it pulled the first train out of Chicago on October 25, 1848.

THE RAIL SPLITTER AT THE CAPITOL

The Union seemed already to be disintegrating, when Abraham Lincoln arrived in Washington, D. C., for his forthcoming inauguration on March 4, 1861. South Carolina had taken the news of his election in November, 1860, as an excuse for secession. Six other southern states had followed her example. Yet there was no war. Lincoln made an earnest appeal in his inaugural address for solving the problem within the Constitution, emphasizing that the Union was older than the states and that no state could lawfully secede. Then came the news of the capture of Fort Sumter.

Since the South committed the first act of violence, since the United States flag flying over Federal troops had been fired on, millions in the North who had been hesitant now declared their eagerness to defend the Union. On April 15, Lincoln issued a call for 75,000 soldiers . . . not to wage a general war, but to re-claim Union forts and property . . ."to be accomplished with the least possible disturbance to peaceful citizens."

Abraham Lincoln arrives in the old Baltimore & Ohio station, Washington, D. C., February 23, 1861. Allan Pinkerton, first of the detective-firm family, is at the extreme rear.

Daily adjournment of the Congress, scene at the Pennsylvania Avenue entrance to the Capitol grounds, Washington, D. C., 1866. The locomotive carries United States Army Railroad marking.

"Leaving the Junction," one of the thrilling
Currier & Ives' "Lightning Express" prints, 1863.

PRINT MAKERS TO AMERICA

The news of the day, wrecks and disasters, naval and land battles, romance of the early river packets and showboats, sporting events, country scenes . . . portrayals of these reached nearly every American home in the form of Currier & Ives' amazingly inexpensive and accurate lithographic prints. Vying in popularity with the prints of the Mississippi and Hudson Rivers, came a dramatic series for the railways: "The 'Lightning Express' Train Leaving the Junction," "An American Railway Scene, at Hornellsville, Erie Railway," "The Express Train," among other titles. These have proved genuine documents of the early American railways, "because of the accuracy and minuteness of their technical drawings," writes Harry T. Peters, in *Currier & Ives, Printmakers to the American People.* He notes that, "In 1834, when Nathaniel Currier formed his first partnership, Andrew Jackson was President . . . Texas still belonged to Mexico, the Great West was a wilderness. . . . In 1888, when Currier died, he left a country spanned from coast to coast by the railroads that had been only a curious experiment in 1834. . . . His lifetime covered the conquest of the West, the harnessing of steam, the rise of industrialism, the Civil War and the aftermath of reconstruction."

"American Express Train"—top, published by
N. Currier, 1855; below, by Currier & Ives, 1870;
outside Jersey City, on the Erie Railroad.

107

Northern troops built five locomotives in Vicksburg, after the fall of that city.

SERVING THE BLUE AND THE GRAY

Just when American locomotives had attained greater size and more power, when the tracks had been laid to the shores of the Mississippi, and the prairies were beckoning with allurement ahead . . . the nation was shocked by the threat of War between the States.

Immediate further development of peacetime comforts was necessarily halted, and the exciting new inventions—the steam railway and the electric telegraph—were promptly pressed into service of war. Troops were rushed to preserve the Union, by all available trains; cars were armored and guns were mounted, for the protection of the workmen repair-

ing tracks and rebuilding bridges put out of commission by the enemy. While the railroads played many vital parts in military exploits, one of the most spectacular was that of the *"General,"* a locomotive of the Western & Atlantic (now the Nashville, Chattanooga & St. Louis) line. An indispensable aid to the Southern Army, hauling supplies between Atlanta and Chattanooga, the *"General"* was captured April 12, 1862, by the daring of Captain James A. Andrews and a score of other Union soldiers. Disguised, they had crept through the Confederate lines, climbed aboard the *"General"* at Big Shanty, Georgia, uncoupled its train and steamed north, planning to rip up tracks, destroy bridges, and render the

Railroad crews pose among Atlanta's ruins for Matthew Brady's camera.

Old roundhouse at Norwalk, Ohio; drivers, oilers, spic-and-span locomotives.

Armored car with cannon protected workmen repairing war's havoc on the railroads.

road useless to the South. A number of the Confederate soldiers, led by W. A. Fuller, gave spirited chase on foot, by handcar, and a trio of engines, keeping Andrews so busy that he could not complete his plan. He was finally overtaken and captured.

A statue, topped by a metal sculpture of the locomotive stands in Chattanooga to the memory of Andrews, erected by the State of Ohio from whose Volunteer Infantry Companies many of the men participating in the raid had come. The *"General"* is still on display at Chattanooga, and has been exhibited many times at fairs and expositions, in various parts of the country.

After the fall of Vicksburg, when Union troops were occupying that city, five locomotives were built by the soldiers under the direction of Colonel Coolbaugh of General James B. McPherson's staff. The shawled and amply-skirted ladies, with their Union officer escort, may be seen at the top of the opposite page, admiring these new locomotives with U. S. Army Corps markings. Drawn by a special staff artist, this appeared in *Frank Leslie's Illustrated Newspaper,* January 16, 1864. A typical railroad battery with cannon, on the Philadelphia and Baltimore Railroad, was designed to protect workmen employed in rebuilding the war-destroyed bridges on that road. The Civil War gave ample demonstration of the railroads' stamina.

The **"General,"** famous locomotive of the South, captured and recaptured, 1862.

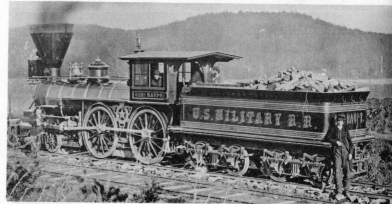

"General Haupt," a Wm. Mason locomotive, confiscated from the Orange and Alexandria.

European and Asiatic laborers mingled in the work of
carrying the railroads over the prairies and mountains.

"I'VE BEEN WORKIN' ON THE RAILROAD . . ."

*"I've been workin' on the railroad
All the live-long day,
I've been workin' on the railroad
Just to pass the time away. . . ."*

Though the name of the author of these lines is not
known, the song has been called the most famous of
all railroad songs. The Republican platform of 1860
had promised free land to any person, "man or
woman, head of a family or twenty-one years old,
either a citizen or an alien who declared his intention
of becoming a citizen." Any one of these could enter
a claim to 160 acres on the public domain and, by
occupying it for five years and making certain improvements, would have full possession of the land.
Congress passed and Lincoln signed this Homestead
Act in 1862.

Then came the laws chartering companies to build
railroad lines to the Pacific coast. *The Beards' Basic
History of the United States* says: "By acts of 1862
and 1864 provision was made for a line in the central region, serving Federal interests. The Union Pacific Company was to start from a point in Nebraska,
later fixed as Omaha, and build westward. The Central Pacific Company was to begin at San Francisco
or a place on the navigable waters of the Sacramento
River and built eastward.

The steel rails were soon to mark the end
of the plains-roving Indians and the great
herds of buffalo and other wild animals.

Blazing new trails to the South and West: timber felled and sawed and laid with the bark on for the early tracks.

"At some spot, to be determined by the speed of construction, the two lines were to meet, thus completing the overland route. In 1864 the Northern Pacific Company was authorized to construct a railway from Lake Superior to Puget Sound by a northern route. To speed up the work of the Union and Central Pacific Companies, Congress granted them an enormous acreage of land in the form of free rights of way and alternate sections on each side of their lines. In addition it lent them a large sum of money for every mile of track laid—a sum varying according to the difficulties of construction. At last the continent was spanned by railways. Manufacturers, merchants, and capitalists were delighted at the prospect. . . . Land-hungry men and women were delighted also: the railways would make it easier for them to go West with their movable property and occupy the now free land; railways would provide transportation for agricultural produce to Eastern markets and would increase the value of farm homesteads. And, what was more, the North would be made stronger in wealth and in ties of communication."

The railways now pushed out over the prairie and mountain wilderness; everywhere new towns sprang up. Immigrants from Europe and the far East worked side by side to blast the roads and lay the tracks.

Railroad construction gang near Greenville, Pa., alongside locomotive of 1876 vintage. Below: laying the track on the route West.

Driving the Golden Spike marked the linking of the Union Pacific and the Central (now Southern) Pacific, May 10, 1869.

THE JOINING OF THE RAILS

The price of railroad progress was the death of hundreds of workers and engineers, for the Indian tribes "made desperate by brutal aggressions of the white race" were on the warpath. On the chance of meeting hostile Sioux, Snakes, Blackfeet, Arapahoes, and Crows, the surveyors, bridge builders, graders, and tracklayers all went armed at their work. Years before, in 1857, the War Department had issued an exhaustive report on "Explorations for a Railroad Route from the Mississippi River to the Pacific." This, comparing the merits of several routes, is starred with the names of young Army lieutenants and captains who later were high-ranking officers in the Civil War. Jefferson Davis, then Secretary of War, warmly praised the excellence of Captain George B. McClellan's report on existing railroad standards . . . McClellan, soon to be in command of the Union Army of the Potomac; Davis, soon to be President of the Confederacy! The Congress of 1862, harried by a fast-mounting national indebtedness due to the Civil War, had allocated very inadequate funds to the railroad builders. The venture was considered highly speculative; incredible construction difficulties loomed, and the hostility of the Indians added greatly to the hazards. With the risks involved, private capital could not be raised. But the Congress of 1864 was in a more generous mood. Much lobbying had been done and the Congress, now accustomed to the spiraling inflation, had greatly increased its grants to the railroads. For each mile of track laid between the Missouri River and the east base of the Rocky Mountains, and from the Sierras to Sacramento, Congress granted $16,000; for each mile from the Rocky Mountains across the Great Basin, $32,000; and for each mile over the mountains—the Rockies and the Sierra Nevadas—$48,000. "Inquisitive persons, noting the huge gifts to the railroads, wondered how much the railroads had given to members of Congress," wrote E. H. Cameron, in "Road to Fortune," *The Technology Review,* March, 1948. For several hundred miles the tracks followed a section of the Oregon Trail. It was the route used for centuries by buffaloes and Indians, and over it

The "Jupiter" and "No. 119" met at Promontory Point, Utah; the present rail route lies thirty miles away.

the Mormon emigrants had made their heroic trek to the West. "With increasing tempo," writes Cameron, "the drama went on; records of railroad construction were shattered, and in the sixth year an audience consisting of all America watched the race of the Union Pacific building westerly, with the Central Pacific laying its tracks toward the East. The climax was melodramatic, when the two lines met at Promontory Point, Utah, on May 10, 1869. Bearded railroad officials drove gold and silver spikes in a tie of polished laurel wood, bearing an inscribed silver plate, while soldiers, Mormon elders, and emigrants looked on. The silver track sledge was wired to make an electrical contact, which operated telegraph receivers in cities and towns from San Francisco to New York." Bret Harte wrote:

> *"What was it that the Engines said,*
> *Pilots touching—head to head,*
> *Facing on the single track,*
> *Half a world behind each back?"*

Crews had laid ten miles of rail a day, placed 25,000 ties, driven 55,000 spikes and fastened 14,000 bolts before the ceremony of the golden spike! There was a "Golden Spike Day" for the Northern Pacific, too, fourteen years later. Lake Superior lay to the East, 1198 miles; the Puget Sound to the West 847 miles, on that gala day which brought cheering crowds to the meeting of the rails, September, 1883. The line roughly followed Lewis & Clark's expedition of 1804-06.

Bands from Salt Lake City, workers, bewhiskered railroad dignitaries were among the estimated 1,500 celebrants.

The Northern Pacific, uniting Lake Superior with Puget Sound, had its own gala Golden Spike day in September, 1883.

Palace hotels on wheels was the proud announcement at a station of the Chicago & Atlantic Railway, direct through route from the seaboard to Chicago

DEPARTURES AND ARRIVALS

Post-Civil War travel was brisk, though many refinements in running the railroads had not yet been achieved. Train attendants were not in uniform; there were no "information bureaus" and no baggage checks.

The many illustrations of the period around 1875 show irate travelers, each claiming the same trunk, and the tact of the baggage-master was put to a severe strain in settling some of these arguments. "The original allowance of fourteen pounds is found to be increased to four hundred pounds," wrote Horace Porter, in his chapter on "Railway Passenger Travel" in *The American Railway,* "when ladies start for fashionable summer resorts." A glance at the draped, padded, and sashed skirts of the day . . . the brimmed hats trimmed with feathered wings and ribbon bows . . . reveals how easily even a few changes of costume and accessories would necessitate several trunks. At this period, the passenger was allowed to pick out his own luggage in the station baggage-room and carry it off . . . a method that resulted in heavy claims on the companies. The rush for the country, circa 1868, presented an even madder confusion than such departures of present day.

The waiting room at a country station, circa 1889, has a contemporary aspect— save for the costumes of the period.

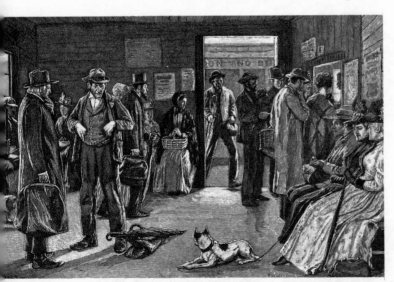

The trials of a baggage-master, in a day of no claim checks and evidently militant females, made heavy demands on a man's tact.

Passengers mingled with trunks and boxes in the baggage room; ladies traveled in costumes elegant in fabric and silhouette.

Week-end in the country: the 5 P.M. crush in the railroad station of 1868 had all the rush and potential hostility of today's hegiras.

The Village Depot, engraved from a painting by E. L. Henry, 1868. The train was met by stagecoach, private carriages, and bullock-drawn cart.

"MEET ME AT THE DEPOT"

Everywhere, the early railways acted like magnets; they drew people—idlers and busy alike—to the depot. From sleepy towns to quick-paced cities, the railway station could usually be counted on as the place where interesting things would be happening. The steam locomotives were exciting enough; and the welcomes to people arriving—the farewells to those departing—on a journey, were as good as a gossip column to keep one informed on the town's doings.

Judge Gillis who, in 1835, took his first train ride behind the *"DeWitt Clinton,"* left additional notes on his experience. "The incidents off the train were

Snow on the Canadian border halts the through train, November 1888.

quite as striking as those on the train; everybody, together with his wife and all his children, came from a distance with all kinds of conveyances, and being as ignorant of what was coming as their horses, drove as near as they could get, only looking for the best position to get a view of the train. As it approached, the horses took fright and wheeled, upsetting buggies, carriages, and wagons . . . and it is not now positively known if some of them have stopped yet." Now, around the seventies, the horses were less excitable, but the depot as a focus of local interest held an undiminished charm.

The old, bulging "balloon" or "diamond" shaped smokestacks were still in use, on locomotives during the Reconstruction era. Never designed for ornament, they served the utilitarian purpose of catching sparks and cinders from the wood-burning engines. When coal succeeded the use of wood as fuel, smokestacks were modified into a straight and narrow shape.

Train conductors wore ordinary clothes and their attempts to collect fares were often resented by inexperienced travelers. A suspicion-ridden Senator from the West, on his first train journey, punched the conductor who tried to take his ticket. The Senator was determined not to be cheated by a railway "sharper." Soon, train employees were required to wear uniforms.

The departure of a train for the West, from Chicago, was high drama . . . shared by Indians, frontiersmen and elegantly dressed passengers

Home for the Holidays. The speedy steam railway brought more frequent reunions, and school recesses spent with one's family.

Boston and Worcester railroad depot
as the "steamboat train" started for New York.

Gables and ornament abounded on the
railway stations, regardless of size, in 1887.

MAIN LINE AND WHISTLE STOP

Railroad mileage had multiplied from 30,000 to
166,000 in the years between 1860 and 1890. Within
a score of years after the Golden Spike ceremony—
joining the first transcontinental railway—three additional railroads spanned the land, and short lines
had been united into systems, linking numberless tiny
towns and villages to each other and to the great
metropolitan centers. Especially during the 'eighties,
much attention was given to the design of railway
depots. Some roads established standard plans for
each class of station. The pages of the *Railroad
Gazette* blossomed with illustrations, from that of
the small, rural, flag-stop category to that being built
at Jersey City, for the New York, Lake Erie, and
Western. The late-Victorian love of gewgaws gave

Left below: **New Union
Railroad Depot** at Worcester, 1876,
replacing the original building.

Turrets sprouting more turrets on a Pennsylvania Railroad suburban passenger station.

rise to an architectural style described as "Railway Gothic." The more ambitious structures had height, arches, towers . . . that at Jersey City, a tower 115 feet high, including a finial of 15 feet. The main waiting room was lighted with stained glass windows in the clear-story and boasted a gallery at the second story level, from which various offices opened off. The railway stations, small and large, were the great meeting and greeting places for aspirants to political honors.

General Ulysses S. Grant who, all his life, had shown little interest in politics, was chosen as the Republican presidential candidate in 1868. He was elected, then re-elected in 1872. After four years, another former Union Army General, Rutherford B. Hayes served as President. James A. Garfield, still another Union Army General, was nominated to succeed Hayes. When Garfield made his triumphant campaign swing into New York City, 1880, flag-waving crowds along the route were wholly masculine. "Votes for Women" lay ahead.

Many-gabled station, 1886, one of the West Shore Railroad's "Standard Class A—Agent" plans.

General Garfield, the Presidential Candidate, speaks to the citizens at Poughkeepsie, 1880.

General Arthur is greeted by General Garfield on the Presidential Campaign Special at Albany.

Grand Central Depot, the first of its name, was built athwart Fourth Avenue at Forty-second Street, New York City. Manhattanites agreed that it was indeed "grand" even if, in 1871, its location could not accurately be called "central."

GATEWAY TO A CONTINENT

In many areas across America, the railroad ran right through the center of town, paralleling the Main Street, and welcomed warmly by the authorities. But New York, with a large share of its transport waterborne, did not manifest any such enthusiasm at the coming of the Iron Horse. "Traffic congestion in lower Manhattan had already become unbearable when New York's first railroad was chartered by the Legislature," say the authors of *New York: The World's Capital City.* "The lines of what are now Fourth and Park Avenues traversed the most difficult terrain in this part of the island. At that time no one thought it practical to open a thoroughfare through this rocky, hilly area, and a franchise was granted to the Harlem Rail Road with permission to lay its tracks along this route." As several of the early steam engines had exploded, the trains were prohibited south of Fourteenth Street. Then, as the population moved north, the railroad's southern terminus was set at Twenty-sixth Street. Later, the trains were not permitted further south than Forty-second Street. Commodore Cornelius Vanderbilt decided to replace the old Twenty-sixth Street station with a handsome new terminal—to be called "Grand Central"—on Forty-second Street. It was opened October 9, 1871, the day of the great Chicago fire. A larger building supplanted it in 1901, to be replaced in turn, February 13, 1913, by the present building with its network of tracks at different levels and its "celestial ceiling" often criticized by astronomers.

Huge glass-roofed train shed, Grand Central, the route to New England, the West, and local stations.

The hiss of steam and chug of engines a constant thrill to passengers in station.

Pride of the Pennsylvania, Philadelphia's once great
Broad Street Depot, rear view. Now demolished.

Forty-second Street wore a crowded look,
outside the Grand Central Depot, even in 1871.

Entrance to trains, Broad Street Station, Philadelphia,
1885. "Show Your Tickets" was now the rule.

Three-tiered berths, wood-stove heat: one of the early Webster Wagner sleeping cars, used on all Vanderbilt railways.

UPPER AND LOWER BERTH

Many ingenious designs were evolved, and various patents were issued, during the evolution of the sleeping-car berth. The railroad companies soon realized that over-night travel—even when not in competition with the large river steam-boat lines which offered patrons sleeping berths, meals served in spacious cabins, and entertainment such as music and dancing —demanded sleeping accommodations for rail passengers. *The American Railway* credits the Cumberland Valley Railroad of Pennsylvania with the first attempt to offer sleeping berths. In the winter of 1836-37, this road fitted up a car divided into four sections, each section fitted with three berths. Though primitive in construction, this car was used until 1848. Various other roads offered cars with berths patterned after those of a steam-boat cabin. But all were crude; only a coarse mattress and pillow were

Fisher's sleeper, an 1860 patent, claimed such ease of operation "attendants could be dispensed with."

Emigrant car fitted up as an ambulance, used during the Civil War. Heating stove at one end, kitchen at the other.

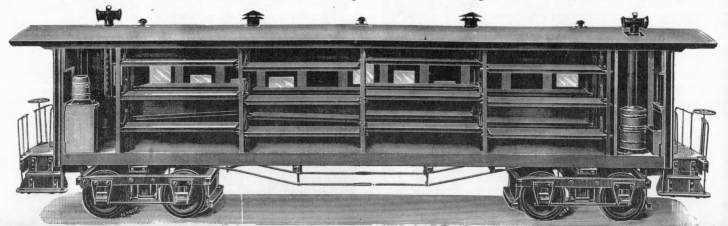

Pullman's first sleeper, a remodelled day coach, had flat roof only six feet from the floor.

Pullman's luxurious through-sleeper on the Transcontinental Route, 1872, offered complete comfort.

supplied; bed linen was not furnished. In 1850, the Baltimore and Ohio road had sleeping cars with berths in three tiers, in which passengers could not sit erect, and from which they often fell to the floor as the cars rounded sharp curves. The first man to work out the design of the upper berth as a hinged shelf was Theodore T. Woodruff. A wagon-builder, with true inventive skill, he scorned the then-prevalent ideas of hoisting the upper berth into the ceiling of the car with ropes. The most creative of his ideas was the hinged upper bed above the windows. By day it was swung up, parallel with the wall of the car; by night it converted into a couch. "While the invention of the sleeping-car is commonly associated with other names," says Sigfried Giedion, "the credit for the original idea, and for the priority of patent and for having constructed under his patents the first practical sleeping-car, belongs to Theodore T. Woodruff." Woodruff patented his invention in 1856.

Kellogg's patent, 1877, stowed folding beds under each sofa; chair pedestals supported upper berth posts.

The "Pioneer," Pullman's first complete sleeper, became President Lincoln's funeral car.

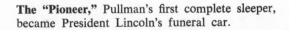
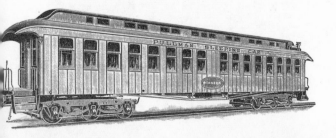

Wagner's Palace Drawing Room and Sleeping Car on the Utica & Schenectady Railroad, 1866.

PULLMAN PROVIDED COMFORT AND LUXURY

George M. Pullman entered a Lake Shore Railroad train at Buffalo, in 1858, to go to Chicago. There was a new sleeping-car attached, and Pullman decided to test it. Much tossed about, he rose early and by the time he had reached Chicago he had "conceived the notion," says *The American Railway,* "that in a country of magnificent distances like this, a great boon could be offered to travelers by the construction of cars easily convertible into comfortable day and night coaches, and supplied with such appointments as would give the occupants practically the same comforts as were supplied by the steamboats. He began experiments soon after . . . and in 1859 altered some day-cars on the Chicago & Alton Railroad." These converted cars were a marked improvement over sleeping-cars then in use.

Meanwhile, Woodruff had organized a company to manufacture what he had patented as a "Seat and Couch Railway Car." The time was 1857; the capitalization was for two million dollars; and young Andrew Carnegie was one of the investors. His original $217.50 returned him dividends of five thousand dollars yearly a few years later, for several years.

Though Pullman's first converted cars were being operated on the line between Chicago and St. Louis, they provided little luxury, and the upper berths were hoisted to the ceiling, manipulated by pulleys and ropes. Pullman went to Colorado, opened a store selling to miners, and in four years had accumulated twenty thousand dollars. With this, he returned to Chicago, determined to build the sleeping car of comfort and convenience he had envisioned years before. Patents had been granted him as early as

1859, and in 1864 the Pullman Palace Car Company was organized. The luxurious *"Pioneer"* was built a year later.

Pullman adopted Woodruff's idea of the hinged upper berth, in place of his earlier method of lowering the berth from the ceiling by ropes. He also eliminated the center tier of berths, making the *"Pioneer"* more spacious than any previous car. Remembering the distress of his own early sleeper ride, Pullman had reinforced the trucks of the *"Pioneer"* with rubber cushions. A foot more in width and two and a half feet higher—due to the change in the upper berths—the new sleeping car, he knew, would require changes in railway station platforms and in bridges. His contribution, Pullman said, was "to build a car from the point of view of passenger comfort." He did not let himself be hampered by standards then current. The remodeling of the early cars had cost him about a thousand dollars each; the *"Pioneer"* was said to have cost $18,000—four times that of sleeping cars being built at the time. Almost as soon as it was completed, the *"Pioneer"* gained national attention as the funeral coach of the assassinated President Lincoln. Station platforms had to be narrowed, bridges had to be raised, to allow the extra-size car to pass from Chicago to Springfield. "A few months afterward," *The American Railway* says, "General Grant was making a trip West to visit his home in Galena, Ill., and as the railway companies were anxious to take him to his destination in the car which had now become quite celebrated, the station platforms along the line were altered for the purpose, and thus another line was opened" to the *"Pioneer"*. . . soon to be operating on the Michigan Central. Berths cost two dollars a

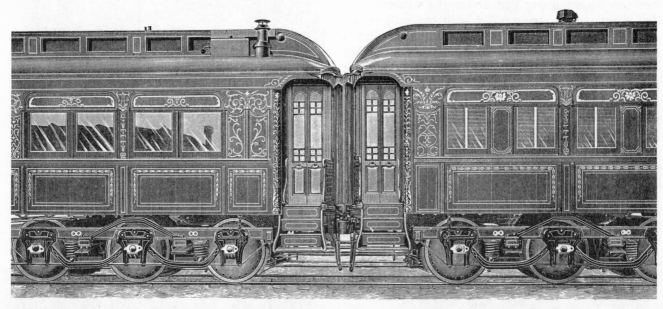

Pullman's "vestibuled limited train," introduced in 1886, had a handsome architectural appearance and the greatest safety device of the era. Passing from one car platform to the other was now made safe.

night. Its glittering chandeliers, its painted ceiling with azure ground, were glowingly described in newspapers of the period. The *"Pioneer"* provided the comforts of a first-class hotel. Its black walnut woodwork and rich Brussels carpets made the added cost —other sleeping cars charged $1.50 nightly—no deterrent to its immediate favor with discriminating travelers.

The early method of coupling cars, which allowed a large amount of slack between one car platform and the next, was one of the chief dangers of railway travel. Pullman's "vestibuled limited trains," patented in 1887, achieved the effect of a continuous train, with all the flexibility needed as the cars rounded curves. It was the most valuable safety appliance yet devised, and appeared first on the Pennsylvania Railroad, 1886. The "vestibuled limited" carried several sleeping-cars, a dining-car, and a car that served as smoking salon, library, writing room, with a bathroom and barber-shop.

The vestibuled car had an elastic diaphragm, a buffer from platform to roof.

Special sleeping car designed and built in 1859 for use by the Prince of Wales.

Wood-panelled car built in 1880, typical of Pullman décor with lavish use of gilt.

REVERSIBLE SEATS . . . RESTFUL RIDES

Many inventions were patented during the 'eighties for the design of car seats. It was observed that, in America, people disliked riding backwards—an aversion not shared by railway passengers abroad. Reversible chair backs were admittedly essential, but there was the problem of making the seat adjustable, so that it would slope backward, regardless of the way the seat-back might face. *The Railroad Gazette,* for a decade from 1882, pictured and described in great detail the various inventors' ideas. There was the *Gardner* reversible car seat, 1882, which adjusted to give the backward inclination of the seat, "the comfort of which was well understood by the makers of old stage-coaches." There was the *Emmert* coach and reclining car seat, with foot and leg rests, used in eleven coaches on the Chicago, Burlington & Quincy road, and in four coaches on the Chicago & West Michigan line, 1888. The *Hitchcock* reclining chair adjusted to a number of sitting and dozing positions, and had a head-rest that was without "annoying springs or catches." Its extension foot-rest was strong enough to bear a weight of 500 pounds.

The most persistent of the patent chair inventors was M. N. Forney, who was the author of detailed articles published in *The Railroad Gazette* in 1886, 1887, and 1888. Mr. Forney observed, June 4, 1886, that "the savage who rested his weary body on the trunk of a fallen tree, or on a rock, probably never

Car seats which converted into couches, forerunners of the sleeping car, were patented as early as 1854. Seats and backs were folded over to form sleeping surfaces. *M. N. Forney's* improved car seat (right) was in use on several Eastern railways from 1886.

This Baltimore and Ohio Railroad coach, c. 1890, was spacious, functional, and lighted by gas lamps.

Hailed as a "considerable improvement," this adjustable car chair was praised for its locking device which was simple, durable, and easily worked. It was manufactured by Scarritt, St. Louis, in 1887.

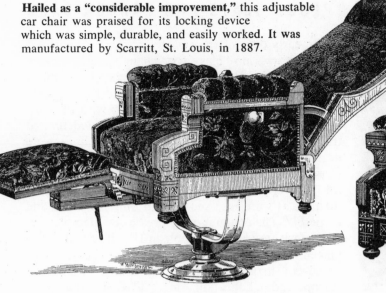

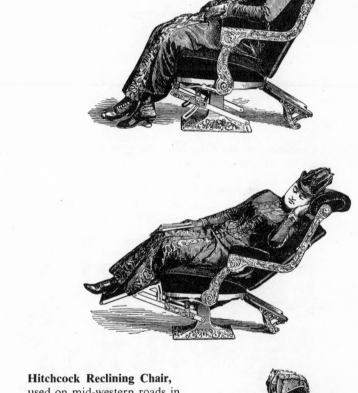

entertained a thought of shaping either of these to the form of his own body. He accepted them both as inevitably uncomfortable, and squirmed into the least painful position he could assume . . . The early car-builders seem to have entertained a similar idea regarding the seats they furnished to the traveling public. . . . If you complained that the seats were uncomfortable, the car-builders were disposed to answer that the discomfort was due to some defect in the occupant . . . and if the passenger wriggled about into every conceivable position, in his efforts to find the least uncomfortable, the cause was attributed to the ill nature of the passenger." Forney's adjustable chairs were closely related to the human anatomy; shoulder blades, lumbar region of the back, pelvis all were scientifically supported and—even when the seat-backs were reversed—the contours of the chair and those of its occupant conformed harmoniously. His sketches bear a close resemblance to those used to illustrate today's body-contour chairs.

From year to year, Forney made adjustments, offering both double seats and single chairs, publicizing each new development with detailed diagrams and intelligent comment. Forney seats were used on the New York & New England, Long Island, and New York Central lines.

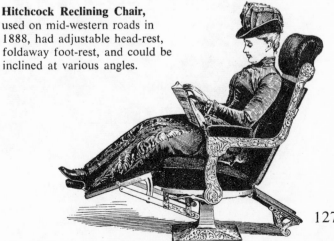

Hitchcock Reclining Chair, used on mid-western roads in 1888, had adjustable head-rest, foldaway foot-rest, and could be inclined at various angles.

127

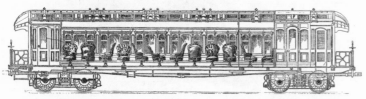

Pullman parlor car with wainscot paneling and wicker chairs designed to give a home-like atmosphere.

PLUSH SEATS AND PARLOR CARS

In the early days of the railways, it was emphasized that there was no "class" system in America; every passenger enjoyed the same type of accommodations . . . a contrast to the first, second, and third classes on British and continental roads. But, with the evolution of special reclining chairs, vestibuled limited trains, parlor cars, and sleepers, sharp lines were drawn between the affluent and the ordinary travelers. Yet it soon became the boast that, in America, for a modest extra fee, travelers could enjoy such luxuries as were reserved abroad only for kings and emperors. The contemporary press presented pictures of the private train of Napoleon III, the royal car of Queen Victoria, among others, declaring that "the height of luxury has been reached by royalty in Europe and nabobism in America." Over-ornamentation was frequently confused as an indication of elegance. The elaborately carved and painted woodwork was re-echoed in the patterned plush of the upholstered chairs. Edward Bok, in *The Ladies' Home Journal,* observed that "women whose husbands had recently acquired means" were selecting "certain styles of decoration and hangings they had seen in the Pullman parlor-cars . . . a veritable riot of the worst conceivable ideas."

It was an era that became devoted to "patent" furniture: chairs that adjusted for sleeping; beds that folded into a wall. But there were some exceptionally handsome drawing room cars, such as the four built for the Boston & Albany road; two had smoking rooms and seats for 27 passengers; two had seats for 36. Each car was 64 feet long. The interiors were designed by an eminent architect, and the decoration was pure Byzantine. They had heat registers, and were lit by electricity.

Exhibited at the Centennial, 1876, this car with revolving seats had two compartments, chairs for 19 and two lavatories.

Large picture windows, overstuffed upholstery, mirrors and ornate decoration designed to make travelers feel at home, en route. (Below)

Club car for smokers—a setting of elegance. (Right)

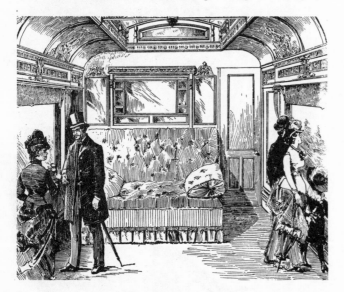

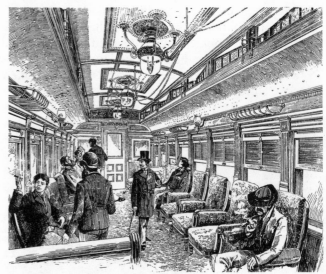

Drawing room car, remarkable for its "refined and restful elegance, free from glitter." Built in 1887 for the Boston and Albany, its colors were low in tone; mahogany interior richly carved, with metal work of statuary bronze.

MEALS ON WHEELS

By 1868, travelers had a wide choice of food *en route,* from ten-course dinners to snacks served hastily at railways stations. Pullman's first dining car, the *"Delmonico,"* made its appearance in 1868. Soon the trains as far west as Omaha carried diners.

In May, 1872, *Harper's New Monthly Magazine* described a trip to California: "Whatever you may think of Chicago in ruins, or the future of that stirring place . . . at Chicago the journey to California really begins. You take up your residence on the train . . . you undress and go to bed as you would at home. . . . From Chicago to Omaha your train will carry a dining car, which is a great curiosity in its way. It is as neat, as nicely fitted, as trim and cleanly, as though Delmonico had furnished it. . . . You sit at little tables which comfortably accommodate four persons; you order your breakfast, dinner, or supper from a bill of fare which contains a surprising number of dishes; you eat from snow-white linen . . . admirably cooked food, and pay a modest price. It is now the custom to *charge a dollar a meal* on these cars, and as the cooking is admirable, the service excellent, and the food various and abundant, this is not too much. You may have a choice in the wilderness of buffalo, elk, antelope, grouse, beefsteak, mutton chops. . . . Beyond Omaha, unless you have taken seats in a hotel car, you eat at stations placed at proper distances apart . . . stations under the supervision and control of the managers of the roads, and at many of them—especially on the Central Pacific road in California—your meals are served with actual elegance. Sufficient time is allowed—from 30 to 35 minutes—to eat; the conductor tells you beforehand that a bell will be rung five minutes before the train starts, and we have always found him obliging enough to look in and tell the ladies to take their time, as he would not leave them.

"Ten Minutes for Refreshments," at a railroad lunch counter. It was often asked why a train should make it necessary for passengers to stop for food at a station, when "steam-boats did not stop and tie up for meals at wharves along their routes."

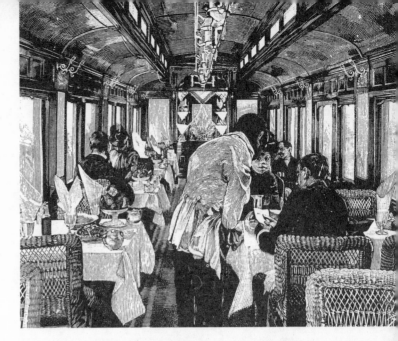

"There is a pleasant spice of adventure in getting out by the way-side at the eating-stations. We saw strange faces, had time to look about us, the occasional Indian delighted the children; we stretched our legs, and saw something of our fellow passengers from the other cars. Moreover, if you have a party desirous to eat together, the porter will telegraph ahead, and reserve seats for you." Pullman had 500 sleeping, drawing-room, and hotel cars on the roads by 1872; was building three new ones a week.

This dining salon of 1869 offered a "choice of buffalo, elk, antelope, grouse, beefsteak, mutton chops" on a *table d'hote* dinner for only a dollar.

Tray service at the station stop offered home-cooked specialties to early Chesapeake & Ohio travelers.

Pullman dining car of 1875 was beautiful, spacious, and inviting with fresh linen, tassel-fringed draperies, leather chairs. Used on the Canadian National Railways.

131

Benjamin Harrison, in the plush grandeur of a
Wagner Palace Car, en route to his 1889 inaugural.

Observation car of the "Legislative Express,"
from Albany to New York. Time: Spring, 1882.

PRIVATE CARS . . . THE ULTIMATE LUXURY

Back in the days of fabulous private fortunes, the insigne of success was the private railway car.

Pullman built these luxuries, 30 years ago, for about $80,000 each. Railroads carried them at about the rate of 25 fares for each trip, plus a surcharge of ten percent. The owner used his private car an estimated 120 days a year; the rest of time it was parked in a railroad yard at the modest cost of $25 for the first seven days; $12 daily thereafter.

In that era of low wages, the services of a chef, steward, and waiter could be enjoyed for about $6,000 yearly. An overall estimate which included furnishings, and food for guests and crew while the car was in use, plus tips to station and yard-masters, totalled about $125,000—including the car's initial cost—for the first year. But not all private cars were for personal pleasure. Though many were maintained to carry their owners to the Kentucky Derby, to Harvard-Yale boat races, to race-week at Saratoga, to Florida or California in season, many also were company-owned and served to carry corporation officers on business trips. Private cars could also be rented for $175 for one or two days. This price included a porter, cook, waiter, and linen. Food, fares, parking—in case you used the car as your hotel—were extra. As early as 1888, *Harper's Weekly* said: "Dramatic companies, hunting parties, political delegates, frequently have occasion to use the same private car for several days, using it as a movable hotel, and to meet this requirement the Worcester Excursion Car Company have constructed very commodious coaches. They are furnished with gun-racks, fireproof safes, stationary bathtubs, electric bells, spacious saloons, berths, etc. Every first class road has one or more cars for the use of its officers."

From the mid-80's to the stock market crash of 1929, the plush private car was the mark of opulence. Morgan, Harkness, Hutton, McLean, Sinclair, Schwab, Ford, Donahue, Brady, Clark, Raskob, Ringling, Whitney, Widener, Woodin, Fleischman, were among the owners. George Pullman owned two—giants in length; one of sixty-seven feet, fitted with pipe-organ, and glittering chandeliers in every compartment.

When presidential candidates toured the country, or traveled to their inaugurations, is was no uncommon courtesy for the railroads to offer the use of a company-owned private car to such aspirants to public office.

The First Fast Mail train between New York and Chicago was equipped with a "catching post," an iron arm that snatched mail pouches from posts at stations en route.

The FLIGHT of the FAST MAIL on the
LAKE SHORE and MICHIGAN SOUTHERN RY.
The Popular Passenger Route between the EAST and WEST.
UNION DEPOTS, NO FERRY TRANSFERS, NO DELAYS.

Postal clerks speedily pulled in the mail pouches at each of the 100 way stations that lined the rails from New York City to Chicago.

MAIL BY RAIL

The first Railway Post Office in the United States was introduced in 1864. It was not the first anywhere, however: Canada had adopted the idea earlier, having emulated England where the mail car had been instituted in 1837. In Colonial days, the postman jogged along on horseback, at one or two miles an hour; later United States mail agents traveled on post-roads by "stages, sulkies, four-horse post-coaches, horseback, packets, and steam-boats," as Thomas L. James, Ex-Postmaster General, notes in his chapter: "The Railway Mail Service," in *The American Railway*. "The growth of the mail service has been coincident with that of the railway itself. . . . Almost as soon as a railroad is fully organized it becomes a mail contractor with the Department." Congress approved the bill making every railroad a post-route, July 7, 1838. Two years earlier, Postmaster General Barry pointed out: "Already have the rail roads between Frenchtown in Maryland, and Newcastle in Delaware, and between Camden and South Amboy, in New Jersey, afforded important facilities to the transmission of the great Eastern mail." A railroad between Washington and New York was being constructed, and it was predicted that this would afford "a speedy service between the two cities . . . the run between them would probably be made in sixteen hours." The first fast mail train over the New York Central and Lake Shore and Michigan Southern Railroads left the Grand Central

Station for Chicago on September 16, 1875, and reached that city less than 26 hours later, which was about 12 hours speedier than the previous month's record. Installed on the train was the system of catching mail bags with an iron arm. The train whizzed by more than a hundred stations, seizing the mail bags, adding them to the 33 tons of mail from New York and a large amount from New England which had been taken on at Albany.

By 1888, mail was distributed on 126,310 miles of railway, and postal-clerks traveled in crews over 122 million miles annually, to sort and pouch the letters and periodicals en route. The New York and Chicago "Fast Mail" left New York nightly at nine. Five hours of intensive work by the sorting clerks in five cars preceded its departure. "Since the removal of the deadly stoves . . . the occupants of the postal cars suffer to no small extent from lack of heat. Steam-heating apparatus is provided, worked by the engine, but the cars are occupied for five hours before the engine comes near them, and the hands of the men become numb with cold," James says. "The salaries of these men . . . of whom so much is expected, range from $900 per annum for the lowest grade to $1,300 for the superintendent." The railroads were poorly paid for the service, often building special trains at no compensation, save the payment made by the Government for so many pounds of freight-mail matter carried. With the mail coaches immediately in back of the locomotives, the postal clerks were among the first casualties in wrecks.

A crew of 19 skilled men, "thorough experts in the geography of the country," was employed on the New York to Chicago Fast Mail train by 1888.

Five mail cars were carried, the one immediately in back of the engine being devoted to sorting letter-mail; the other four to packages and papers.

THE CENTENNIAL . . . MAGNET FOR MILLIONS

More than eight million people visited Philadelphia for the nation's Centennial celebration in 1876, and most of the visitors came by railroad. From North, South, East, and West the crowds poured in . . . over the Delaware and the Schuylkill bridges, on the railways, until every available piece of rolling stock was pressed into service. The Pennsylvania Railroad deposited the milling crowds at its enormous station built on the Fair grounds. From converted freight cars, regularly used for carrying the Jersey peach crop, thousands debouched to view the exhibits. It was a splendid display case for America's . . . and the world's . . . progress; a retrospective view of the nation's growth since the Declaration of Independence in 1776; a look at breathtaking developments in the making. Thousands were thrilled by the exhibits of art and science; of discovery and invention. President Grant and the Emperor, Dom Pedro of Brazil, opened the Exhibition; foreign delegations and commissions attended in gala uniforms; Wagner had composed the music for the Centennial Inauguration March. France—where the Statue of Liberty was then being sculptured—shipped the hand up-

Passenger depots, during the Centennial, took their toll of the traveler's tempers, as this sardine-pack in a station on the New Jersey Central Railroad suggests.

The Delaware River Bridge at Yardleyville gave the New Jersey road a new approach to Philadelphia.

The Bridge over the Schuylkill afforded Fair visitors a first glimpse of the Exposition buildings.

holding the torch, for special display. A gold and silver model of a Pullman Palace Sleeping Car was on exhibit in one area; two of the Pullman Car Company's newest designs—the Drawing Room Car, and the Hotel Car—were displayed in another. Everywhere there were wonders, long remembered . . . subjects for years of discussion with family and neighbors . . . when the crowded trains, the strained

hotel accommodations, and the fatigue were forgotten.

Coming in over the Schuylkill River bridge at West Philadelphia, thousands of the railroad passengers caught their first glimpse of the Centennial Exposition buildings, among which the Main Hall was the largest in the world. Exhibits of steel, machinery, and petroleum held particular fascination for many.

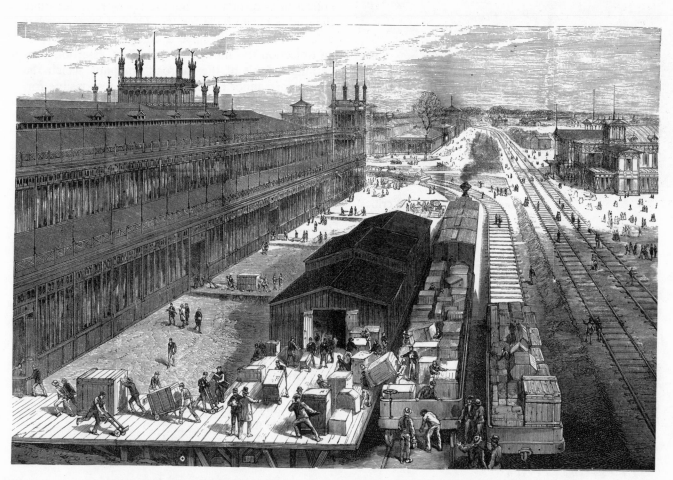

Foreign lands shipped many precious old treasures and wonderful new inventions for exhibit at the Centennial, adding to the extraordinary demands made on railroad equipment.

TRIALS OF THE CONDUCTOR

Tact and patience—essential qualities.

Passengers were portly and critical.

A penny a mile bought few comforts; mixed pipe-smokers and babies.

"The very best and most intelligent people in the community (excepting those who travel much) are among those who oftenest leave their wits at home when they take a railroad trip," says B. B. Adams, Jr., in his chapter, "The Every-day Life of Railroad Men," in *The American Railway*. Adams analyzes the various qualities needed in a conductor:

"The passenger-train conductor has in many respects the most difficult position in the railroad ranks. He should be a first-class freight conductor and a polished gentleman to boot." Emphasizing that many passenger-train conductors are promoted from the freight service, Adams pointed out that on a freight train, "he has very likely been learning how *not* to fulfill the requirements of a passenger conductorship. In the freight service he could be uncouth and even boorish, and still fill his position tolerably well; now he feels the need of a life-time of tuition in dealing with the diverse phases of human nature met with on a passenger train.

"He must be good at figures, keeping accounts, and handling money, though the freight-train service has given him no experience in this line. . . . Every day, and perhaps a number of times a day, he must collect fares of fifty to a hundred persons in less time than he ought to have for ten. Of that large number a few will generally have a complaint to make, or an objection to offer, or an impudent assertion concerning a fault of the railroad company which the conductor cannot remedy and is not responsible for.

"A woman will object to paying half-fare for a ten-year-old girl or to paying full rates for one of fifteen. A person whose income is ten times larger than he deserves will argue twenty minutes to avoid paying ten cents more (in cash) than he would have been charged for a ticket. Passengers with legitimate questions to ask will couch them in vague and backhanded terms, and those with useless ones will take inopportune times to propound them. . . . All these people must be met in a conciliatory manner, but without varying the strict regulations in the least."

Where the train conductor's contact with many passengers required tact and patience, he had need of severity and strength with others, sometimes "drunk and disorderly," who were more ready to fight than to pay fares. "Care must be taken," Adams cautions, "with this sort of character not to punish him or use the least bit of unnecessary severity, for he will, when sobered off, quite likely be induced by a sharp lawyer to sue the railroad company for damages by assault."

Incidents of travel on the railroads in 1873 have their counterparts today.

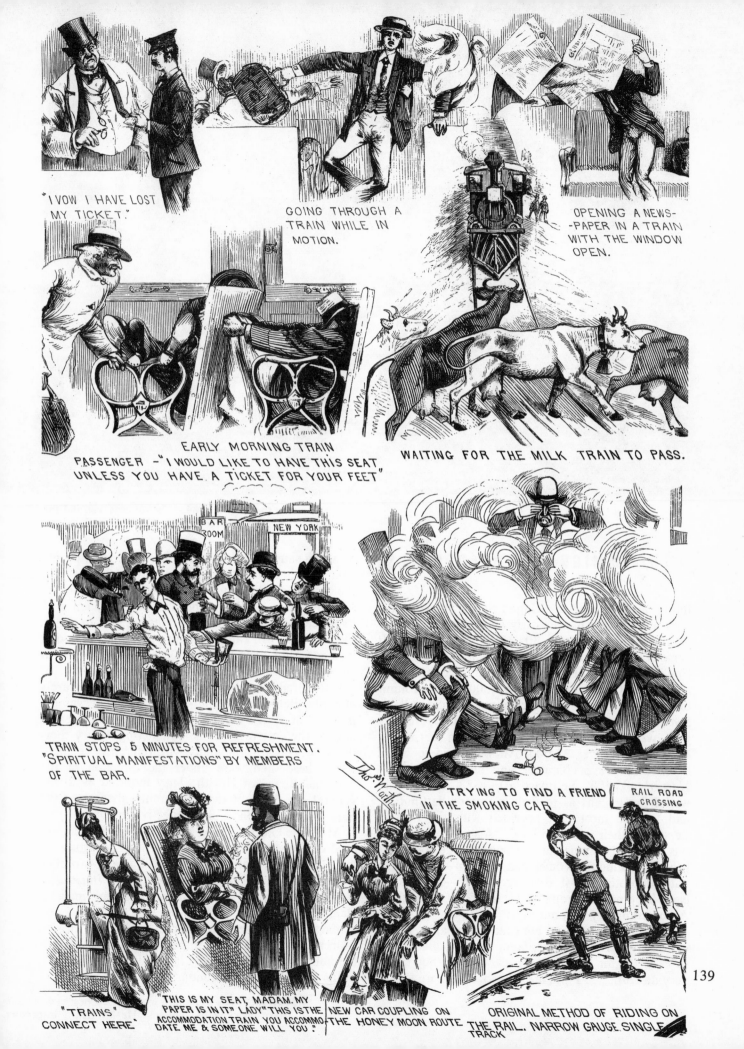

"I VOW I HAVE LOST MY TICKET."

GOING THROUGH A TRAIN WHILE IN MOTION.

OPENING A NEWS-PAPER IN A TRAIN WITH THE WINDOW OPEN.

EARLY MORNING TRAIN PASSENGER – "I WOULD LIKE TO HAVE THIS SEAT UNLESS YOU HAVE A TICKET FOR YOUR FEET"

WAITING FOR THE MILK TRAIN TO PASS.

TRAIN STOPS 5 MINUTES FOR REFRESHMENT. "SPIRITUAL MANIFESTATIONS" BY MEMBERS OF THE BAR.

TRYING TO FIND A FRIEND IN THE SMOKING CAR

"TRAINS" CONNECT HERE

"THIS IS MY SEAT, MADAM. MY PAPER IS IN IT" LADY "THIS IS THE ACCOMMODATION TRAIN YOU ACCOMMO-DATE ME & SOMEONE WILL YOU?"

NEW CAR COUPLING ON THE HONEY MOON ROUTE

ORIGINAL METHOD OF RIDING ON THE RAIL. NARROW GAUGE SINGLE TRACK

Crossing the Plains, 1886. "The *tay* was wet and the lager foamed," and pipe-smoke mingled with garlic odors.

THE IMMIGRANTS HEADED WEST

Immigrants reached the United States in extraordinary numbers during the early and mid '80's. In the fiscal year ending June 30, 1882, nearly 800,000 persons had arrived, about 35 percent of whom were English-speaking. England, Ireland, Scotland sent nearly 180,000; Canada over 98,000. Next in number were the Germans—nearly a quarter of a million. Sweden was represented with about 64,000; Norway with over 29,000; the Celestial Kingdom sent nearly 40,000; Italy over 32,000. All were said to be of excellent average character and many arrived, as *Harper's Weekly*, February 10, 1883, said: "with well-defined plans as to their places of destination, and for the most part provided with the railway tickets for their journey inland." Agents for the various railroads immediately took charge of these groups, placing the women and children—"with their natural protectors, if they have any"—in separate cars; keeping the "rougher persons" by themselves. A contemporary account says:

"At the start the cars are rude but cleanly. Plenty of fresh water is supplied. Some effort is made, too, to keep the air fresh and the car decent, but this is very difficult. . . . Pipes are lighted; meals are spread in which sausage, garlic and sauerkraut form prominent elements, and the mingled odors combine with the smoke of cheap tobacco to render the cars insupportable. . . . When the train stops, laden with its miscellaneous freight, the adults are glad to alight; the children rush eagerly about gathering the oddest mementoes of their journey. Occasionally a kitten is captured to the delight of the whole carload. . . . It is petted, fed, put to sleep in dinner pails, and rarely abused." Before arrival at Chicago—which was the main point of distribution—sanitary inspectors came aboard the emigrant trains, conducting a very thorough inspection, principally with reference to smallpox. These men were under the direction of the National Board of Health. They inquired as to the general condition of the immigrants, then as to the date of vaccination, and its effectiveness.

At Castle Garden, in New York—between the arrival of the steamship and the evening departure of the West-bound trains—the colorful array of foreign costumes was described in *Frank Leslie's Illustrated Newspaper*, May 1, 1880: "The quaint costumes of Danish and German villages, the rich colors of Connemara cloaks, the hues of the beribboned lassies from many climes, blend in glowing contrasts, while the immigrants sit or sprawl in indolent nonchalance in the Castle Garden rotunda."

Immigrants' beds were hard wooden benches; vaccinations were checked by National Health Board inspectors.

A Stop on the 'Road
"Get on Board there!"

Rogers.

Immigrant Inspection Service.

The Youngsters.

141

INTO THE CLOUDS BY COG

It required almost two decades for Sylvester Marsh to obtain a charter from the state of New Hampshire for his proposed cog railway to the top of Mount Washington. Practically every mention of Marsh includes the statement that the legislators laughed, and suggested that he apply also for a charter to build a road to the moon. But, in 1857, the charter was granted and Marsh purchased 17,000 acres of land from the base to the summit, broke ground, and built a mile of the road to prove that such a venture was practicable.

Mount Washington Cog Railway was formally opened in July, 1869. Its construction had required nearly eight years.

Jacob's Ladder. The trestle-work, in places more than twenty feet high, made passengers feel "entirely severed from the earth."

A company was formed, and the road progressed slowly, for—as *Harper's Weekly,* August 21, 1869, says: "There were very few weeks of each year in which any work could be done. The men were driven away from their work in the early fall, and were not able to recommence it until another summer was almost at hand."

The Superintendent of the road, J. J. Sanborn, took pains to explain to the first fearful visitors the means by which the little train was hauled to the top of the 6,288-foot mountain, and the various devices for the passengers' safety. "A third track, laid between the customary two, was fitted with cogs. The engine and the car each had a third wheel, also fitted with cogs. The teeth of the one fitting into those of the other propelled the car and engine steadily up the steepest grades." It differed from the Mount Holyoke Railway, where a stationary engine pulled

The center rack rail, into which the cogged wheels of locomotive and platform car locked with reassuring accuracy.

Tip-Top House at the summit, where winds as strong as 200 miles an hour might be met. Nearby, the U. S. Meteorological Station.

Among the clouds: views over a one hundred mile radius, into Massachusetts, Vermont, Canada, and out over the Atlantic Ocean.

Nearing the summit. The sharp grades made passengers grasp the seats of the crude little platform car.

the cars up by a long rope. "The road is really as steep in some places as a flight of stairs," an early visitor wrote. "But we think of the atmospheric brakes, of the friction brakes, of the ratchet wheel, and the cogs. . . . The stoutest of the party looks a little pale; but we feel the firm grip of cog upon cog; we remember that the wheel is so clamped upon the pin-rigged middle rail that the engine nor the car can be lifted or thrown off; that the pawl dropped into the ratchet-wheel would hold us in the steepest place; that the shutting of a valve in the atmospheric brakes effectually stops the wheels from moving. . . . We seem to go up from the middle of a great valley; there are no level places. The mountains about us shrink into small hills. Now, no trees. Now, only rocks. Now, we are at the top, cloud-wrapped.

"We scramble to the Tip-Top House and by its fire have time to consider what we have done. In an hour and a half we have climbed by steam a ladder nearly three miles long . . . we have passed from the atmosphere of July to that of January. We return with less of a tremor than we experienced on the top of an old-fashioned stage among the precipitous hills of Maine."

En route to Crawford Notch, White Mountains, high trestle on the Portland and Ogdensburg Railway.

Steam inspection car, Kalamazoo-designed for use of division superintendents and track masters, carried seven persons, and burned ordinary kerosene as fuel.

Velocipede hand car, propelled by one man. Its back seat could carry another who was free to give his entire attention to inspection of the track.

LITTLE CARS THAT RODE THE RAILS

The little cars used for inspection of track conditions, transfer of work crews, maintenance of telegraph lines, and other purposes varied greatly in style, weight, and means of propulsion—but all had a debonair air suggestive of speed and freedom. Throughout the '80's, the *Scientific American* and the *Railroad Gazette* frequently featured the latest designs: fast-running velocipedes, inspection cars, push cars, cars for track laying, light double-frame section hand cars, heavy extra-strong construction cars—many of which were on display at the Chicago Railway Exposition of 1883. Their weights varied from 1000 pounds driven by a kerosene engine— to 120 pounds, propelled by the hand-and-foot power of one or two men. All were said to be easily removable from the tracks at any desired point; and each could be divested of extending parts for convenience of shipment and storage. The Providence & Worcester road used a number of the light section hand cars, propelled by two men, which could carry a third man on the back seat, and a fourth in the platform car, "by use of a camp stool or chair." On the prairies, the sail-car—once discredited in the South, in the '30's—was used on long sections of tracks by the Kansas Pacific Railroad. It was cheap to build and to maintain and was praised in that the wind saved the labor of men, involved in running a hand car.

Sailing car on tracks over the Western plains. Used for years on the Kansas Pacific Railroad, the sail saved man power, and rivalled fast express train speeds.

Three men and their tools, or a fourth man, could ride on this light hand car, for telegraph line repairs.

Lightness, simplicity, speed, and cheapness were offered in Stock's hand car. Hourly speed—20 miles.

New Year's, 1864, a Michigan Central train remained in a snowdrift over eight hours.

Even in the East, where tracks were easier to clear, snowstorms often disrupted train service.

Early snow-ploughs were not always effective. Snowed-in on the Union Pacific, train passengers shot wild game, and searched for food at settlers' cabins.

LOCOMOTIVES AGAINST BLIZZARDS

Passenger trains to the West have been snow-bound, sometimes for days, even in the current decade. The shortage of food, of blankets, of heat fills newspaper readers today with horror. Nearly a century ago, the stories of trains "lost" for days, even forever, sent chills down the spines of citizens by their home fires.

In December, 1872, about 350 passengers occupying several cars on the Union Pacific were snowbound for over two weeks, between Percy and Cheyenne. But more real hardship occurred on the prairies only seven miles from Chicago, January, 1864, where a Michigan Central train ran into a snowdrift. "There were about 100 passengers aboard, many of them women and children. Some had light lunches with them; some not even a cracker," W. S. Kennedy wrote, in *Wonders and Curiosities of the Railway.* As the day wore on, fences were torn up for fuel for the stoves; these, over-heated, set the car roof afire. Against the gale, the fire was extinguished with great difficulty. Eight hours later a Michigan Southern train appeared on a crossing 400 yards away, and the passengers from the first train were transferred, through drifts ten feet deep, with cold so intense that almost everyone was badly frostbitten. Now, the second train was buried in the drift; its engine frozen. A beacon was set out and seen by a station agent. He arrived by ten P.M., bringing food and blankets. After a fairly endurable night, the passengers were taken back to the city by sleighs the next day.

Kennedy tells, too, of a locomotive at Kiowa, Kansas, in 1878, swept from a railroad embankment by a waterspout and lost in a quicksand; and of an entire freight train lost, near the town of Monotony, on the Kansas Pacific, probably buried under a land-slip.

The Rotary steam snow shovel was widely used on the Trans-continental lines of American and Canadian railways by the winter of 1888.

As the railroads multiplied and spread into new territory, old bridges had to be strengthened and many additional viaducts and trestles constructed . . . over ravines, rivers, and valleys. To the wooden bridge and the wooden trestle, American railways owed much of their progress. Two Pennsylvania carpenters, Burr and Wernwag, developed the wooden truss bridge. Wernwag in 1803 built a highway bridge across the Delaware that served for 45 years. Then, strengthened, it was used as a railway bridge for another 27 years.

The old builders were very selective as to the quality of the timber they used, making sure that it was at least two years old. But, in building the railways, nobody wanted to wait for seasoned wood. The desire for speed led to Howe's invention of a truss bridge which could be adjusted by bolts and nuts, to absorb shrinkage. This Howe truss bridge was used satisfactorily on all railways for about 30 years, from 1840. Its vulnerability to decay and fire hastened the advent of iron and steel bridges. Such materials—essential on spans of 200 feet or more—would otherwise not have been so much in demand, since American railway spans—in the greatest number, were less than 100 feet long. The Howe wood truss bridge was used on all new lines in the West, to be superseded by iron and steel, after the roads were in operation. A civil engineer of 1888 said: "The American way is to get the road open for traffic in the cheapest manner and in the least possible time, and then complete and enlarge it from its surplus earnings, and from the credit which these earnings attract. . . . It speaks well for the skill and honesty of the American bridge engineers that many of their

Conewago Creek bridge of the Pennsylvania Railroad. Wooden truss supports rest on stone pylons.

Conemaugh Viaduct of the Pennsylvania R. R. . . . a graceful stone arch substantially built, still standing.

Timber viaduct on the Erie at Portage, N. Y., 800 feet long, over the Genesee River.

Curved viaduct of the Union Pacific, at Georgetown, Colorado.

old bridges are still in use, some 80 years since they were built, designed for loads of 2,500 pounds per linear foot, and now carrying loads of 4,000 pounds and more per foot. Sometimes the floor has been replaced with a stronger one, but the trusses still remain and give good service."

The first iron bridges, modeled after their wooden predecessors, had short panels and high trusses. Riveted connections were avoided, and every part was designed so as to be quickly erected upon staging or false works, placed in the river. The long time needed for riveting all the connections—the practice in England—was considered financially impracticable here. A railway bridge contractor outlined his formula: "Our practice is to put in temporary trestle work of timber resting on piles, which trestle work is renewed in the shape of stone culverts covered by embankments, or iron bridges on stone abutments and *built after the road is running.*" D. J. Whittemore, the Civil Engineer for the Chicago, Milwaukee, and St. Paul system explained: "Everything not covered with earth, except cattle guards, be the span 10 or 400 feet, is called a bridge. Everything covered with earth is called a culvert." In the United States, by 1888, there were 61,562 iron and wood truss bridges, and 147,187 wooden trestles. Some of the early railway bridges were of exceptional beauty, that of the Erie Railroad over the Genesee River at Portage, New York, being "unsurpassed by any wooden structure erected for a similar purpose anywhere in the world." Opened in 1852, it was totally destroyed by fire in May, 1875, immediately rebuilt of iron, and opened to traffic in July of the same year. Everywhere—over the Hudson, the Missouri, the Ohio—notable bridges and trestles were built in the post-Civil War years.

Torrington truss bridge, Naugatuck Division, N. Y., New Haven and Hartford, built on stone pillars from an earlier bridge.

The largest drawbridge in the world, in 1889. New London railway bridge, over the Thames, replaced the Groton Ferry.

The St. Charles railroad bridge over the Missouri. River currents and subaqueous terrain created difficult problems.

A wreck hidden by a sharply curved track, but the timely warning of one saves many.

At the brink of danger, the train is saved, "thanks to the quick action of a hero of the track, and the brave, quick-acting men of the engine."

The signal to stop was indicated by a lamp swung across the track.

To move ahead, the signal was a lamp raised and lowered vertically.

DANGER AHEAD!

Old-timers' railway lore abounds with tales of brave deeds, not only of heroic engineers and firemen but of ordinary citizens who risked their lives to warn approaching trains of unsuspected danger. Rising waters, a bridge washed away, a track in serious disrepair or other catastrophe that might have brought death to hundreds, was happily averted by daring and quick action.

"A vivid picture of a railway train in the extremest peril . . . a heroic man on the spot, aware of the nearness of the approaching train, dashes forward to meet it . . . wildly waving hat and handkerchief, and calling at the top of his voice," so *Harper's Weekly*, February 10, 1872, presented a dramatic incident in railway travel. "The signal of death is seen and, quick as thought, both engineer and fireman are engaged in a mighty effort to stop the train. The engineer is shown with one hand on the lever which shuts off the steam, the other on the lever which reverses the action of the driving wheels; while the fireman gives the 'Down Brakes' signal and, with lightning

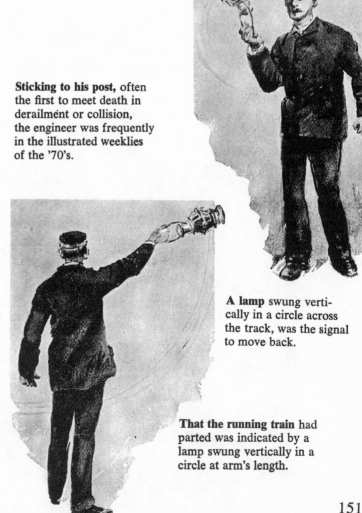

Just time to jump, and often not that, when two engines approached head on, on one track.

Sticking to his post, often the first to meet death in derailment or collision, the engineer was frequently in the illustrated weeklies of the '70's.

A lamp swung vertically in a circle across the track, was the signal to move back.

speed, seizes the wheel of the engine brake." The legend of Kate Shelley, a fifteen year old girl who saved a through train on the Chicago and North-Western railroad, when a bridge had been carried away by a raging Des Moines river flood, is one of the spectacular deeds of daring often re-told, though it occurred in 1881.

For all foreseeable emergencies, for handling extra trains, for routing trains on single tracks, for delays which force trains off their regular schedules . . . rules, usages, and signals had been adopted which were in general use over the United States by the mid-'80's.

State legislatures established, many years earlier, codes for the operation of railroads. New York State's code of 1856 declared, among its many hundreds of admonitory paragraphs: "The Safety of Passengers is to be regarded as the highest and most important duty . . . Flags are to be used, at drawbridges when open . . . Lamps are to be used for the same purpose after sundown . . . When on the road the train will be under the direction of the conductor . . . The engineman must always run on the assumption that at any station he may find a train out of place."

That the running train had parted was indicated by a lamp swung vertically in a circle at arm's length.

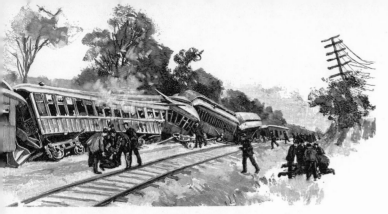

Front view of the wrecked train, which was carrying happy vacationists from Wood's Hole and Nantucket to their homes in New York, Ohio, and Kentucky.

Accident at Prospect Station, Penna., where passenger cars set afire from over-turned stoves left the bridge, and fell bottoms up to the frozen creek below.

Wreck near Quincy, Mass., August 19, 1890, caused by a ratchet jack left on the rails.

RAILROAD DISASTERS

In the early days of the steam railroad, accidents were few. The light rolling stock, the slow rate of travel, kept serious disasters to a minimum. In his *History of Travel in America,* Seymour Dunbar says:

"Speaking in a broad sense . . . the first twelve years of the history of American railroads—covering the period from 1829 to 1841—were distinguished by a most remarkable absence of heavy calamities . . . Traffic over the roads was insignificant when compared with the proportions it afterwards assumed, and the average length of a journey was very short. There was scarcely any travel at night, and when a passenger train was run during the hours of darkness it was usually preceded by a pilot engine intended to discover whether or not the track was in proper condition. If a defect in the road did exist, then the pilot locomotive, instead of the train itself, suffered the penalty . . . Even a collision between two trains running in opposite directions did not produce a memorable catastrophe during the first decade or more of railroad operation."

But, as speed developed—from the 12 to 18 miles an hour of the early trains to the 35 or more miles an hour later—and as heavier locomotives were built and put into operation on tracks often intended only for light equipment, grisly wrecks began to occur

with shocking frequency, from about the middle of the century. A great many more trains were in operation, and the journals of the period reveal horrifying casualties.

"Every man who leaves the city by a train must cast a lingering look behind, in sober sadness, doubting whether the chances of a safe arrival are not entirely against him," *Harper's Weekly,* June 21, 1858, said in commenting on a recent disaster on the Erie Railroad: "Boilers are bursting all over the country —railroad bridges breaking and rails snapping— human life is sadly and foolishly squandered." It was a ratchet jack—in use by a repair crew, which could not be extricated from the rails in time, as an express train from Wood's Hole rounded a curve—that caused a frightful wreck on the Old Colony Road, near Quincy, Massachusetts. The engine struck the upright jack, reared, left the rails, and ran against the side of a 12 foot cut. The train of baggage, smoking and Pullman car, and six ordinary coaches carried 391 returning vacationists from New England's seaside resorts. Fifteen passengers were killed outright; forty-six were seriously injured, of whom six perished later from burns. Whether it was an obstruction on the rails, or a bridge that dropped crowded cars to the beds of icy creeks, escaping steam from the locomotive boilers and fires from overturned stoves added to the terror of railway accidents.

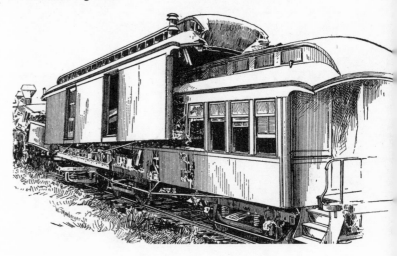

The baggage car telescoped the smoking car, in the Silver Creek disaster, due it was said to the fact that the baggage-car draw-bar was higher than that of the smoking car.

Frantic rescue work at Jackson, Michigan, after a crash on the Michigan Central Railroad, October 1879. The dying were pinioned beneath the frightfully wrecked cars.

153

FLOODS, WASHOUTS AND BREAKDOWNS

Any one who turns back to the illustrated weeklies of the '70's and '80's must be impressed with the high incidence of accidents on the railways. Not all of these could be attributed to human carelessness, or shoddy materials. Admittedly, inferior workmanship and flimsy equipment played their parts, but it was those so-called "acts of God"—floods, washouts, wind-spouts, tornadoes—which frequently levied the most terrifying tolls in dead and injured, on the railways. A substantial Howe truss bridge, built entirely of iron, and previously tested under the weight of six locomotives, was the scene of a gruesome accident near Ashtabula, Ohio, on December 29, 1876.

Drawn by two engines—the *Socrates* and the *Columbia*—a train of 11 cars with 175 passengers approached the bridge at eight P.M., in a violent snowstorm. As the *Socrates,* the first engine, was passing over the bridge, running slowly, the engineer felt a sudden settling of the structure. He was about two car-lengths from the western end and instantly opened wide the throttle. The *Socrates* shot ahead, but the draw-bar connecting the two engines snapped, and the *Columbia* plunged through the bridge, followed by the express, baggage, and passenger cars. The sleeping car swung over to the side

Flood in Alabama. Flares give warning of washed-out track, train at a standstill.

Breakdown on the road. One of the happier incidents that brought a respite to train-wearied bodies, and acquaintance with new country.

Washout on the New York Central. Passengers, luggage, and mail sacks are transferred over hills and across water by improvised planks 'and "Shank's Mare."

and a moment later caught fire from its stove. Only the engineer of the *Socrates* could report the disaster in all its terrible details. Fed by a fierce wind, the fire soon made the cars a mass of flames, lighting up the ravine and drawing people from the depot a quarter-mile away, and from the town. Rescue groups conveyed survivors to nearby hotels and surgeons arrived, on a train from Cleveland. Identification of most victims was impossible. Fifty were dead; as many more seriously injured. The engineer of the *Columbia* was thrown head first from the window of his cab and, though badly wounded, miraculously survived.

In many sections of the country, raging flood waters carried huge trees and buildings down stream, pounding against and weakening bridge and trestle foundations. Sudden washouts, detected in time, forced train loads of passengers to walk over improvised wood planks to stations on a river's opposite bank. Occasionally, a defect in equipment, an empty watertank, or a roadbed made perilous by a washout halted a train in open country, sometimes providing a welcome interlude to passengers fatigued by several days' travel. Broadsides, depicting the most terrifying railway disasters, were widely printed and eagerly bought after these lamentable events. Still, ever more thousands of people traveled by train.

Forest Hills disaster. Extricating the dead and dying, Boston and Providence Railway.

Wreck of a bridge. Flood waters, laden with debris and a wrecked locomotive, batter the stonework masonry of a railroad viaduct.

155

SWITCHES, SEMAPHORES AND SAFETY

Devices to assure greater safety in railway travel came into almost general use in the last quarter of the Nineteenth Century. The switch-tower with its signal man at the interlocking switches, the semaphores with their warnings, the split-switches which reduced the dangers of derailment . . . all were being adopted by the larger railroads and many of the smaller ones. Foreign visitors to the Centennial were fascinated by the railway exhibits, especially the safety devices which were not then in use in other lands. At the time, 1876, George Westinghouse was only 30 years old, yet his air brakes were on 38 per cent of America's locomotives and passenger cars. Westinghouse had perfected his compressed air brake when he was only 23. Eleven years later, he founded the Union Switch and Signal Company, to make devices that would keep trains moving safely.

Interlocked levers to operate switches and signals eliminated the chances of human error, so that movements could be made only in prearranged sequences. It had frequently happened that a switch, thrown under a moving train, had split and resulted in the derailment of some of the cars. This inspired the invention of a detector-bar which, placed along the rail and carried on swinging links, made it impossible for the switch to be moved so long as there was a wheel on the rail above the bar. A wide variety of signals had been in use, before the semaphore signal was generally adopted.

A board called the blade or arm, pivoted on a post is, briefly, a semaphore. In horizontal position, the blade indicates danger; when it hangs at about 60 degrees from the horizontal, it indicates safety. A lantern is hung on the post. In back of the pivot is a lens of colored glass, either red or green. As the blade is moved, it reveals red, or green, or the white (safety) of the lantern light. The use of torpedoes, to explode when struck by a car wheel, brings warnings in fogs or in areas along the road not protected by semaphores.

Split switches and detector bars. The rod at the right of the track is the connection to the signal tower by which the switch-locks and bars are moved.

Railway crossing gate, often ignored by the public. In Massachusetts alone, in 1888, 11 percent of all deaths on railways occurred at the grade crossings. 47 percent of the deaths were of track-trespassers.

Semaphore signal with indicators. One arm governed several tracks. The number of the track which was clear was shown on the indicator disk. The blade in a horizontal position indicated danger.

Night approach to Philadelphia on the Pennsylvania Railroad. Joseph Pennell's engraving suggests how much the safety of passengers depended on the signal man in his tower, the vigilance of track employees.

Portal of a finished tunnel in the Colorado Rockies. The background peak is Cameron's Cone.

TUNNELS, GRADES AND SWITCHBACKS

Building a railway over varied terrain—from rolling valleys to steep mountain peaks, through deep gorges and narrow canyons—demanded the best judgment of trained engineers in locating the line. Land that looked the easiest sometimes presented the greatest problems. Many heights were too steep for direct ascent or descent . . . so the practical and economical ideal of the shortest distance between two points had to be abandoned for circuitous switchbacks. When a line could be run through a narrow pass, its location was relatively simple. Inequalities in land levels frequently demanded enormous trestles to raise the tracks over low country; walls of rock which blocked the proposed route had to be tunneled, sheared down, or encircled; often the procedure was to cut niches into the rock, leaving projecting cliffs over the roadway. In 1887, sure-footed donkeys carried the ore from certain mines in Colorado—to which access could be attained by no other means; a year later a railway was in construction to those mines.

"No heights too great; no valleys too deep; no canyons too forbidding; no streams too wide" was the high resolve of the ambitious railroad builders. In

Stout timbers served for temporary supports in the process of constructing a tunnel.

Circuitous loop of track over trestle and bridge, Georgetown Branch of the Union Pacific.

A gallery or shelf, cut into the side of mountain pass, successfully avoids the use of a tunnel.

constructing a line of railway through rock, the engineers found that tunnels were generally to be preferred to making a deep cut or trench. Cuts often resulted in the crumbling of the side walls, causing pieces of the upper rock to fall onto the track, with the possibility of accidents. While the tunnels cost more to build than the cuts, they eventually proved the more economical. Despite the customary belief, constructing tunnels through solid rock offered few difficulties. Soft shale and erratic seams in the mass demanded an extra measure of resourcefulness, calling for temporary supports to prevent what was to be the roof of the tunnel from falling into the already excavated areas. Seasoned timber of exceptional strength was generally used for the temporary supports.

The skill of the engineers—their ability to meet and conquer seemingly impossible obstacles in the way of new roads—merits the highest praise. With full regard for amazing engineering feats of earlier centuries . . . from the days of Pericles to those of Da Vinci . . . the engineering profession, before the building of the railways, scarcely existed. Certainly, as the great lines were flung across mountain and valley, gorge, canyon, and river . . . the versatile capacities of the American engineer were demonstrated to the world.

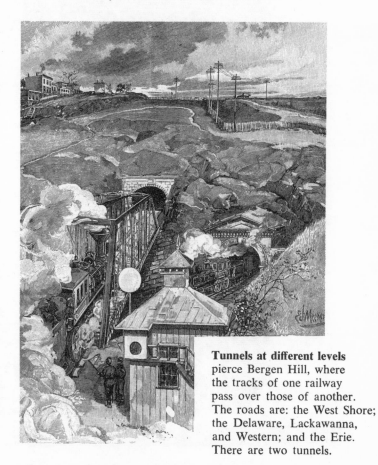

Tunnels at different levels pierce Bergen Hill, where the tracks of one railway pass over those of another. The roads are: the West Shore; the Delaware, Lackawanna, and Western; and the Erie. There are two tunnels.

159

Fast passenger locomotive, with a single pair of driving wheels, Baldwin-built for the Philadelphia & Reading, 1880.

Fontaine locomotive of the Canadian Southern Railway. Built by Grant, Paterson, N. J., 1881. Reputed speed: 90 mph.

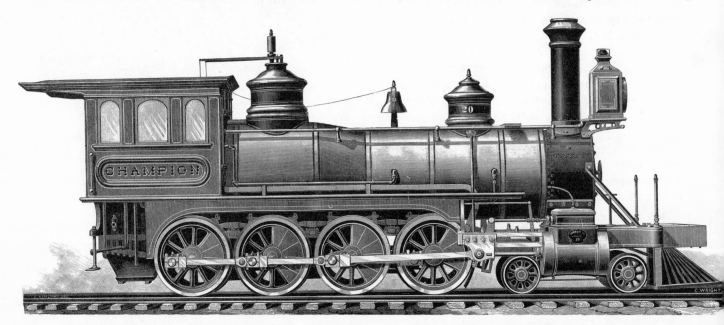

Champion, twelve-wheeled locomotive of the Lehigh Valley Railroad, was built in its Weatherly, Pa., shops, 1882.

Tank engine from the Central Pacific Railroad's shops, Sacramento, 1882.

FULL STEAM AHEAD!

America's first invention applied to a locomotive was the swiveling truck which, placed at the front end of an engine, enables it to run around curves of almost any radius. Equally valuable improvements were made in railway cars, both for passengers and for freight. Ross Winans of Baltimore devised a *pair* of fourwheeled swiveling trucks, one under each end of the car, enabling it to accommodate to the inequalities of a rough track and to follow the locomotive around the sharpest curves. On many American lines, the curves were of less than 300 feet radius, while in Europe there were few curves of less than 1,000 feet radius. The flexibility of the American machine increases its adhesion, equalizes its pressure on the track, prevents shocks and blows, enables it to draw greater loads, and to keep out of the repair shop. Locomotives are designated by the number of their truck and driving wheels.

Reference may be made to a locomotive as a 4-6-2 *Pacific* type. *Pacific* is a popular synonym for 4-6-2 and those numerals are easy to explain. The first and last figures relate to the number of small truck wheels at front and back respectively; the center figure refers to the number of the driving wheels. So, a 4-6-2 engine has a four-wheeled truck immediately in back of its cowcatcher; followed by three pairs of driving wheels, and a two-wheeled truck at the back under the fire-box. There are about forty different types of locomotives by wheel classification, and other distinctions such as compounding and single or double expansions. A locomotive is, essentially, a simple mechanism . . . a boilerful of water, a fire to heat that water, and some cylinders and pistons to apply the steam thus generated to the wheels. Among the most famous types of locomotives, in the past or now in use, are the *Consolidation, American, Mogul, Prairie, Atlantic, Decapod, Santa Fe, Mikado,* and *Pacific*. Types from the '80's show the interesting variations made in one decade.

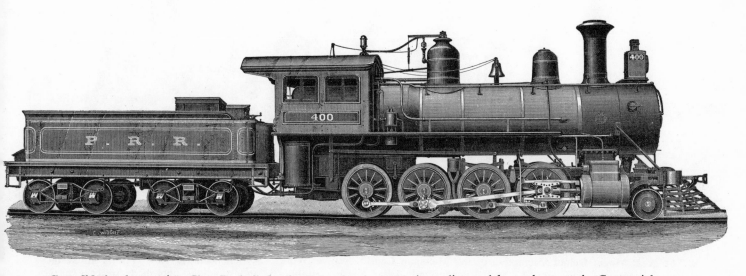

Consolidation locomotive, Class R., built by the Pennsylvania, 1886. An earlier model was shown at the Centennial.

Powerful twelve-wheeled locomotive, built in 1882 at the shops of the Central Pacific Railroad, at Sacramento, California, still retained the flared smokestack and some of the decorative scroll-work of earlier engines.

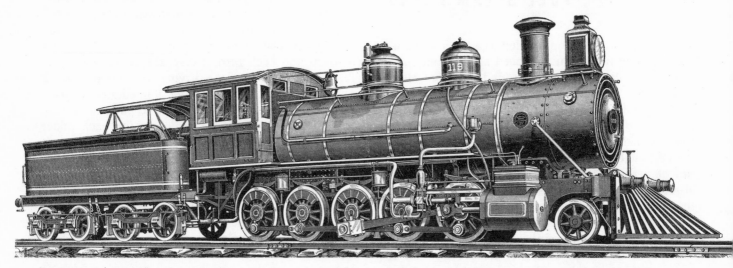

The famous Decapod from the Baldwin Locomotive Works. It and the Southern Pacific's "El Gobernador" were the two most powerful locomotives in the world. Built for working a mountain grade on a Brazilian railroad, in 1885.

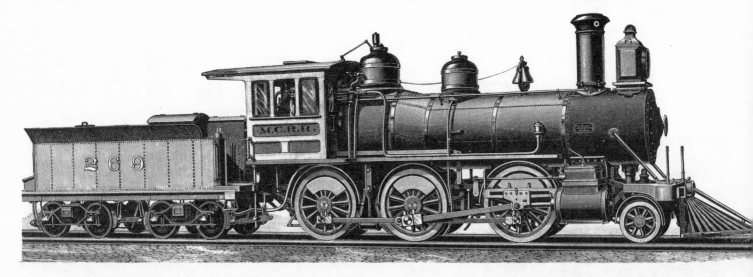

The great Mogul freight locomotive of the Michigan Central Railroad, was built in 1887 by the Schenectady Locomotive Works, at Schenectady, New York. Smokestacks were simplified, and moldings abolished for easy curves.

Freight locomotive of the Baltimore & Ohio. It reveals the increasing trend to functional design, as seen in today's monster locomotives. By 1885, the combined weight of a powerful engine and tender was about 224,000 pounds.

Compound express passenger locomotive, built for the Central Railroad of New Jersey, successor to the road for which George Stevens had obtained, in 1815, the first railroad charter ever granted in the United States.

Compound freight locomotive, with eight driving wheels, for the Norfolk & Western Railroad. It had been found better to increase the number of wheels, rather than to enlarge their diameter, which placed the engine too high.

163

The freight brakeman's work, when the weather was good offered many pleasant interludes.

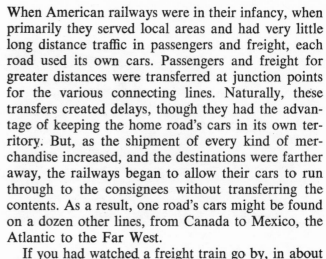

F. O. B. . . . U. S. A.

When American railways were in their infancy, when primarily they served local areas and had very little long distance traffic in passengers and freight, each road used its own cars. Passengers and freight for greater distances were transferred at junction points for the various connecting lines. Naturally, these transfers created delays, though they had the advantage of keeping the home road's cars in its own territory. But, as the shipment of every kind of merchandise increased, and the destinations were farther away, the railways began to allow their cars to run through to the consignees without transferring the contents. As a result, one road's cars might be found on a dozen other lines, from Canada to Mexico, the Atlantic to the Far West.

If you had watched a freight train go by, in about 1890, you might have seen cars marked *Railway Despatch, Fresh Meat Express, Traders' Despatch, White Line, Blue Line, Armour Refrigeration Line, Swift's Refrigeration Line, Union Line, Red Line, Export Refrigerator, Star Union, Merchant's Despatch Transportation Company,* in addition to the names or the initials of many of the established railroads. Some of the names represented cooperative lines owned by the railway companies. Each road assigned a certain number of its own freight cars and the expenses and the earnings of the line were prorated. The special cars—such as those used for dressed beef and those for livestock—were usually owned by the firms who shipped in them. Coal had its special cars; coarse lumber and stone moved in flat or platform cars. Other cars had carefully controlled temperatures: refrigerated to maintain 40 degrees—used for dressed meats, fruit and provisions. Potatoes in bulk were brought in great quantities to the East, in box-cars fitted with an ordinary stove in which a fire was maintained or an automatic self-feeding oil stove that would function for ten days or two weeks without attention. Special freight cars were equipped with water troughs and hay racks for the shipment of horses and cattle; there were express cars also, for more valuable horses, and these could be coupled to passenger trains.

California fruits, Kansas wheat, Michigan pine, West Virginia and Pennsylvania coal, Southern cotton . . . all poured into the cities, while finished merchandise from the factories and shops was sped to the merchants throughout the country. "A package of merchandise can be transported from New York to Chicago in two days and three nights," was the railways' promise in 1890, and shippers and consignees arranged their sales and stock of goods in accordance with the maintenance of this schedule. Already, "freights" of 50 or more cars were not unusual.

Braking in wintry weather meant braving the worst of snow and sleet on icy freight tops.

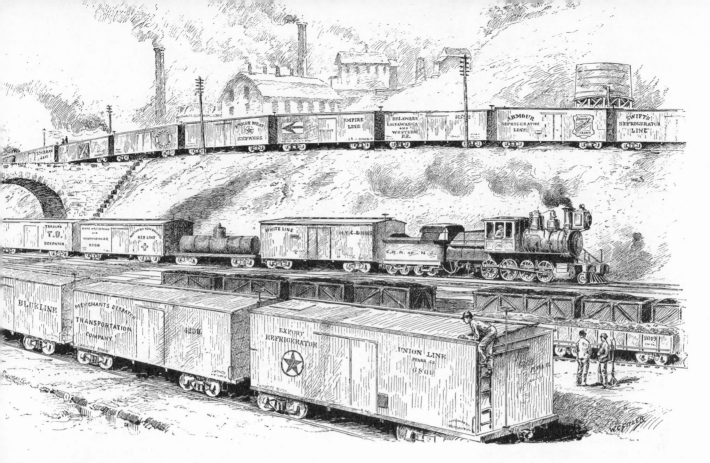

The long lines of freight cars, with names and symbols, were like a catalog of the nation's railways.

Traveling car of a tobacco company, "strictly pure."

Dump car. Some were operated by steam from the engine.

The Burton stock car could carry 20 cows, or 18 horses.

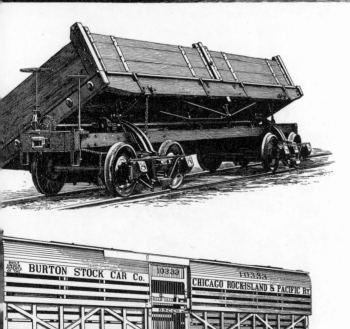

In the freight yard at night the brakeman's signals were interpreted by switchman and engineer.

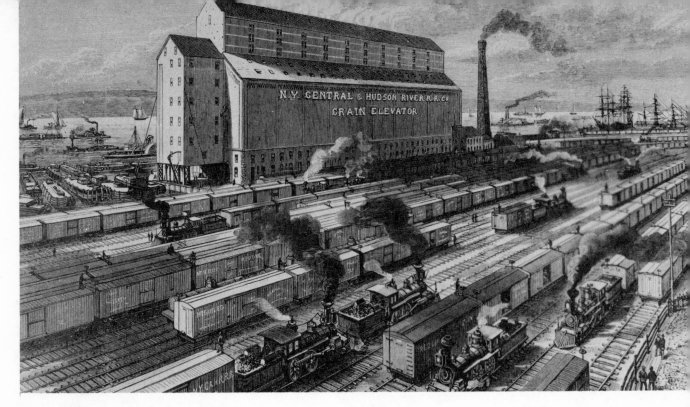

The great freight yards with their elevators and countless tracks—like this of the N. Y. C. & H. R. Railroad on the North River—received such enormous shipments of grain that many of the freight trains were nearly a half-mile long.

FREIGHT YARDS AND RAIL JUNCTIONS

The yardmaster was expected to know the contents of each freight car, its destination, and the track on which it stood. He had assistants and the foremen of yard crews, each crew having charge of one road engine, and going out with it.

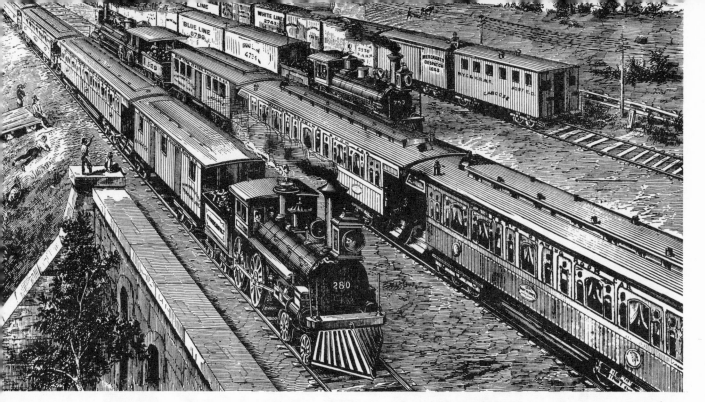

Drawing room cars and sleepers, day coaches and baggage cars swept along on the New York Central—"the great four-track railroad of the world" —beside endless lines of freights and cabooses from all the railways of the land.

Rail junctions, with their complex system of interlacing tracks, had nearly as many engines used for shifting the cars, as there were road engines used for moving the freight trains. The unloading and loading went on, day and night.

FARES,
PLEASE

THE HUMAN TIDES *of city-dwellers, hurrying, homeward-bound, horse-cars, like snails inching along . . . heyday of the hay-burner; trolley travelers standing, squeezing, squirming at close of day . . . these joys of urban locomotion, the penality of proximity.*

"DON'T TALK TO THE MOTORMAN" *. . . a forbidding sign seldom heeded; in the good old Summertime . . . open cars with reversible seats and running boards. What a thrill to "hit the breeze" on family outings to some distant park . . . a nickel a ride to quarters little known. "Take me out to the ball game" . . . a day to remember, now all but forgotten.*

RAPID TRANSIT, *never solvent . . . searching, groping for a way of life, as city streets grow ever more populous. Overhead . . . noisy, rumbling railways on stilts girded by sinewy ribbons of steel encircling the city . . . or burrowing underground where millions move like moles . . . rushing, crushing, pushing, shoving . . . "Take the express, then change for a local."*

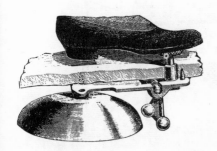

CLANG! CLANG! CLANG! *The horse-car's gone, the trolley gong is heard no more . . . the El is razed, its tracks uprooted, reaching the end of the line . . . point of no return.*

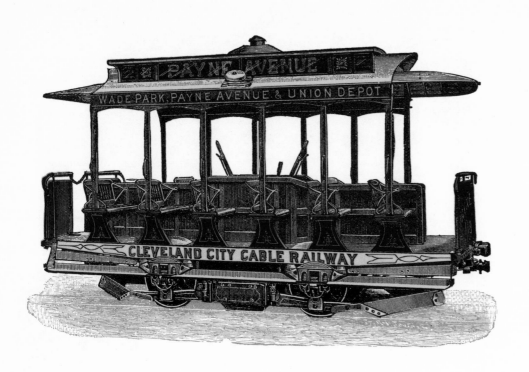

OPEN GRIP CAR

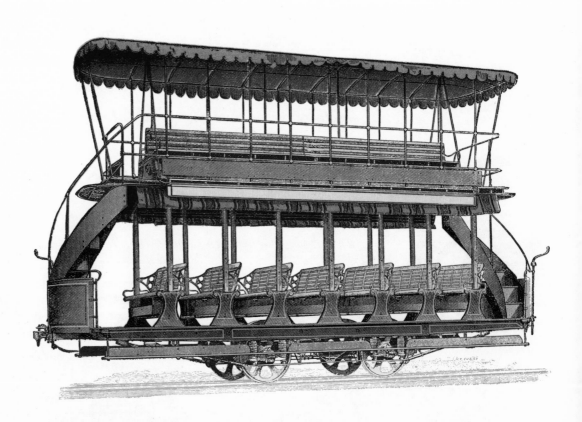

DOUBLE DECK CAR WITH CANOPY

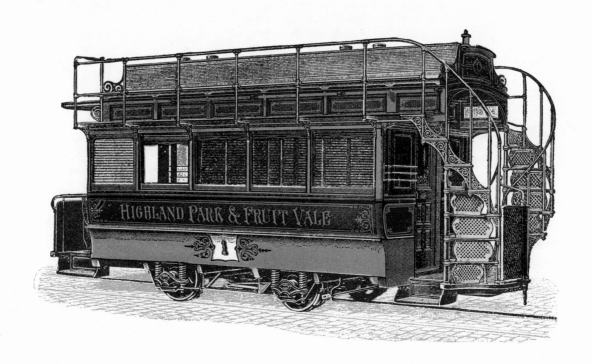

DOUBLE DECK CAR

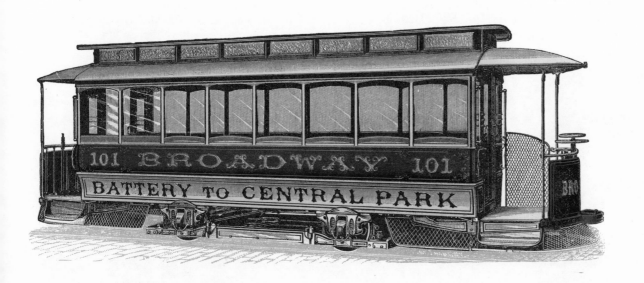

CLOSED ELECTRIC CAR

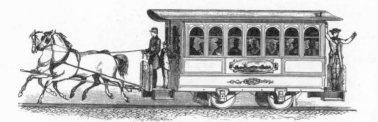

Early horse cars resembled the pioneer railway carriages which, in turn, reflected stage coach design.

OMNIBUSES ON IRON RAILS

Manhattan's traffic jams of today are actually less acute than those which existed in downtown New York streets 125 years ago, according to contemporary accounts and pictures. Horse-drawn omnibuses—which had superseded the earlier stage coaches—intermingled with private carriages, until it was declared impossible to accommodate any more traffic. Yet only seven years before the first "horse railway" cars appeared in 1832, there had not existed even a local omnibus service. In this city of nearly 200,000 people, the inhabitants walked to their places of employment, unless they were affluent enough to own or hire carriages. Infrequent stage coach service existed to Philadelphia, Albany, and Boston and, more frequently, the buses ran to New York's "suburbs," Yorkville and Harlem.

Then, in 1827, an enterprising resident, Abraham Brower, had ordered a stage coach type of vehicle built with open sides and seats arranged crosswise, to carry twelve people. Called the *"Accommodation,"* this was operated on Broadway. In 1829, Brower had another vehicle built, with seats running length-

Thousands came by the horse railway cars to the famous Crystal Palace where New York's first World's Fair was held in 1853 . . . on the present site of Bryant Park. A colorfully costumed foreign cavalry detachment thrills the well-dressed sidewalk throngs, including small boys at the curb.

Jefferson Market, on New York's Sixth Avenue horse car line, 1857. The cars were filled, day and night. The Market's huge wooden tower held a fire-alarm bell.

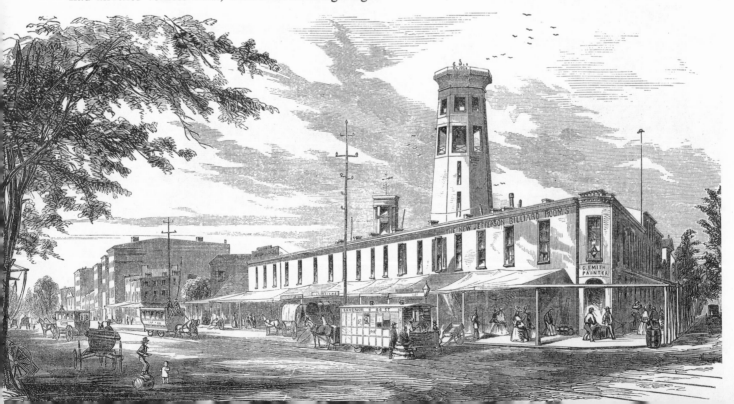

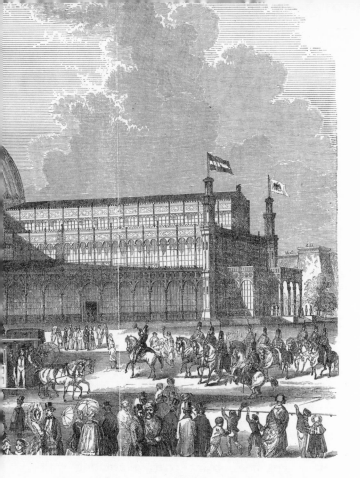

wise. This, bringing the passengers face to face, was named the *"Sociable."* Two years later, Brower ordered of John Stephenson—a recently established coach-maker—a larger, heavier vehicle, which carried the name *"Omnibus"* on its side panels. From that beginning, over a hundred omnibuses—most of them independently owned and operated—were running on New York streets by 1835.

Inspired by the new railroad locomotive, the *De-Witt Clinton,* John Mason—a prominent banker, merchant, and citizen of New York—envisaged a new kind of street railway with "coaches mounted on iron wheels drawn by horses over iron rails" laid in the middle of the street. This was an idea never before considered but a charter was granted by the state legislature for a single or double railroad between Twenty-third Street and the Harlem River. Since this was thinly settled, mostly farm territory, permission was obtained to carry the line from Fourth Avenue and the Bowery to Walker Street. John Stephenson constructed the two cars for the street railway. Each car, with seats for 30 passengers, was divided into three compartments each with its own entrance door, so that the effect was similar to that of three stage coaches linked together.

There were gala ceremonies, speech-making, and a trial run with city and New York and Harlem railway company officials filling the two cars on opening day, in November, 1832, when the first mile of track had been laid from Prince to Fourteenth Streets. Another mile had been added, by another year, and the route extended to four miles by 1834. Expansion was halted for a time but, by the early 1850's, the Second, Third, Sixth, and Eighth Avenue lines were established, and others were being built in Brooklyn.

Below right: **United States Pneumatic Postal Dispatch** opposite the offices of many publications, patent attorneys, and an early advertising agency. The horse car ran from City Hall to Central Park, on Third Avenue— the route of the Harlem and Yorkville line.

New York Times Building of 1857, newly erected in "Printing House Square," where the City Hall, Bowery and Third Avenue horse railway cars rolled briskly along, passing the surviving omnibus.

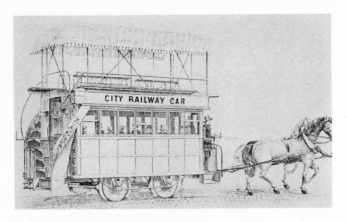

Elegant double-decked horse railway car, Boston 1857.

New Orleans Street Railroad car, 1855,
said to have been converted from an omnibus.

STREET RAILWAYS SPREAD

New Orleans was the next city to lay tracks for a street railway. The original plan was to construct four and a half miles of tracks from Canal Street out to the small suburb of Carrollton but, before the line was laid, a branch was started on Magazine Street. In December, 1834, a contract for two horses and a driver—for the Magazine Street line—was signed. After New York built its extra lines, and Brooklyn had horse cars making continuous runs from Fulton Ferry to Greenwood Cemetery, while another route connected Brooklyn with Williamsburg, cars on rails appeared on Boston streets.

Though it was hoped that Boston and its suburbs would soon be connected by the horse railway, doubts were expressed that such transit could ever enjoy a solid success because, as *Ballou's Pictorial,* June 7, 1856, said: "The founders of this village, never dreaming of its possible magnitude, were excessively economical in laying out the town thoroughfares, now too contracted for the vehicular tide which flows through them already." New York's broad and spacious streets were referred to with open envy. Boston's Tremont Street track had been laid experimentally; if the system did not work to the public satisfaction, the tracks were to be removed. Yet the obvious advantages of the horse cars were glowingly set forth: "Street surfaces are full of irregularities . . . passage over them in an ordinary conveyance reminds one of a run across a 'chop' sea.

All this jolting is avoided on the rail. The cars glide as smoothly as a rowboat over a quiet stream."

By 1857, Boston was making horse car fashion news with an open car on the Metropolitan Horse Railroad. The month was April; the car, "very pretty, with elaborate paintings," and the passengers' attire were well described: "The new open car offers a very novel appearance as it moves through our streets filled with ladies and gentlemen, presenting a variety of costumes, black coats alternating with gaily colored silks and satins, collapsed frocks contrasting with expanded crinolines." Though the cars had been running for two years, each new one attracted crowds of onlookers along its routes. The Metropolitan Horse Railroad—with 500 horses, about 50 open and top-seated cars, 50 omnibuses, and 80 closed and open sleighs—announced its intention to provide enough cars, each of which seated 24, for every passenger to have a seat. Added allurements were offices in the Metropolitan Hotel, "fitted up very liberally with a complete suite of apartments for the ladies, provided with all modern conveni-

Open and roofless, this Metropolitan horse car attracted staid Bostonians in front of the Winthrop House, April 1857.

First City Railway horse cars appeared on Boston streets, 1855.

The **Metropolitan Horse** Railroad's cars in Tremont Street, Boston and Roxbury route, 1856.

Early Boston and Cambridge New Horse Railroad car to Mount Auburn, 1856.

ences." So short a time before, people who lacked private carriages had been forced to walk, even to the suburbs. Then came the Omnibus "Hourly" on wheels or sleigh-runners, according to season.

About 1858, Philadelphians were heatedly for, and against, street railway construction though even its opponents conceded that the laying of the tracks was perhaps inevitable. The *Sunday Dispatch* warned readers that "In New York City they kill one person each week on city railroads and mangle three or four on an average in the same time." Baltimoreans next made ineffectual efforts to prevent the coming of the horse cars on rails. By 1859, Pittsburgh, Cincinnati, and Chicago had street railways and, in 1869, the first street car line outside America was started in England, at Birkenhead, built by George Francis Train, an American.

The "drawing-room companions" and scientific journals of the day constantly illustrated and described the new horse cars as these appeared in various cities. One from New Orleans, double-decked and gay-awninged, had a flight of steps accessible

from both sides . . . doubtless a problem to the crinoline-skirted Southern belles.

Certain class distinctions existed. Some horse cars, on which extra fares were charged, were reserved for ladies—assurance against exposure to ribald words, foul whiskey and tobacco odors! Poor country-cousin types were the humdrum horse cars with straw on the floor, liberally dampened with tobacco juice. Though men seldom smoked, except on car platforms, tobacco chewing was a favorite pastime. Ventilation, especially in cold weather, was poor; the air malodorant.

By 1886, 100,000 horses and mules were in use on the more than 500 street railways in over 300 United States' cities. The cars served many uses, often being rented privately for wedding parties, Sunday school and lodge picnics, and other excursions. It was not unusual, in a number of cities, for car lines to maintain a horse car hearse, suitably sable-curtained, and complete with lugubrious driver . . . so that mourning families and their friends could journey together to the cemetery.

First horse car of the Baltimore City Railroad, July 20, 1859 . . . its introduction was attended with much opposition.

Busy scene in Fulton Street, Brooklyn, from the Ferry, 1857. Four horse cars in one block, shared with an omnibus, carts, and carriages.

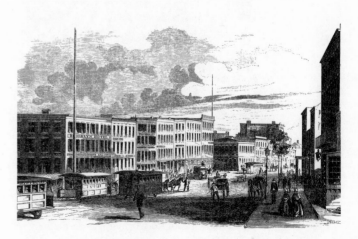

Street Car Accommodations . . . ironic reference to the overloads during the Centennial Exposition, 1876. Contemporary sketch of a Philadelphia horse car.

PITY THE POOR HORSES

Since horses were in their stables about 20 hours of each day, many more horses were required than cars. The ratio varied in different cities with five to nine horses to each car. Selection, care and feeding of the animals being weighty matters, the success of the horse railway depended in no small measure on the intelligence and ability of the stable superintendents, their managers, foremen, veterinarians, farriers and hostlers. In the purchase of the right type of horses

or mules for car use, weight, build, height, color, disposition, gait and age were carefully considered. Mules were preferred for use in the deep South, being able to endure extreme heat. They also cost less but seldom had any appreciable re-sale value.

In his chapter on Horse Traction, in *Street Railways,* published in 1892, C. B. Fairchild suggests that: "As to build, a good blocky horse without too much 'daylight' under him or, rather, not too long-legged—say from 15½ to 16 hands high—usually gives the best satisfaction. The feet and muscles of the legs are the mainstay of a railroad horse and should be carefully noted in the selection . . . a good disposition and easy gait are absolutely necessary." The best weights, when horses were driven in pairs, were about 1100, while approximately 1200 pounds was suggested for single driving. For use operating sweepers and snowplows, heavier horses were recommended. "Mares," Fairchild observed, "last longer than horses, but are not usually so docile."

Newly purchased horses were rested for a day or two; then they worked a fourth or half the usual time, driven by men who painstakingly broke them in, generally harnessed alongside an experienced car horse. They were considered "seasoned" in about a year.

Started at Last . . . horse car passengers often helped to whip the horses and free the cars from heavy snow-drifts that covered the tracks.

Ninety in the Shade . . . hard-worked horses died so fast on Chicago streets that "authorities lacked the means to remove their bodies with necessary promptness."

Always Room for One More . . . though the horses were ready to fall. *Harper's Weekly*, September 21, 1872, editorialized on the "scandalous conditions."

Car horses were fed three times daily and emphasis was placed on the choice quality and careful preparation of the feeds—10 or 12 pounds of cut hay with 14 pounds of ground oats and corn being suggested as an adequate and economical daily ration. Single horse cars averaged a daily journey of 10 miles; 15 miles was considered standard for a pair of horses. Horses were usually rested one day in seven. Wherever possible, a driver was assigned to the same team, as the horses responded better and kept in better condition than when driven by different men.

The importance of proper shoeing—for cobblestone and dirt roads, for wet weather and frozen ground, and the animal's individual gait—led to the publication of many books on the subject. Fairchild advised of the "books in language so simple that anyone may learn to practise humane treatment of this most faithful and patient servant of man, the street car horse." Railway managements tried to maintain model conditions—as to stalls, ventilation, water-troughs, rest periods and grooming—to protect their investments in horse-power. Yet, simultaneously, on city streets, horrifying spectacles of cruelly over-worked horses were seen daily.

A Pail of Water . . . for a deserving dobbin. The pleased man in the cutaway may have been a representative of the local humane society.

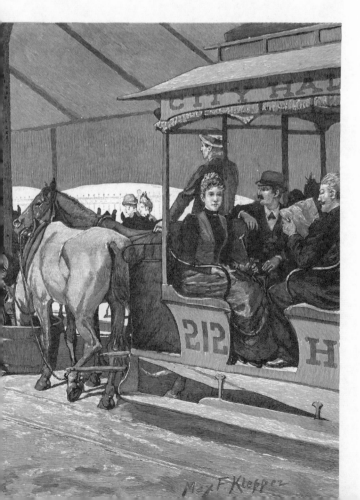

The Running Horses . . . the ride in the open air, brought obvious pleasure to corpulent driver and his passengers of the late 1880's.

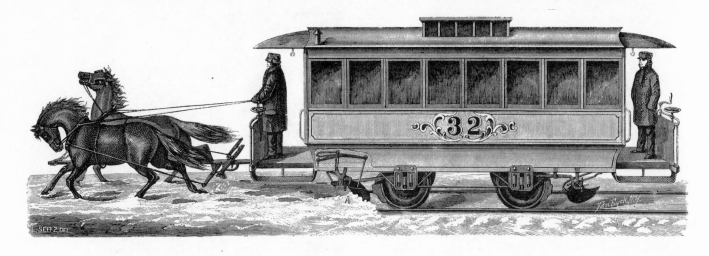

Snow plows, attached to both ends of a horse car, were tested in several New England towns, also Albany, Troy, and Philadelphia, 1866-7.

DEEP SNOW MAKES THE GOING SLOW

Uninterrupted operation of the street railways, during Winter weather, created heavy problems. With snow on the tracks, street car wheels could make no contact and the usual practice would have been to clear the tracks, by snow plows or manpower. But in many cities, especially in the earlier years, horse car operators were prohibited from this, since the city fathers decreed that snow must be allowed to remain on the streets—for the pleasure and benefit of those who traveled in sleighs—until it melted away.

Boston's mayor and aldermen suggested that the horse railway companies could substitute sleighs for their cars, and charge the same fares. That this advice was followed is indicated by the listing—among the Metropolitan Horse Railroad's assets—of 80 closed and open sleighs. In other cities, when horse car operators attempted to melt the snow by the use of rock-salt, the residents and pedestrians along the car lines protested that the salt cooled the air to a dangerous degree, creating an extra crop of coughs and colds. The heavy blizzards—that were talked about for fifty years after, by those who experienced them—were pictured in many periodicals, showing New York street car operators struggling to keep routes open. As in stage coach days, men passengers often had to join the straining horses to free street cars from the snowdrifts.

Car heating was another worry for the street railway managements. Small heaters set under the floors of cars, with pipes to conduct the warmth upward, often also set the cars on fire. If fires did not occur, a stuffy atmosphere did. On certain lines, the heaters were installed on the car's front platform, from which the warmth was wafted into the car by registers. But with the uncertain ventilation, the often overheated air, and the passengers' damp clothing . . . riding the horse cars in Winter held few charms for the fastidious.

The great blizzard of January, 1877, created staggering problems for street car operators. As the snow prevented all contact of car wheel with the tracks, despite the power of ten horses the work cars could be moved only with the utmost difficulty.

Centre Street, New York City, February 1857. A long string of horses was harnessed in single file to haul an equally long street car from snowdrifts.

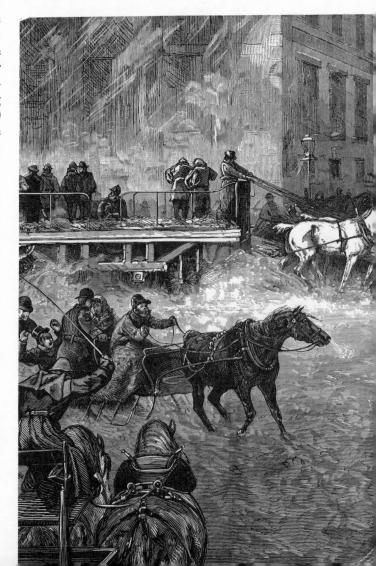

178

Men and horse teams, pitted against slush, snow, and blocked traffic under one of Manhattan's elevated street railways, January 1884.

Long noose-like ropes anchor side-platform standees on a New York Railroad car, 1867. Artist's prediction or actuality, captioned: "What are we coming to?"

ALWAYS ROOM FOR ONE MORE

Introduced with a decent regard for the passengers' comfort and the animals' pulling power, street railways soon became so popular that efforts to control the number of fares broke down. It was not unusual for cars with a seating capacity of 22, to carry 85 or 90. Yet the passengers continued to climb aboard, packing themselves in the car's interior, on the roof, or on front or rear platforms . . . evidently convinced that, if one could establish a toe hold, the horses would be equal to the load. *Harper's Weekly,* September 21, 1890, observed: "The car is packed and jammed until there is scarcely room to breathe . . . They manage such things much better in France. A Parisian omnibus or car is permitted to take the exact number of passengers for whom seats are provided, but not one more."

Contemporary art and editorials tell the tragic facts: horses dropping dead from heat and overwork in the summers; passengers out in slush and snow helping to keep the cars rolling in winter. Though most of the New York car companies had established relief stations along their routes for the horses, public

and private agencies had also erected nearly 150 drinking troughs for the horses, and the Society for the Prevention of Cruelty to Animals had a force of ten men, posted where they would be most effective for the prevention of abuse.

Heating of the horse cars was a problem in cold weather. Floors of the early cars were usually spread with hay to about mid-calf of the average passenger and it was not unusual for some of this hay to cling to neat trouser legs and sweeping skirts as men and women left the cars.

Horse car revenues were increased by the sale of space for advertising posters. First inspired by the requests of women passengers for public notices of their favorite charity, church bazaar, or similar event, the notices developed into a lucrative source of extra income for the car companies and a point of focus for gentlemen passengers' eyes which previously had concentrated on the ladies to, it was said, much feminine embarrassment. To reduce the number of accidents in boarding and alighting from the cars, newspapers carried many articles of advice.

Nearly 60 years after the first horse railway had appeared on Fourth Avenue, sketches showing how to get on and off a car were published in the *New York Sun,* and reprinted in the *Scientific American* of April 2, 1892. "Thousands of women," the *Sun*

THE WAY TO GET ON

HOW NOT TO GET ON   RESULT OF GETTING ON BY REAR HANDLE

said, "ride in horse cars in New York every day, of whom ninety-nine hundredths, or nine hundred and ninety-nine in a thousand, are in a state of next to complete ignorance of the scientific laws which dictate the mounting and descending in safety, and threaten disaster upon those who violate them. As a rule the cars are stopped and started properly, so that a woman can step on or off as though she were on her own staircase. But occasionally the horses will start a moment too soon or the impatient female will attempt to step to the street while the car is still moving, and then there comes calamity, perhaps humiliating and embarrassing, and always dangerous."

Baskets, shovels, valises in mad confusion on a rear car platform.

STREET-CAR SALAD

Never full! pack 'em in!
Move up, fat man, squeeze in, thin.
Trunks, Valises, Boxes, Bundles,
Fill up gaps as on she tumbles.
Market baskets without number,
Owners easy—nod in slumber.
Thirty seated, forty standing,
A dozen more on either landing.
Old man lifts the signal finger,
Car slacks up—but not a linger—
He's jerked aboard by sleeve or shoulder,
Shoved inside to sweat and moulder.
Toes are trod on, hats are smashed,
Dresses soiled—hoop-skirts crashed.
Thieves are busy, bent on plunder,
Still we rattle on, like thunder.
Packed together, unwashed bodies,
Bathed in fumes of whisky toddies;
Tobacco, garlic, cheese, and beer
Perfume the heated atmosphere.
Old boots, pipes, leather and tan,
And if in luck, a "Soap-Fat man."
Aren't this jolly? What a blessing!
A Street-Car Salad, with such a dressing.

Reprinted from *Harper's Weekly*, March 23, 1867

Some held to poles, some, it was said, sat on laps of others. Interior of a New York horse car, 1867.

SOMETHING LIKE THE CONSEQUENCES

HOW TO GET OFF

HOW NOT TO GET OFF

BUILT IN NEW YORK ... BOUGHT BY THE WORLD

Few lives in retrospect appear more admirable than that of John Stephenson, coach and car builder. Commissioned by A. Brower to build New York's first vehicle bearing the name *"Omnibus,"* in 1831, he also designed and built the first two horse cars for John Mason and the opening of the Fourth Avenue horse car line in 1832. The next year, Stephenson took out his first patent for improvement in car design. After building the first Fourth Avenue cars, Stephenson's enthusiasm led him to enlarge his plant. Then the depression of 1837 halted expansion and Stephenson was in a bad spot financially. He settled as best he could with his creditors, sometimes building vehicles for those to whom he was indebted. He had presented a four-horse truck, in lieu of cash, to one creditor, John Malt, who paraded the truck on Broadway, displaying the sign: "This is the way one bankrupt pays his debts; his name is Honest John Stephenson." Meanwhile Stephenson continued to build omnibuses and wagons. In 1852, when New York's horse car lines were extended to additional avenues, Stephenson once again was building street

Car building works of John Stephenson Company, Limited. A car for the Kansas City Cable Railway Co., 1889, stands at the arched gateway.

Stephenson-built in the 1880's for use on a horse car line in Baltimore, running from Columbia & Park Avenues to Druid Hill Park.

Eloquent evidence of the good taste and honest design expressed in all John Stephenson's coach and car building, this interior of the 1870's.

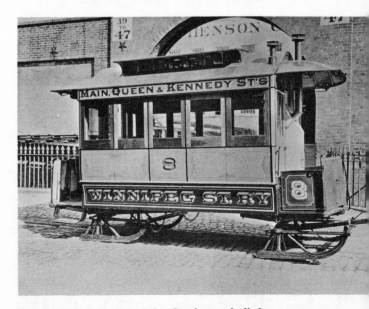

For forty below zero, John Stephenson's little street car on sleigh runners, with a stove on the front platform, built for use in Winnipeg, Manitoba.

Few business men of a century ago had Stephenson's foresight. Each car he manufactured was photographed before shipment, a priceless record for historians.

Beautiful painted panels, a car to view with pride, destined for the streets of Buenos Aires, in the 1870's . . . with scenes symbolic of the Argentine.

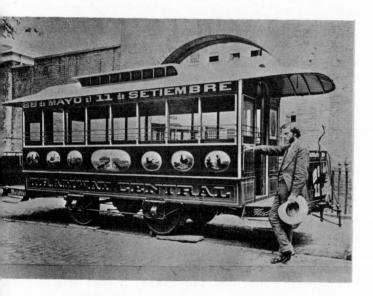

Out in China, too, in the 1880's, the "Company of the Iron Road Horse Car" placed its orders with the John Stephenson Company of New York.

Special private car designed by Stephenson in the 1870's . . . its chastely elegant interior a happy contrast to many ornate private cars of its day.

cars . . . eventually developing into the world's greatest designer and manufacturer of these vehicles.

In an interview with the *Scientific American*, August 24, 1878, John Stephenson—being asked how he had just won an order for 25 cars from the North Metropolitan Tramway of London, against 19 competitors—said: "Our cars weigh less by one-half than those made in Germany. They can be procured for £35 less than Birmingham can quote. The cars we furnished Glasgow can be operated from a stable one-third smaller than their own cars require. The nature of American woods has much to do with our success. The selection and preparation of material are no light jobs; the process of preparation requires three to four years. American irons are tougher than the English and we can get the required strength with less weight. We use white oak, white ash, poplar, basswood, hickory, beech, maple and pine—woods all easily procurable by us, while the English are obliged to use teakwood. Because their woods are inferior, they find it necessary to reinforce with iron, at the expense of lightness. . . . We meet with considerable opposition abroad, and the press is used to raise a cry against any corporation sending money away from home, especially in the present hard times." The cost of a modern car, ready for use, in 1878, was from $1,000 to $1,200.

Foot of Market Street, San Francisco, where street cars met passengers from sailing ships.

Valencia Street horse car line, San Francisco.

HEYDAY OF THE HORSE CAR

In many cities, the omnibuses continued to serve certain routes long after horse railway cars were well-established. But reckless driving was frequently charged against the bus drivers, New York newspapers declaring them "dangerous," "brutal," racing up and down streets with the "utmost fury." Carriage drivers and pedestrians were in peril of their lives. Hackney-coaches and gigs were crushed between two racing omnibuses . . . which had plenty of space elsewhere in the streets. "A ferocious spirit appears to have taken possession of the drivers," one paper added, "who defy law and delight in destruction." As the horse cars were restricted to their tracks, their drivers could not dash into other traffic lanes. This dependable quality of the railway cars, plus their capacity for carrying a greater number of passengers over longer routes, led to their growth.

Practically all cities and towns in the United States, most leading cities in Canada, as well as in Europe, Mexico, South America, Australia, and New Zealand, had their horse railway cars. In 1878, the Stephenson works had orders for London; Paris; Port Adelaide, Australia; Lima, Peru; St. Petersburg, Russia; Hull, Swansea, and Liverpool, England; Bahia, Brazil; Berlin; Jalapa, Mexico; Amsterdam, Holland; Wellington, New Zealand; Christiania, Norway; Rio de Janeiro; Hamburg; and a score of other places. America's wheels were rolling, not only across the face of the nation but over every continent on the earth, for the British colonies in South Africa also had American horse railway cars.

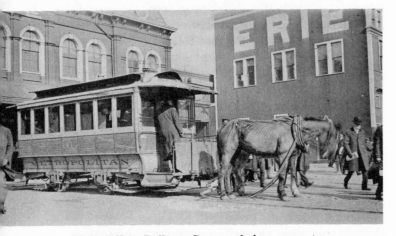

New York's 42nd Street, 1884, with view of the 6th Avenue El, and the horse cars.

Metropolitan Railway Company's horse car at the Erie Railroad's ferry terminal, 1917.

Central Park, North and East River Railroad's horse car at West and Liberty Streets, 1906.

Horse Car on West Street, at Chambers, 1916.

By 1888, many horse car lines converged on New York's "Printing House Square,"
bounded by Park Row, Nassau, Centre, Spruce, Frankfort and Chatham Streets.
The Sun, The Tribune, and the "new" *Times* buildings then dominated the area.

IT STARTED IN SAN FRANCISCO

The years succeeding the Civil War were a time of many inventions, of brave new efforts for improvement in various fields, including that of city transit. The overcrowded horse railway cars, their overworked horses and slow rate of travel inspired ideas for other methods. One of the simplest and most appealing was that of the cable. It had the virtues of cleanliness, safety, speed . . . and the cars glided along with an almost eerie smoothness that added to their fascination. San Francisco, in the flamboyant days of its gold strikes and quick wealth, enjoyed the first cable cars, just as today it is one of the last cities still to use them. A manufacturer of wire rope, Andrew Smith Hallidie, is credited with surmounting problems of cable car design and operation. Said to have witnessed a frightening horse car accident on a steep hill, in which with one horse fallen and brake broken the badly overloaded car slid to the bottom, and the panicked horse had to be destroyed, Hallidie gambled all his own money and all he could borrow —close to 100,000 dollars—on a cable car line. Troubles such as the builders of the Els encountered, in excavating for their deep pillar supports, also harried Hallidie in digging his cable-vaults.

The first line was constructed in Clay Street, a half-mile stretch under which was a double set of gas and water mains, not to mention ancient cisterns and some sewers. Discouraging delays and high costs

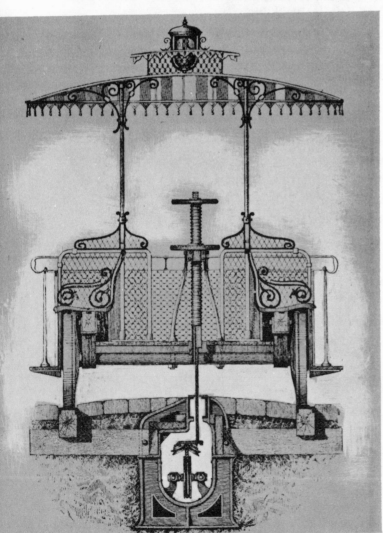

Hallidie's first screw type grip control was soon supplanted by Casebolt's lever-operated grip, the type in use today.

Tracks were laid at the bottom of the tunnels and at intervals along the sides pulleys were placed on which the cables traveled

Balloon car brought Baroque distinction to the Market Street Railway, in 1872. Bright idea of San Franciscan Henry Casebolt, inventive blacksmith. The carriage body due to its pivot mounting could be swung around with the horses in a half circle, without turning the trucks, when ready for the return trip.

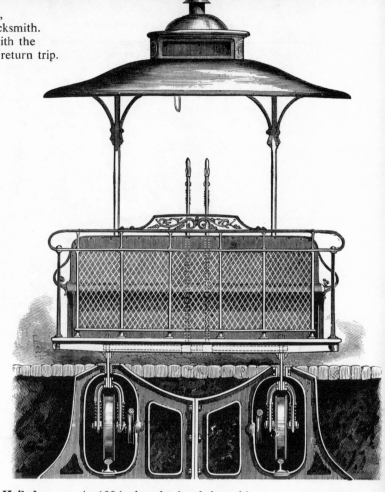

added to Hallidie's worries. On the very last day when his franchise stated that the experimental operation must be started, August 1, 1873, the cable car was tried out, Hallidie at the hand wheel. His workman, after one look at the steep hill, had refused to handle the grip. Though a number of minor emergencies developed in the test run, nearly a hundred people managed to climb into the grip car and its trailer, which had a combined seating capacity for thirty, on a trip later in the day.

Hallidie's success led to the building of a half dozen other cable roads. Henry Casebolt, a competent blacksmith with a talent for invention—he who had already built the umbrella-like balloon cars for the horse railway—devised a grip mechanism that supplanted Hallidie's cable-grip. Cable car transit soon attracted a number of investors. At a cost of nearly half a million dollars, the California Street line opened formally after several years a-building in April, 1878. Its cars had a florid Baroque splendor, a glittering of gold ornament and stained glass. This line is still in operation. Cable cars were already serving a number of United States cities by the early Eighties. Passengers grew to know and enjoy sharing the ride with the grip man, as they had with the horse car drivers. In fair weather, the grip car was a thrilling spot.

Hailed as new in 1884, the wheels of the cable cars were placed underground in the same tunnel as the cable. Slots in street replaced tracks.

BUT...WILL THE CABLE HOLD?

"We cannot attempt an exhaustive treatise on cable traction," C. B. Fairchild says in *Street Railways,* the practical handbook for railway men, published in 1892, "for we have in our office a list of 1,000 patents, issued in the United States alone, on this one subject." The idea of cable traction was not new when Hallidie applied it to the first San Francisco cable line in Clay Street. Hallidie's own super wire cable—which he manufactured in a modest factory —was being used in a number of industries, particularly for the aerial tramways bringing down gold and silver ores in the high Sierra. Its strength and practicality had first been demonstrated on a 200 foot stretch; then later for an ore tramway almost six miles long. He knew that hotel and building elevators were suspended from wire cables, and the hills of San Francisco suggested an extra opportunity to the keen-minded Scot. Just as, in New York City, the Society for the Prevention of Cruelty to Animals had intervened on behalf of the overburdened railway car horses, in California this same Society was calling the attention of the Legislature to the cruelly

brief life of the street car horse as compared with that of horses otherwise engaged. Hallidie's musings —the horse accidents he had witnessed plus his natural interest in finding more uses for his superior wire cable—dovetailed with the S.P.C.A.'s protests. Each supported the other.

Fairchild had emphasized that, in treating of cable railways, it was proper that early workers in the field should receive due credit for their ingenuity. The principle had, he explained, been employed in mines for many years and suggestions as to adapting the idea to street railways had been made by E. S. Gardiner of Philadelphia, and others, but there was no evidence that the men who made the first practical test, in San Francisco, in 1873, had any previous knowledge of such suggestions. Andrew S. Hallidie

Three Sutter Street dummies with car loads of ladies at the corner of Sutter and Larkin, in 1881.

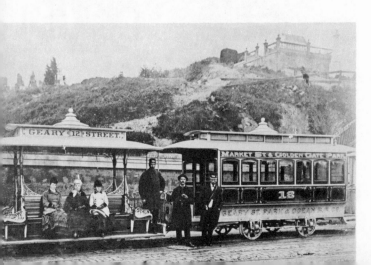

Even with the ladies, the grip car of the cable lines was first choice in fair weather, Mayor Adolph Sutro holds the grab handle of the trailer; Samuel Clemens (Mark Twain) is among the notables.

Andrew Smith Hallidie, pioneer in the construction of the California Street Railway, donned top hat for the spot of honor in the center of the front seat, for the opening day's formal run of No. 10 dummy on San Francisco's Clay Street Cable Line.

and his associates were acknowledged as the pioneers in operating street cars by a cable, slotted tube and grip. Hallidie had explained that he would substitute for the horses an endless rope, concealed underground, to which the cars would be connected much as were the ore buckets to the endless cables used in the mines. There would be one difference—the car could be detached from the moving cable, and reattached, as required.

People liked the grip cars. No dirt and cinders, no danger of explosion—as from the steam locomotives; no stable stench; no cruelty to man's most faithful friend, the horse. No tracks to catch and snap the wheels of carriages. But there were some apprehensions.

Would the endless cable remain strong, or would it ravel and break? The cables sometimes were exceptionally long, one used in Denver almost seven miles in length; three- and four-mile cables were more or less a commonplace. Hallidie's wire cable consisted of six strands of nineteen steel wires each, with a rope center. There were ropes with a wire center which, it was claimed, made them stronger but they lacked the desired flexibility and were not considered best for street railway use. Some workmen claimed that every rope had an individual personality . . . some being well-behaved, others an endless nuisance.

It was on the cable that the greatest care was lavished. At night, when the cars were not running, every inch of the wire rope received the close inspection of maintenance crews. The standard type of cable was expected to last about 75,000 miles, giving probably a year's use on some lines. While the ropes seldom broke, the occasional wearing through of one strand sometimes tangled in the grip, making it impossible for the gripman to stop his car. This led him to sound his gong in raucous, steady warning, often overtaking a car in front discharging or taking aboard passengers. Its gripman then would depart with speed, fearing a collision. Folk of the '80's claimed that they'd seen a half-dozen cable cars, gongs strident, all charging madly down a street running away from the car that couldn't be halted. In such an emergency, the conductor of the luckless car was expected to make a flying leap, reach a call box, and order the power house to halt the cable.

Thrilling new way to travel. Even those, bound for a cemetery visit, took the cable car to connect with the steam dummy to Calvary Cemetery Park.

189

CARRYING THE CROWDS BY CABLE

Alexander S. Hallidie's invention was in the high noon of success. Londoners were reading, in January 1883, about the new system of working tramways. "By it horses and locomotives are done away with, the carriages being propelled by an endless wire rope placed under ground, and worked from a stationary steam engine from either end of the line. The advantages claimed for the system are that it is perfectly noiseless, very cleanly in consequence of the horse being dispensed with, and the cruel process of dragging cars by horses is removed." The great nuisance to private carriages "skidding" by coming in contact with the grooved rail of the horse system would be eliminated, for the Cable proposed to "put down flat rails or bands of steel only just wide enough to clear a smooth road for the cars close to the pavement, and there will be nothing to impede in any way the free use of the road by other conveyances." In the United States, in the decade after Hallidie's first trial run in Clay Street, cable lines were operating successfully in eight other cities.

Everywhere the cable lines were carrying crowds. Once again, as with earlier means of city transit, property owners who had bemoaned the cable's approach were rejoicing at the increased value of their real estate, and workers—due to the increased speed of the cable cars—could live further away from the city without spending an interminable time in travel. Soon, too, the car horses could retire to the country.

On San Francisco's steep hills, riding a cable car was as much fun as a roller coaster. Although Cali-

fornia was just recovering from a tight money market, there was no difficulty in finding plenty of financing for new cable companies. Between 1880 and 1883, a number of additional cable lines had been established. In 1886, the Omnibus Railroad Company, one of the city's first public utilities, disposed of all its horse cars. San Francisco was embracing the cables with gusto.

Between the millionaire and the poorest worker

Small girl shares breeze with tall-crowned hats and elderly beards on San Francisco Cable Line for Central Avenue Market Street, and the Ferries.

Worked without horses or locomotives, Hallidie's Patented Cable Tramway, featured in *London Graphic* as "very renumerative, paying dividends up to 30%."

in the City of the Golden Gate there had never been the sharp class distinctions encountered in Eastern cities. If any had existed, the cable car became the great democratizer. It was the gayest way to attend the grand opera, weddings, a picnic, outdoor dinner, or ball game. The cables carried high and low to every form of sport and entertainment, creating a friendly openheartedness that immeasurably enriched the city's charm.

Safely handling large crowds, Market Street, San Francisco, Cable Railway, Haight St. Branch Line, at its terminus at Golden Gate State Park.

"The days of old, the days of gold, the days of '49" . . . California celebrated its Admission Day, anniversary of Statehood, with triumphal arch over cable car marked "To Cliff House Park and Ferries, via Haight Street."

Eight other cities had cable lines, four years after San Francisco's first—Chicago, Brooklyn, Kansas City, Mo., St. Louis, Los Angeles, Oakland, Hoboken, and Omaha. Chicago's State Street Route was converted from a horse car line in 1881.

EDISON ELECTRIFIES THE RAILS

"The practical application of electric current—as a motive power for railways—seems never to have had a prospect of success," observed *Scientific American*, June 5, 1880, "before the experiments of Dr. Siemens in Berlin, in 1879, and the present extended experiments of Mr. Edison." The difficulties were great, the cost of experiments a deterrent to most inventors. But, as the *Scientific American* pointed out, "Mr. Edison, more fortunate in this way than many of our experimenters, has not been hampered by monetary difficulties. Having ample means for carrying out his ideas, he has been enabled to develop his inventions more rapidly perhaps than any man living."

The little electric railway at Menlo Park was a half mile in length—soon to be extended to a mile circle—and had been built on natural ground with no regard for curves or grades, and little or no grading. "The motor," a visitor was told, "is precisely like Mr. Edison's electrical generators, and the motive power is supplied by his stationary engine, the power being converted into electrical energy by a single generator. The current thus created is conveyed to the track by two copper wires, one wire connected with each rail. The machine is managed about like a steam locomotive, and it pushes ahead with wonderful power."

Many among the first 12 or 14 passengers recalled, years later, that the early trial to which Mr. Edison had invited them had scared them almost to death . . . they had traveled at breakneck speed up and down grades, around sharp curves, over humps and bumps, at a terrifying speed of 25 to 40 miles an hour. The reporter for a scientific journal commented: "Our experiences were sufficient to enable us to see the desirableness of a smoother road, and to convince us that there is no lack of power in Mr. Edison's machine."

Edison's Railway, 1880: one electrical locomotive, one open car.

Earliest version of Edison's electric locomotive provided no protection against bad weather.

THE ELECTRIC RAILROAD.

INTERIOR OF THE CAB.

Two years later, the driver's house was enclosed and had a contrivance in front to carry a headlight, giving a steam-locomotive look to the electric wonder.

"Without puffing or snorting, without smoke or cinders," reported an impressed visitor, "the train left the shed and was switched on to the main track, taking the curve into Menlo Park woods with no noise except that made by the running of the wheels."

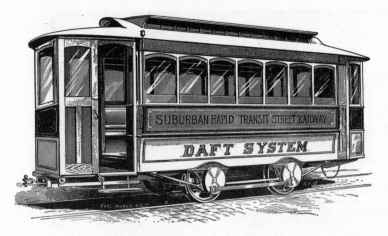

New Daft Electric car in Pittsburgh, Pa.

Daft Electric Railway at Asbury Park, N. J., 1886, had 11 open cars, 4 closed, each with sufficient power to tow another ordinary car fully loaded.

THE DAFT TROLLEY SYSTEM

Many other men, besides Edison, had been experimenting with the application of electricity to street car operation. Important among these was Leo Daft, who had come from England to the United States in 1866, at the age of 23. After operating a photographic studio in Troy, New York, he turned to the greater fascination of electricity. In his small electric light plant in New Jersey, he mounted a motor on wheels and tested it, using rails as one of the conductors for the current, with low voltages to guard against shock. In May, 1883, Daft built the *Ampère*, a two-ton working locomotive, with a 25-horsepower motor drawing current from a third rail, returning it by the running rails. Though the trial test before bankers and reporters wrecked the *Ampère*, Daft soon built two other locomotives, the *Volta* and the *Pacinotti*, operating them in Boston and at Coney Island's Iron Pier. At the latter spot, the general manager of a Baltimore horse car line became interested in the electrical locomotive, deciding to give it a trial on the Baltimore car line's sharp, hilly branch. Despite stiff conditions, Daft welcomed the trial. Passenger service started August 10, 1885, making the three-mile Baltimore branch line the first electric railway in regular operation in America.

The third rail gave trouble; rains created short circuits, holding up service, and when Daft stepped up the voltage to 120, complaints about shock and the occasional electrocution of small animals poured in. Though the Baltimore branch line reverted to horse-drawn cars, Daft by that time was busy perfecting his *Benjamin Franklin* electric locomotive for use on New York's Ninth Avenue El. From 1886, Daft electric cars were running in a number of cities . . . the controversial third rail abandoned for two overhead wires, the separate locomotive supplanted by electrified horse cars with trolleys. Daft lived until 1922 . . . to see electric trolleys in the high tide of their popularity.

Daft's double trolley road, Cincinnati, O., 1889, part of its route over cable car tracks. The electric line towed in the cable cars when these broke down.

Passenger carrying capacity was doubled, 1886, by Daft's Baltimore and Hampden Electric Line. It used new overhead conductor attachment.

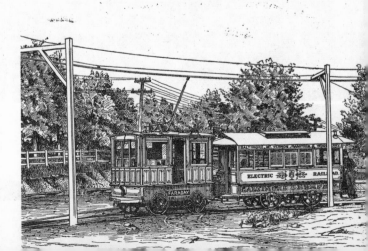

Van Depoele's Scranton Suburban Railway, 1886, opened with snow and ice on tracks, attained hourly speed of 12 miles, each car running 100 miles daily.

TROLLEYS BY VAN DEPOELE

A lengthy list of "electricians," mainly self-taught, had busied themselves producing electric locomotives. The Americans—blacksmiths, farmers, academic professors, several former examiners of the United States Patent Office—did not make much practical progress.

Charles J. Van Depoele, born in Belgium in 1846 and, like Daft, coming in his early years to America, was not content with the flourishing business he had established shortly after his arrival. Leaving his Detroit woodworking shop and several hundred employees to the management of his father, he went to Chicago, forming an electric arc-light company. At 36, he was experimenting with electric cars and, a year later in 1883, showed a small car at the Chicago Industrial Exposition. Reports of Siemens' two-horsepower dynamo drawing three tiny cars for months at the Berlin Industrial Exhibition in 1879, hauling 80,000 visitors, apparently suggested to Van Depoele the value of showing such a car at Chicago's Exposition. In 1884, Van Depoele operated another electric car at the Toronto Exposition. Both these show cars were powered by current from a wire in a slot between the tracks. For his first city street cars, Van Depoele used up to 1,400 volts, with little overhead *travelers* . . . which Daft called *trollers* . . . and which for both inventors caused many operational headaches. He and Daft feuded verbally over their respective ideas—Daft placing his motor under the cars, Van Depoele his on the front platforms. Though Van Depoele lines were operating in five cities, by 1886, the heavy motors—too great a load for the platforms of the light horse cars—soon shook the cars to the breaking point. Many predicted that electric power could never supplant horses for smooth-running city street transit.

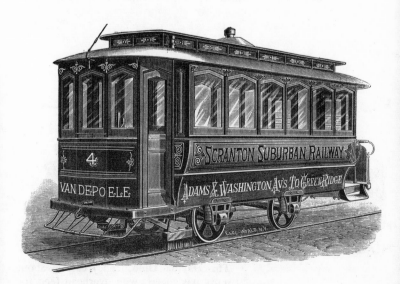

Street car operating successfully in Scranton, Pa.

Windsor, Canada, had its Van Depoele Electric Trolleys, running two miles to Walkerville; using an overhead conductor, the current conveyed to the motor by a *traveler*.

In Minneapolis, 1886, the Van Depoele Electric Railways carried crowds to grand open air concerts Sunday afternoons and evenings.

Cleveland passengers, in 1889, found it a "delightful sensation" to ride on the Sprague Road on Euclid Avenue.

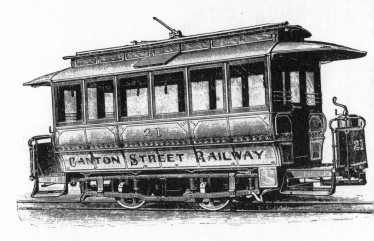

Canton Street Railway, electric-powered, was one of the first electric systems in Ohio.

SPRAGUE SPARKS ELECTRIC TRANSIT

Born in Connecticut in 1857, Frank J. Sprague was a wizard in mathematics at 16, a graduate with high honors from Annapolis Naval Academy at 21. After graduation, during his first cruise, Sprague came ashore with nearly 60 preliminary applications for patents, ideas produced during his off-duty hours. At the Torpedo Station at Newport, Rhode Island, his thoughts were directed to electric transportation and—though then most interested in improving the dynamo—Sprague produced an invention for speed control of electric motors.

In 1882, the Crystal Palace Exhibition in London prompted Sprague to obtain a three months' leave at his own expense. He haunted every electrical exhibit, wrote a detailed technical report thoroughly documented with drawings, charts, and performance tests and—though he had long overstayed his leave and was threatened with a court-martial—had the satisfaction of having his report published by the Navy, and the court-martial canceled. During his rides on the London tubes, then drawn by coal-burn-

ing engines to the near-asphyxiation of passengers, the idea of a "self-adjusting, upward-pressure contact" trolley came to Sprague, but he neglected to apply promptly for a patent and, as he wrote nearly 50 years later, "About the same time, but I think later, the idea of a trailing trolley occurred to Charles Van Depoele in the United States, and when . . . we both later began to use it, a patent interference resulted. . . . The United States dates slightly favored Van Depoele, and a patent was finally issued to him, but with arrangements made for mutual use."

After Sprague resigned from the Navy, he worked for less than a year at Menlo Park for Edison. He saw the rebuilt little Edison locomotive which to Sprague possessed little or no novelty. Sprague worked on installing electric light systems and often found himself with men, including Edison, who worked by trial and error methods, not too much impressed by academic training. Sprague's expert knowledge of mathematics and engineering, plus his fine tact, enabled him to make some contributions in overcoming certain roundabout methods. While in-

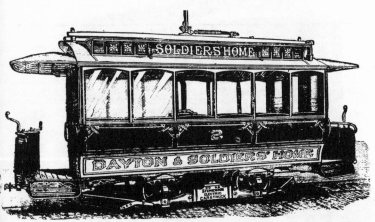

This Dayton, Ohio, trolley carried about twenty passengers, with overhead feed for power. Body by Stephenson, New York builder.

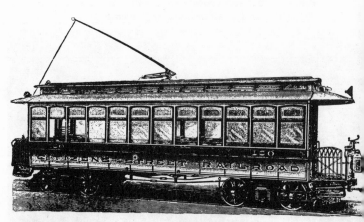

In the Nineties the smaller trolleys were replaced with cars better equipped and spacious enough to accommodate fifty passengers.

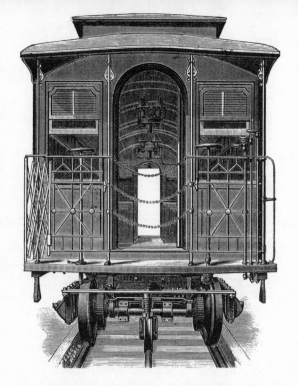

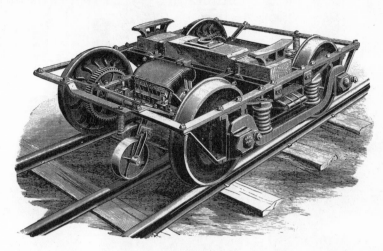

stalling an electric light system in Brockton, Massachusetts, Sprague spent spare hours working in a little shop on a model for his first railway motor.

With practically no capital, in 1884, Sprague formed his own Electric Railway and Supply Company, obtaining small sums of money from E. H. Johnson, an associate of Thomas A. Edison. Sprague's motors were excellent and orders flowed in, from Europe as well as from all over the United States.

Now Sprague concentrated his attention on electric railroads. Experimenting on a 200-foot length of track in a New York City alley, he worked with an ordinary flat car to develop an electric motor which he hoped would be used on the Elevated. Sprague attached two gear-driven motors in one truck in what he described as "wheel-barrow fashion." The axle supported part of the motor, while the truck frame held the other part, spring-mounted. This enabled the motor safely to bounce over bumps

. . . a vast improvement on the designs of Edison, Daft, and Van Depoele. In May, 1887, Sprague undertook to supply a complete electrical street railway for Richmond, Virginia. Though scores of problems arose, Sprague and his assistants eventually solved them, and the Richmond Union Passenger Railway attracted the inspection of street-railway dignitaries from everywhere. By 1889, over half of the street car systems in this country were equipped by Sprague, and over 90 percent used his patents. In 1893, he was building high-speed elevators; in 1895, he started his greatest achievement—multi-unit control; and in 1902 invented the "dead man's button" on the controller, which shuts off power and applies brakes automatically, should a motorman faint or doze-off . . . saving entire trainloads of passengers from injury or death. Had his inventions not been sold to General Motors, Westinghouse, Otis Elevator, and others, the name of Frank J. Sprague would now be as well known as that of Edison.

Sprague electric two-car train, designed for use on New York's elevated tracks.

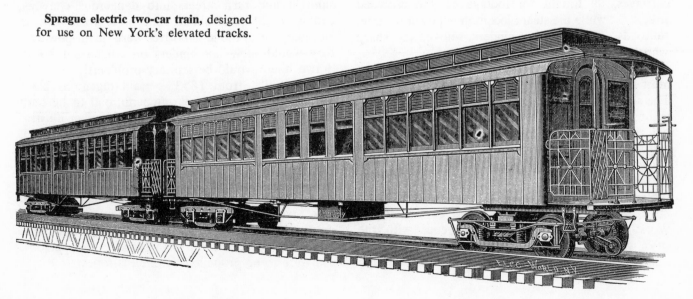

NEW YORK PLANS AN ELEVATED

From the mid-1850's, appalling traffic jams continued to harry New Yorkers. Horse railways, omnibuses, drays for freight, provisioners' carts, private carriages, all fought for footage on the crowded streets . . . while the steam-locomotive-powered street railroads contributed hot cinders, smoke, and sharp whistles, to the terror of restive horses.

It became obvious that the use of other roadways must be explored, either underground or overhead. The slow pace of horse-drawn vehicles was another galling fact. Manhattan, with a speed that staggered old residents, was stretching northward; additional and speedier transportation had to be evolved.

Consideration of underground routes was hindered by the great property owners who insisted that any subterranean burrowings would endanger their buildings; and by the objection of the Croton Water Works' officials who feared interference with the city's water supply. New Yorkers, forbidden to consider the earth beneath, looked to the sky—at the

second story level. Proposals for elevated roads filled the scientific journals, while furious protests from shop keepers and residents along the contemplated routes erupted in letters to the editors of newspapers. Elevated roads, it was claimed, would shut off the sunlight and turn streets into dangerous canyons; people would be afraid to shop on a street with an elevated line. If the locomotives were steam-powered, they would spew hot cinders on citizens; if horse-drawn, there would be sanitary problems!

Meanwhile, from 1853, certain ingenious plans were published for the elevated railroad to be built on Broadway. P. Andrew's design, from an illustration in the *Scientific American,* September 9, 1865, shows four tracks supported by a single row of pillars . . . with two tracks each on two separate roadways, the cars on the lower roadway suspended by wheels attached to their roofs. In place of conductors on the cars, two persons were to be at each station—one to stop and start the cars; the other to collect tickets. The cars were the width of a seat for two persons, and were to be propelled by endless ropes.

Elevated railroad terrace proposed by Wickersham for use on Broadway, 1854. The cars were to be horse-drawn until "some new plans are developed for propulsion by atmospheric pressure." For easy access to the terrace, stairways were to be constructed inside nearby buildings, proprietors of which would be "amply repaid by the resultant publicity," said *Gleason's Pictorial.*

"**Except for the smoke** of the locomotive, the annexed engraving tells its own story," said the *Scientific American* of this plan of James Swett, October 15, 1853. "No wood as fuel is to be used; it might set fire by a stray spark to one of Stewart's bales of fine French muslins. . . . The locomotive is to run on the rails, and carry a suspended car."

Deitz proposed elevated rails, with cars propelled by an endless rope, supported overhead.

Two sets of double tracks, the lower cars suspended by wheels on their roofs, was Andrew's plan.

Proposed Broadway Overground Railroad, 1866. It promised that "there would be no more going out into a filthy, dangerous street for a bounding, thundering omnibus . . . it would cost nothing for extra lighting, warming, or police—like the underground plan." Patented by William Hemstreet.

Approached by balconies from shops, museums, "tenements" along its route, the proposed Overground was to span and roof the street, saving many thousands of dollars in street cleaning "by catching the rain and snow which would run off through the iron pillars," reported *Leslie's*.

"Being of iron and glass," *Leslie's* editor, in an issue of March 3, 1866, enthused: "it is imperishable; requires no preliminary surveying; can be set up or taken down in a day and, in a failure, the material is good for other use."

The decorated cable cars, with curtained windows, retained a coach-like elegance. "There is no more a necessity of consuming a quarter of a business-day, going to and from residence and place of business. This lowers rents in town, and builds up the suburbs."

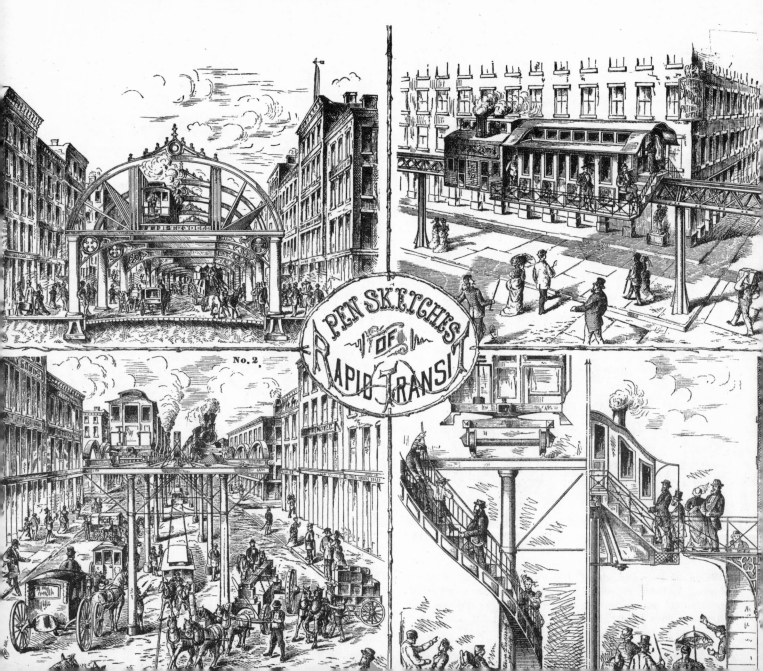

Combining elevated and overhead trolley circuit in a single structure, the Clarke system carries two tracks supported on a central colonnade, saving much space for street traffic.

RAPID TRANSIT INSPIRES INVENTORS

For a decade or more after the close of the Civil War New Yorkers were intensely preoccupied with problems of rapid transit. The pages of the daily newspapers, the leading weeklies, *Harper's* and *Leslie's* and technical journals like the *Scientific American* reported on the various plans submitted by an ever-increasing number of imaginative inventors. These plans were interpreted for the periodicals by enthusiastic draftsmen and rendered capable of reproduction by a staff of wood-engravers. More than a mere record of attempts and failures in the transportation picture, these fantastic illustrations are infinitely more interesting than the realistic portrayals of the elevated as reduced to actual practice. Colorful lithographs were also published and sold to an eager public.

PEN SKETCHES OF RAPID TRANSIT

Atmospheric pressure, to propel trains on tracks over city streets, was incorporated into an elaborate scheme for rapid transit, proposed by R. H. Gilbert in 1872. The cars were to be eight or nine feet in diameter, the Gothic arch spans fifty or a hundred feet apart and the stations a mile from one another. Passengers were to be carried aloft to the stations by pneumatic elevators. Gilbert's Elevated, considerably altered in design, was built in 1878 on New York's West Side.

Rapid transit proposals took many forms as indicated in the accompanying sketches by Gustave Dieterich, appearing in the *Scientific American*, April 1, 1876. Upper left shows a modified version of Gilbert's El (compare with opposite page). Upper and lower right, Gen. Le Roy Stone's plan for a saddle railway to run on a monorail. This was built in England and also adopted for the Centennial Exhibition, but never in New York. Lower left, the Hanna plan calling for a single track horse car line between central pillars below.

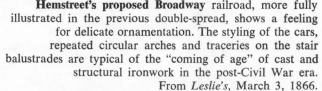

Streamliner of the '80's, the Meigs Eleveated Railway system was actually built and operated in an experimental section, in East Cambridge, Mass. The leading car was a steam locomotive whose horizontal wheels pulled the trains by side pressure on the rails. The oblique wheels maintained balance and ease of riding on the unique monorail construction.

Hemstreet's proposed Broadway railroad, more fully illustrated in the previous double-spread, shows a feeling for delicate ornamentation. The styling of the cars, repeated circular arches and traceries on the stair balustrades are typical of the "coming of age" of cast and structural ironwork in the post-Civil War era. From *Leslie's*, March 3, 1866.

THE WORLD'S FIRST ELEVATED

Weird and wonderful designs for an elevated railway continued to flood the public press and to be described with ardor until, on a day in July 1867, one hundred thousand dollars was subscribed for erection of the elevated invented by Charles T. Harvey. The undertaking was spoken of as an *experiment;* the track was to run from Greenwich Street, Manhattan, up Ninth Avenue to 30th Street—a distance of 26 blocks. Five months later, Harvey—in frock coat and top hat—piloted the first cable car over what was then the world's first elevated track.

Just a year later, July 1868, *Harper's Weekly* reported the trial trip of the new elevated railway in Greenwich Street: "The rapid speed attained . . . leads the friends of the enterprise to hope that the problem of rapid and safe locomotion through the crowded streets of the city has been solved. . . . It is now in running order from the Battery to Cortlandt Street and, with the present machinery, the cars can be propelled with little jar and oscillation at the rate of fifteen miles an hour."

Hope was expressed that certain improvements would enable the projector to run the cars at a much more rapid rate. The State Commissioners, July 1, 1868, having declared the road to be a success, the Governor authorized its completion from the Battery to Spuyten Duyvil. The Directors promised that the road would be finished, up to the Thirtieth Street Depot of the Hudson River Railroad, by January 1869. Harvey—evidently not only an inventor, but a genius at getting things done—also built the Soo Canal. In three rigorous Northern winters, driving immigrant workmen, he linked the West's great iron-ore mines to the foundries of the East.

By 1876, the single track New York Elevated Railway had been extended, running on Greenwich Street and Ninth Avenue from the Battery to Central Park, a distance of five miles. *Scientific American,* April 1, 1876, said: "The question of rapid transit in New York has for a long period perplexed our citizens; has had a curious history; and is now nearing a curious solution.

"Public opinion as to the particular system or form of transit best suited for our community has greatly varied. Twenty-five years ago the elevated railway plan was greatly favored. That was a time when money was scarce; people felt poor; and wanted a cheap form of railway, cheaply built. . . .

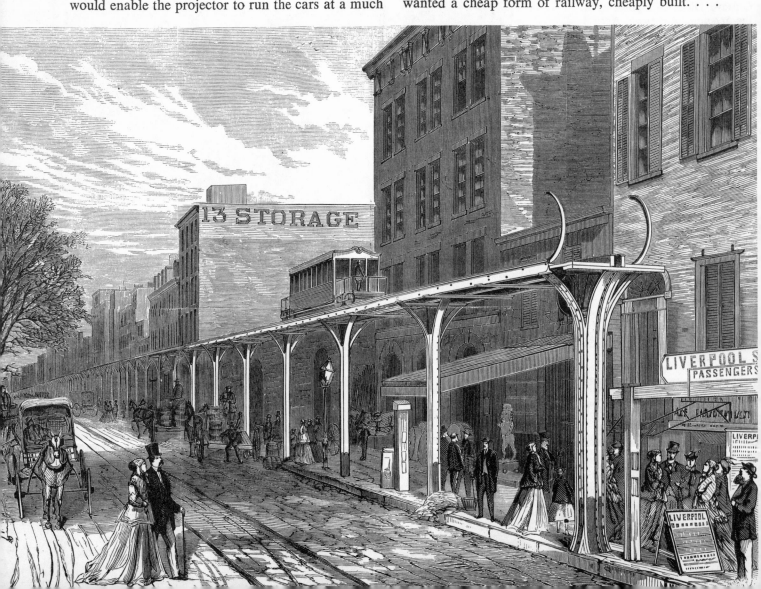

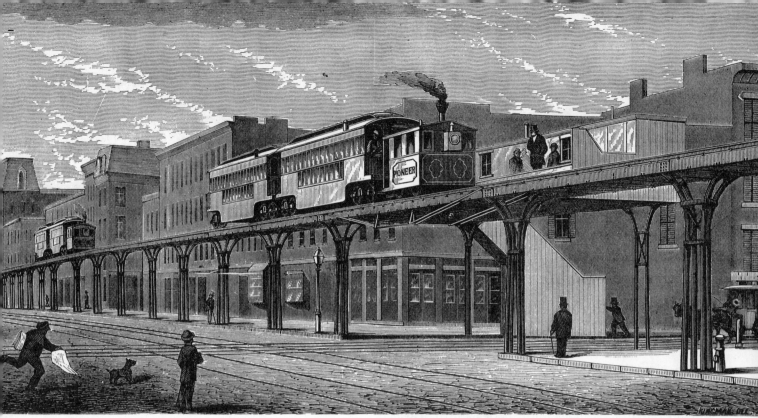

As times improved and money became more plentiful, the *underground* railway . . . became the favorite, and the bare suggestion of filling our streets with elevated railways was hooted at and set aside. Underground roads were declared to be the only proper means of rapid transit. . . . Then, the financial revulsion of 1873—the effects of which still prevail—made our citizens again feel poor, and revived the cry for a cheaper means of transit, on the elevated system." As a result, the State Legislature appointed five commissioners to authorize certain lines and determine routes for these *bridges,* if they thought it advisable. In 1876, a favorable report was made.

As a result, a spate of suggestions for new Els appeared in the newspapers. What opposition existed came from property owners and occupants of buildings on a street where the El might be constructed. These people did not want the "ornamental structure or big bridge" in front of their doors, saying it was equivalent to roofing over of the street, cutting off their air and light. Defending one design—somewhat similar to that patented by William Hemstreet—with stairways in the inside of buildings, it was claimed that the landings would soon become known by the names of the owners of the premises in which they were constructed, and that the resultant publicity would be a rich repayment.

Greenwich Street, New York El, sketched in 1868. A double row of seats placed back-to-back, lengthwise down the center of the car, doubled seating capacity.

Forty-Second Street spur of the New York El, looking west from Third Avenue, was opened formally, 1878, to enthusiastic crowds.

The Inventor of the El, Charles T. Harvey, drove a cable car over the first section of the first tracks laid in Ninth Avenue, New York (1867).

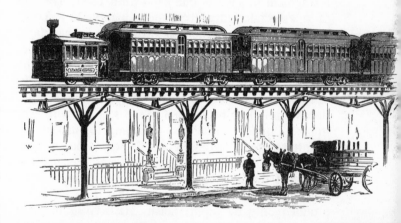

Dr. Rufus H. Gilbert

FROM SURGEON TO EL BUILDER

A remarkable man, Dr. R. F. Gilbert was successful in many fields—as a physician of unusual ability; as a Civil War army surgeon; as the Medical Director at Fortress Monroe; and Director and Superintendent of the United States Army Hospitals until the war's end, when he resigned to return home to recuperate from arduous war experiences. He had performed the first amputations under fire on the battlefield; horses had been killed under him; he carried a fragment of shell in one hand until 1871. The son of an associate judge in Steuben County, New York, he had had limited schooling; worked as a drug clerk; studied classical literature, mechanics, and mathematics at night; later prepared himself to enter the College of Physicians and Surgeons in New York.

Popular and competent, he enjoyed a large practice when failing health and the loss of his wife sent him to London and Paris, intending to inspect the hospital systems of those cities. He came home, convinced that more than medical skill was needed; that tenement dwellers had to have better living conditions, sunlight and purer air, and that these could be attained only by rapid transit. He arrived in New York as the country was on the verge of the Civil War, and enlisted at once as a surgeon in a regiment of Zouaves. When he returned to civilian life, he became assistant to Josiah Stearns, Superintendent of the Central Railroad of New Jersey.

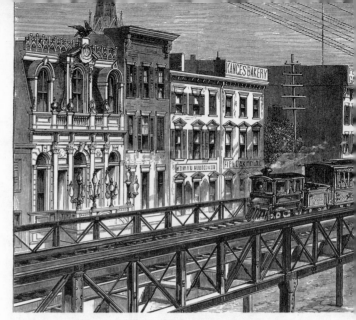

Sixth Avenue Station, at Broadway and Thirty-fourth Street, on the Gilbert Elevated Railway. Steam locomotive propels coal car and two cars for passengers.

Station in Ninth Avenue, near Forty-second Street, New York Elevated Railroad. Horse-railways, private carriages, teams hauling drays with freight, cluttered the street below.

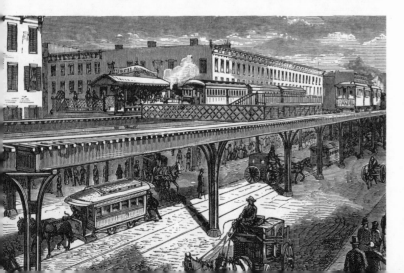

Forty-second Street and Sixth Avenue, Metropolitan (Gilbert) Elevated. At this station passengers who lived in the country left for Grand Central Depot.

Battery Station, on the New York Elevated. In 1878 this road carried four million passengers; with the addition of its Third Avenue branch, a half year later, 14 million.

Beyond Central Park, Gilbert's road on posts 57 feet high. This high level transit terrified many as the train swept "out over the valley in its sinuous course in mid-air."

Dr. Gilbert's early interest in the elevated railway as the best means for rapid transit—from his 1872 proposal for the use of "atmospheric tubes"—continued to occupy his time and energies. He resigned from the New Jersey Central and, by 1878, with modifications as to the motive power, the Gilbert Elevated Railway—"admirably arranged"—was running successfully on Sixth Avenue from the Battery to Central Park. With the west side of the city supplied with elevated railways, the public now watched a new road that was to accommodate those living on the east side. Track for a great part of the line, from Whitehall Street to Yorkville, had been constructed. It was pointed out that the population of the east side, being much greater than that of the west side —where the territory was smaller and more of the buildings were devoted to storage and such purposes —the new railroad would be of even more benefit. Timid souls were assured that, though the height alone of the structure along Pearl and Front Streets was enough to alarm an onlooker, "each of the frail trusses had been subjected to a test of six times the weight that it is intended shall rest upon it." Cars of the finest type and 60 dummy engines—"triumphs of the locomotive art"—were promised.

FROM THE BATTERY TO HARLEM

Construction of the Gilbert Elevated Railway had been approved by the New York State Legislature in June, 1872, and work was begun four years later. Then it was halted by court appeals from various property owners and the *jealousy and opposition* of the horse-railway companies. By October, 1877, the injunctions were dismissed and active construction was resumed. The *new aerial line* was said to be little more than an iron bridge, built as lightly as possible for its purpose, and entirely lacking in any ornamental charm. Though the builders had hoped to make the El unobtrusive, it still darkened the lower stories of dwellings in narrow streets and people were saying that a gracefully arched structure would have been preferable and much more pleasing to the eye.

Declaring that the new El looked more like an endless bridge or immense tunnel, *Harper's Weekly* of February 9, 1878, continued: "It cannot be pleasant to have trains of cars whizzing by one's second story windows every five minutes, even though the rate of speed precludes a too-curious scrutiny of private apartments; and it must be confessed that the tracks . . . do not improve the appearance of the street. But private objections must always yield to the greatest good for the greatest number."

The grievances of the few would be as nothing compared to the benefits which countless thousands would enjoy on completion of the elevated roads.

At Battery Park, N. Y. Elevated. The tracks described a sharp sweep traversing the Park.

The vast tenement population in lower New York would be the first to profit as rapid transit, it was thought, would lead many to move to the suburbs, allowing more space for those who elected to remain. The partial disfigurement of a few streets, by the El, would be compensated by the great improvements in living it would bring to many "now abandoned to misery and squalor." New York's citizens were clamoring for more speedy and convenient means of getting to and from their business than the horse-cars and stages afforded, and more cheaply than the cheapest lines of hacks could offer. The Els held the promise that the working classes would not have to leave their homes so early, and the *weary ride when worn out with the day's toil* would be shortened. No longer would people have to shiver in a crowded, cold, ill-smelling horse-car in winter; they would ride in a comfortable conveyance, without jolt or jar.

Lengthy accounts appeared in the daily papers and illustrated weekly supplements to keep the public abreast with the progress of the Els . . . the Gilbert

West Broadway and Canal Street, Gilbert Elevated. Girders between supporting columns were said to rob the structure of grace.

South Ferry Station, N. Y. Elevated viewed through the ferry gates. Its arched supports were greatly admired.

208

Station at 23rd Street and Sixth
Avenue, on the Gilbert line. The tasteful
design of these buildings was praised.

Railway, afterward called the Metropolitan, and the
New York Elevated Railroad. Maps indicated the
routes already in service and those under construction. *Scientific American*, June 15, 1878, said:

"When the elevated railways, now in progress of
construction in this city, are completed, four great
iron bridges will run lengthwise over Manhattan
Island. When finished, they will aggregate in length
between 60 and 70 miles and there will be two on
each side of the city. On the East side, the New York
Elevated Road runs a double track from White-hall
through Front and Pearl streets, Bowery, and Third
avenue to the end of the island, at Harlem. The Gilbert Road has a circuitous route from Bowling Green
to Second avenue, and along the latter street to Harlem, where it traverses the island over to Eighth avenue. On the West side, the Gilbert line extends along
Eighth, has its longest stretches on Ninth and Sixth
avenues, and finally reaches Bowling Green by way
of South Fifth avenue, West Broadway, and some
of the smaller streets. The New York Elevated Road,

on the West side, extends chiefly along Ninth Avenue, and has its lower terminus at the Battery."

The ills inflicted by the Els were already being deplored. Trains thundered overhead; thoroughfares
were blocked with great iron columns; ash, oil and
sparks were distributed impartially over pedestrians
and on awnings—several awnings had been set on
fire; dirt floated into upper windows; life was endangered from runaway horses; carriage wheels were
broken against the El columns; streets were so
shaded they remained damp, long after wet weather
had cleared. "The ancient story of the intruding
camel, who begged shelter for his head in his master's
tent and ultimately crowded in his unshapely body, to
his master's great discomfiture, is parallelled," said
the *Scientific American* of October 25, 1879, "in
the history of the elevated railways of this city. The
main reason for the adoption of this form of transportation was the cheapness with which it could be
supplied. The camel's head was not attractive, but
it was easily let in, and promised easy removal should
such an issue prove desirable." In five years the Els
had expanded from 4 or 5 miles of light construction,
to ten times as many, and 20 miles more were approaching completion. The massive structures represented an investment of $43,000,000, and almost
monopolized four of the principal avenues and several downtown streets. The annoyances were many,
though the Els were only in their infancy.

Type of Construction used by the N. Y. El
on Third Avenue, called more graceful
than Gilbert's girders.

Sinuous sweep at 110th Street and
Eighth Avenue, on the Gilbert El, hailed
as bold, clever, original engineering.

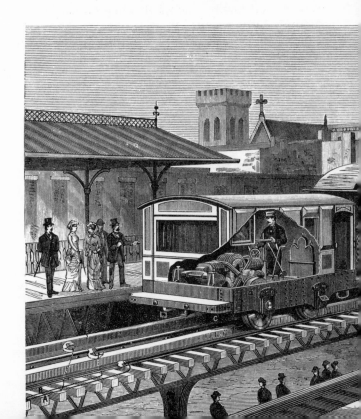

Steam Locomotive, at Franklin Square on the New York El. Imposing building, left, is that of Harper and Brothers, publishers.

OVERHEAD . . . THE ROAR OF THE ROAD

Some docile flesh-and-blood horses promptly adjusted to the early (1878) elevated railways, as depicted in contemporary engravings; but more of the horses continued to cavort, plunge, buck, or madly run away. Many people declared that the weirdly shaped El locomotive, with its cow-catcher, would be less terrifying to living horse-power if it were concealed in a dummy car. A number of these locomotives had been in use for several months on the Gilbert Elevated Railway and were said to be giving good service. Scientific weeklies printed detailed descriptions of the cylinders, driving wheels, truck wheels, and total wheel base; the boiler made of steel with 125 flues; the size of its fire box, the capacity of its water tank, and weight of the engine loaded: 32,500 pounds. No statistics are quoted as to whether the number of runaways was reduced.

An automatically controlled railroad gate, designed especially for the platforms of elevated roads, was one of the inventions for which patents were issued to Mr. John B. Carey, a stenographer of Brooklyn, N. Y., late in 1887. This gate was said to be self-opening and self-closing with the movement of the cars on and off the track at stations. A vertical sliding gate, it was connected at each end by a weighted lever fulcrumed on a post or bracket . . . the lever so formed as to be acted on by the larger tread of the locomotive wheels, and not by those of the car wheels. As the train moved up to the platform, the

Daft Electric motor engine had its trial run on the Ninth Avenue line of the Gilbert Elevated Railway. 1888.

Dummy Car camouflages steam engine on the Metropolitan (Gilbert) Line. This car was considered to be less terrifying to horses.

tread of the first locomotive pressed the front lever down, and the gates followed, until each was flush with the platform. As the train moved away from the station, the treads of the locomotive wheels moved off the rail lever, and the gates went up.

But the greatest interest was being concentrated on the *Daft electric motor engine,* called the "Benjamin Franklin," weighing about ten tons. This was demonstrated on the Gilbert Elevated Railway, on Ninth Avenue, a rainy night in November, 1888. "Notwithstanding the driving rain," *Scientific American* of December 8 reported, "it hauled a train of three regular elevated cars very easily up heavy grades for a mile and a half. At the end of the route, the motor switched off, backed, and hitched on to the other end of the train with the same facility as with a steam locomotive; in fact, it seemed to be done with greater ease. The total weight of the train was estimated at 60 tons. The current was supplied from dynamos located in a station in Fifteenth Street. The electrical current is conveyed from the station and alongside the track by a copper rod ⅝ of an inch in diameter. The current is taken into the motor by a metallic brush which presses upon and slides along the rod. The trial was undoubtedly a severe one, inasmuch as the rails and connecting rod were saturated with water. A number of prominent railroad engineers, officials, and electricians were present and were perfectly satisfied as to the result of the trial. It appears to be only a question of time when our city elevated trains will be hauled as rapidly by electricity as by steam."

Bringing cars up to the track, over an inclined plane, on the Gilbert Elevated.

Typical interior reveals seats arranged vertically and horizonally; tufted upholstery; and arm rests dividing the seats near the doors. Gilbert passenger car.

Exterior of car on the Gilbert El. Spacious size gave wide center aisle.

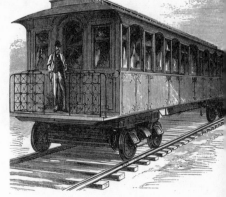

"Palace cars in the finest style." In workingmen's hours, 2 in the morning, 2 in the evening, passengers rode ten miles for five cents on the Gilbert El. At other hours, the fare was ten cents.

FRANKLIN SQUARE

NEW YORK ELEVATED RAIL ROAD

283

TWO CITIES . . . LINKED BY STEEL

Once called the "Eighth Wonder of the World," the Brooklyn Bridge joining New York and Brooklyn was the inspired design of John Roebling. Thirteen years were taken in its construction and, in May 1883, residents of the two independent cities on the shores of the East River—which the bridge spanned with surpassing grace—celebrated its public opening by crossing and recrossing from one city to the other all night, in a continuous procession. There had been colorful formal ceremonies with the President of the United States, members of his Cabinet, Grover Cleveland, then governor of New York, and Mayors of New York and Brooklyn in a glittering parade of 25 carriages . . . salutes from Naval vessels and, in the evening, fireworks: "a display of pyrotechnics absolutely indescribable, of a magnificence never before seen in this country." The elevated trains, first drawn by steam, were soon being hauled by grip cars, the operation of which was described in great detail.

Two cars served adequately at first but, by April 1884, the bridge trustees had already adopted plans for a structure to extend from the New York City end of the bridge into space at the junction of Chatham and Center Streets, so that more cars could be switched during hours of the heaviest travel. It was explained that any system of tracks, girders and columns could never be a thing of beauty or a "welcome ornament" to a neighborhood but that the structure, which must be utilitarian, should be made as unobtrusive as possible. Two stairways led from the Center Street sidewalk to the new platform, sparing passengers for the bridge from the west of City Hall from having to pass through the mass of cars, wagons, and people in the street.

Brooklyn Station on the Brooklyn Bridge, 1833. At left —the Franklin Square Street station, New York side. Though the engravings show steam locomotives, the El trains were soon hauled by grip cars.

"As they will be"—artist's version of elegant equipage . . . resplendent with coachman, footman, and parasoled lady . . . as it appears to outdistance an elevated train on the new Brooklyn Bridge.

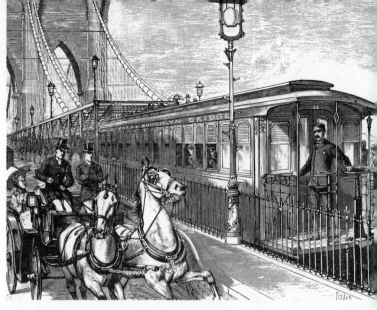

Upper deck promenade, roadway, and elevated railroad on the Brooklyn Bridge, one week after it had been formally opened by the President of the United States and other high officials, May 24, 1883.

New York Terminus of the Brooklyn Bridge, for which increased facilities were already being planned, April, 1844, to extend across space formed by the junction of Chatham and Center Streets, Manhattan.

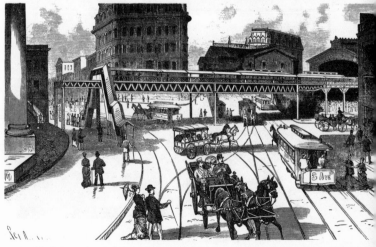

The timid held back, as others fought for space on the already-jammed platforms. Manhattan Elevated Railroad, 1890.

THE CRUSH AT RUSH HOUR

The sky at the second-story level was now no longer the uncrowded area it had once appeared, when the crush on the horse-railways had sent men's minds to devising the elevated lines. In a few years, the El station platforms and stairway approaches were jammed, and the cars were packed to their platform edges. If, as an El passenger, you weren't threatened—as were the riders in horse-cars—with having to trudge through mud, slush and storm ("so detrimental to the health of frail and poorly clad women and girls,") because of the frequent snow blockages, you were likely to find yourself part of an ever-swelling crowd on a platform awaiting an El train long overdue and already bulging with passengers. Though one editor predicted that the business population on some avenues would soon be "trodlodytes—dwellers in dark and shaded caverns—while the other portion would be aerial," none apparently speculated on the effects on future generations of the sardine-pack method of both elevated and surface transit.

In May 1879, the Metropolitan (Gilbert's) Railroad and that of the New York Elevated had been leased to the Manhattan Company, which operated both roads under one direction, merging one line with the other in some localities, and making extensions to the system. Some of the difficulties in excavating for the masonry towers—on which the elevated posts rested—were published in detail. At 110th Street, where the tracks curved from Ninth Avenue eastward to Eighth Avenue, the masonry supports were twenty feet above the original level of

The timid held back, as others fought for space on the already-jammed platforms. Manhattan Elevated Railroad, 1890.

Danger of collision was practically abolished, *except among the passengers* on the narrow stairways. Opening of the Second Avenue El, 1880.

the land which had been filled in to that height, and the masonry rested on a foundation of piles driven in to the depth of forty feet. A network of gas, water and sewer pipes had been encountered, for a distance of four miles, requiring a special plan for each foundation. The greatest difficulty had arisen at 108th Street, where the center of the pier was directly over a huge sewer with two inlets, and the work was further complicated by the proximity of a thirty-inch gas main and two Croton water pipes. Though ordinarily twenty piles would have been enough to give proper support, eighty-two piles had had to be used in this space, with 130 cubic yards of cement, a massive cast iron bed plate, and 80,000 bricks. A thousand tons of iron had been required to arch over the pipes in the 2,400 foundations for the piers. Five steam pile drivers were used in driving the 300,000 lineal feet of piles for the foundations in marshy places.

One could travel from the Battery to Harlem, eight and one-half miles, on the Third Avenue road in 42 minutes; and from Rector Street to 58th Street, about five miles, in 20 minutes. Trains on the Sixth Avenue line were scheduled to run to 58th Street at intervals of two to four minutes, depending on the hour, and to 104th Street and beyond at intervals of six minutes.

With countless millions being invested, certain sections at busy hours were already proving inadequate to the popularity the El had established.

A bitter night at an elevated railway station. Snow, wind and sleet
harried the waiting crowds. Women in fur-trimmed suits, hands in muffs,
and men in fur-collared coats . . . huddled against the cold.

Packed crowds from City Hall Station, New York Elevated, near the
proposed extension of the East River Bridge. In the busy street, pedestrians
rushed to cross before an approaching horse-car and teams drawing drays.

A RAILWAY ON STILTS ON THE BOWERY

In the late Seventies New York's East Side was a beehive of turmoil and excitement . . . a thriving community of many nationalities, bursting at the seams. Waves of immigrants arriving by the boatloads daily made their way into the already crowded tenement slums. To accommodate this phenomenal increase in population the trend of expansion pointed northward. It was only natural, therefore, that the Elevated, already successfully operating on the West Side, should be erected along the course of the Bowery, the very heart of the East Side—and a wide arterial thoroughfare ideal for heavy traffic. Pictured above, from Charles Magnus' *Views of New York and Environs,* published in the late '70's, is the Thalia Theatre, formerly the old Bowery Theatre at Canal Street. The photograph below, taken by J. S. Johnston, looking north from Grand Street in 1895, shows

that the horse cars have already been replaced by cable cars at a time when the dinky steam locomotives were hauling full-sized trains north and south. At Chatham Square, above, several divisions of the New York Elevated Railroad converged, while on the street below many crosstown and Third Avenue horse car tracks criss-cross in all directions. The famous serpentine "S" curve of the Elevated, also from Magnus' *Views,* winds its way through the picturesque waterfront section near Coenties Slip.

The Bowery, fed by the El, was famous in song and fable. Cheap lodgings, flop houses, beer gardens and hostelries catering to the hordes of hoodlums and vagrants who frequented the area, made it "out of bounds" for folks who valued their lives and pocketbooks. Yet the color and glamor of the Bowery attracted many a respectable citizen, and its shops offered prices generally below those of the more sedate uptown establishments. After serving the Bowery for close to seventy years, the El was dismantled.

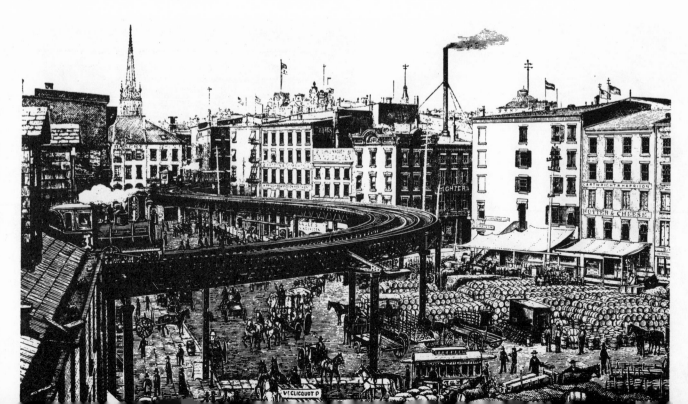

MILLIONS RIDE UNDERGROUND

The out-of-town visitor to New York, taking his first subway ride for a taste of underground thrills, is startled at the congestion and bedlam of rush hour crowds . . . the push-and-shove technique of the average rider . . . the strong arm tactics of station guards jamming dozens more into non-existent space. Blasé New Yorkers have been exposed to such treatment since the present lines opened in 1905 and 1906, yet almost a century ago one could ride underground in comparative comfort for the price of a quarter.

As early as 1858, the forward-looking *Scientific American* published plans for the linking of New York and Brooklyn by excavating under the East River. "Bridges cannot be erected without impeding navigation. Ferries are hazardous due to intense fog, dark nights and fearful collisions with floating ice during winter months. The tunnel is the only safe means of transit."

The State Legislature granted a charter, in 1868, permitting a tunnel under Fourth Avenue for the running of horsecars to Grand Central depot. In 1869, A. E. Beach designed a subway running from Warren to Murray Street. A single car was driven by pneumatic pressure, and eager New Yorkers gladly paid the price for this novel excursion in the nether regions. The line was abandoned in 1872.

First underground railway in America was opened to the public on February 20, 1870. *The Evening Mail* reported "The problem of tunneling Broadway has been solved. There is no mistake about it."

Under Broadway by underground, planned to run from the Battery, north to Central Park. Project described and illustrated in *Scientific American*, April 1, 1876.

Sinking the tracks of the N. Y. and Harlem R. R., under Park Avenue was a great improvement. Portions of the railway ran underground while others were carried in open cuts or over stone viaducts. Built in 1873-74.

Proposed arcade railway and avenue under Broadway, illustrated in *Scientific American*, Feb. 9, 1867. Provisions were made for gas mains, sewerage and water conduits, but no illumination relieved the Stygian darkness of the lower level.

A-WHEELING

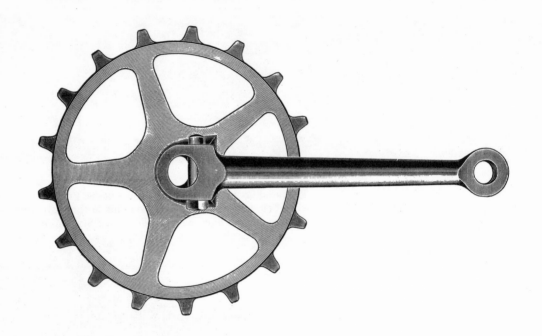

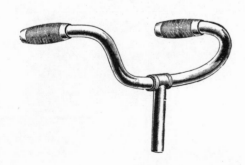

FROM "BONESHAKER" to high-wheeler, hobby-horse
to "safety"... the wheel goes 'round and 'round...
the cyclist rides his hobby, feet close to the ground,
head high in the clouds.

WE'LL GO

GOING PLACES on his own...pushing his way along
city pavements, out on the open road, intent on
exploration and discovery. The wheelman's horizon
widens...revealing new vistas of vale and meadow.
The speedy "scorcher" out to burn up the road...
the six-day rider crouched over handlebars,
bent on doing a hundred in nothing flat.

RAMBLING on "a bicycle built for two"...a boy
and a girl gliding along oblivious...pedaling
the path to romance. Bicycle belles in bloomers...
swains in fancy togs...a picturesque era,
the "gay Nineties"...now vanished forever.

In 1819, British dandies sported the fashionable "pedestrian curricle" built by Denis Johnson, coachmaker.

STRADDLE YOUR SADDLE

As with other means of transportation adopted for use in America, it is necessary to explore the European ancestry of the bicycle to understand the various bizarre forms it took, and the many men who were responsible for its evolution through many centuries. Before the final appearance of the pedal-propelled cycle, there had been countless attempts to employ human muscular energy on a personal means of locomotion, to save walking.

Manumotive vehicles were known in the Middle Ages, attested to by frequent literary and artistic references, both in England and on the Continent. Germany and France share the honors for early experimentation. In France, as early as 1791, the

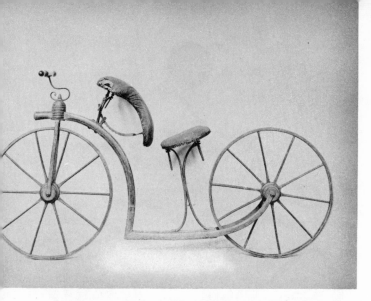

Ladies' Hobby-horse, with wooden wheels and frame, adjustable seat and cushion. Built in London, 1819.

Draisine or Hobby-horse, wooden frame and wheels, wrought iron supports and steering mechanism. 1818.

Chevalier de Sivrac devised a crude prototype which he called a "célerifère," later renamed the "vélocifère." Equipped with a padded saddle, this was mainly a wooden bar supported on two wheels. The rider, by pushing along with his feet, gained speed but as there was no swivel action at the front wheel, it was difficult to steer, except by banking the body to one side. Many Parisians took to propelling these curious contraptions; they even organized a club and held races on the Champs Élysées.

It was Baron Karl von Drais of Mannheim, Germany, who put this form of locomotion to practical use, lifting it from the level of fashion and novelty it had briefly enjoyed in Paris, several decades before. In 1816, the Baron startled the people of the little town of Karlsruhe, as he scooted about on his machine . . . a two-wheeled rig joined by a springy, connecting bar which supported a saddle in the center. This Draisine (named for the Baron) or hobby-horse—as it was popularly known—reached America about 1819. *Harper's Weekly* later reported: "On their introduction into New York our excitable citizens went into an ecstasy of astonishment and delight. The manufacturers for a time could not apparently meet the demand. Very desperate persons at nightfall used to run them up the Bowery to Vauxhall Garden, and . . . from Chatham Square to City Hall Park."

The *Ladies' Literary Cabinet,* of New York, said of the newly-invented velocipede: "It is to have beams, or bodies on springs, and four wheels which will insure its safety. It is to quarter on the road like other carriages, and with four *impellers* it is supposed that it will proceed with astonishing rapidity; but its particular recommendation is to be the conveyance of two ladies and two *impellers* at the rate of six miles an hour."

"Pedestrian Hobby-horse" or Draisine bicycle, 1819. The earliest print with clear details of the hobby-horse.

Draisine or Dandy-horse, with wooden wheels and iron frame-work, c. 1816. Leather saddle mounted on wrought iron piece provided springy ride.

The New Invented Sociable" or "The Lover and is Hobby," title and sub-title of this colored quatint, published in London in 1819.

The Hanlon Brothers patented this "improved" velocipede in 1868. It featured a slotted crank, extensible seat supported on flexible steel for ease of motion. It was made by Calvin Witty, New York carriage builder.

Pierre Lallement, a Frenchman, came to the United States and received the first patent, in 1866, for a rotary action, crank-driven velocipede. This he rode in the streets of New Haven, Conn.

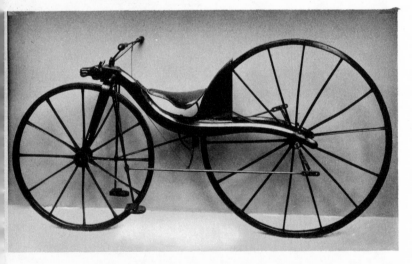

Macmillan's rear-drive bicycle, 1839, the first successful method of continuous propulsion by treadle action. It was widely copied over the next twenty years.

MORE POWER BY PEDALING

As soon as the Draisine appeared in numbers on the streets of London and New York, mechanics set to work making improvements and modifications. Denis Johnson, a British coach-maker, copied the two-wheeler he brought back from Paris, added an elbow and body rest and renamed it the "Pedestrian Curricle." The sporting aspect of the machine took hold and it was a common sight to see young men pedaling along the streets or in the parks. Riding schools were established and women's wheels were provided with special frames that permitted flowing dresses to be worn. The caricaturists such as Leek, Cruikshank, Alken and Rowlandson had a field day poking fun at what John Keats referred to, in 1819, as the "nothing of the day."

In 1820, Lewis Gompertz, of Surrey, replaced the push-and-coast method of propulsion with a manual action—a front wheel handle which operated a rack and pinion at the hub. A pedal-propelled quadricycle was built by the Rev. Edmund Cartwright, about 1819, and other forms of "pedomotive carriages" appeared in rapid succession. Kirkpatric Macmillan built a machine, in 1839, that had iron rims around its wooden wheels, a forked frame and a pair of treadles up front which transmitted foot-power to the rear wheel. It took fifty years for these improvements to be adopted by other inventors.

The "Boneshaker" by Lallement was a true pedal and crank operated bicycle—the forerunner of the "ordinary" of the late 1870's.

Gallic excitement reached feverish heights, resulting in many velocipede races, such as that pictured above, in Paris, 1868. The place: the Champs-Élysées. The time: Sunday afternoon.

wis Gompertz invented this contraption in 1821. Manual action on the front handle bar actuated a rack and pinion device, supplementing foot-power. This engraving appeared in the first issue of *The Velocipedist*, as well as in the *Scientific American* in 1869.

Ernest Michaux, the Frenchman who became the celebrated inventor responsible for bicycle improvements. In 1861, he fitted a cranked axle and pedals to the front wheel hub. By 1865, the Michaux firm was producing 400 vehicles a year.

Home-made velocipede constructed in 1823 by a young man in Norfolk, Conn. It was built of odds and ends of lumber from a woodpile and would, according to a contemporary account, "go like fun."

225

Improved velocipede, patented January, 1869 by Tomlinson, Demarest, carriage builders in New York. From an advertisement in *Harper's*.

"BONESHAKER" INTO BICYCLE

The emergence of the velocipede or "boneshaker" in the form finally known as the bicycle was the result of gradual modifications by many inventors and mechanics. An anonymous writer, in the *English Mechanic* of April, 1866, advocated an endless chain for driving purposes. This forecast the present form of the bicycle. Metal rims with steel spokes were also suggested, in the same year, an indication of advanced thinking which anticipated modern improvements by a generation or more.

The Hanlon Brothers, a troupe of gymnasts and acrobats with a flair for publicity, did much to popularize interest in the cycle. They toured America in 1868 and later, giving exhibitions of death-defying exploits at country fairs, and so revived an interest in velocipedes that had waned. Fancy tricks and stunts were performed before capacity crowds across the nation—their riding school in New York attracted many—and all this did much to focus attention on the two-wheeled machine. "The riding of Fred Hanlon was quite remarkable, being that of an excellent gymnast. He leaped on and off the saddle of the velocipede when in rapid motion, carried his legs over the leading wheels, preserving his equilibrium with the rudder-post, and rode side-saddle-wise with grace, illustrating the ease with which ladies may ride," reported the *Scientific American*.

Riding schools sprang up in the larger cities and, for a fee of about fifteen dollars, one could learn to ride and enjoy the use of the bicycle. One school in New York called itself the Gymnocyclidium. What with wooden wheels and iron tires, the "boneshaker" amply justified its name.

Buell's spring velocipede it was hoped, would smooth rough riding and allay memories of the boneshaker. The four elliptic springs at crucial supports were designed to "relieve the body from the effect of frequent concussions."

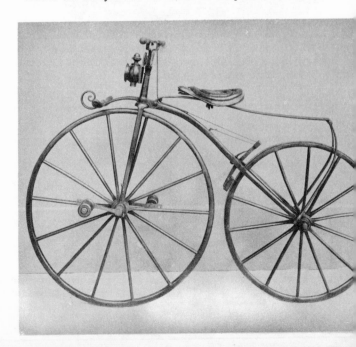

Hedges British boneshaker bicycle contained some improvements, such as headlamp, delicate frame and provision for resting the feet while coasting downhill. 1869.

Outdoor riding school, as sketched by Theodore R. Davis, for *Harper's Weekly*, December 19, 1868. One month's lessons, with wheel supplied, cost the beginner about fifteen dollars, and guaranteed complete satisfaction. Three-wheeled machines were available for ladies, if preferred.

Boneshaker by J. Shire, Detroit, patented in 1879, about the time the high-wheeled "ordinaries" were already appearing. Constructed of wood with iron reinforcements, and many refinements.

Van Anden "Dexter," patented in 1869, was equipped with ratchet device for "free wheeling," similar to present-day coaster-brake bicycles.

VELOCIPEDE MANIA TAKES HOLD

Admittedly, the "boneshaker" was a noisy, rattling, wobbling two-wheeled machine that astonished all who saw it for the first time, during the 1860's. To Pierre Lallement, a French mechanic employed by Pierre Michaux, goes the honor of inventing this velocipede, though a considerable controversy raged as to which man was actually the inventor. While working in the Michaux shops, building three-wheelers and perambulators, Lallement is reputed to have fitted the front wheel of a hobby-horse with pedals, about the year 1863.

Lallement is next heard of, living in Ansonia, Conn., where he proceeded to build what became the first velocipede in America. He fitted pedals to the front-wheel hub and rode this machine around the streets of New Haven, coming to the attention of James Carol. These two men jointly patented their wheel in 1866. But the mercurial Frenchman soon sold his interest to his partner and returned to his native France. With his departure, the invention

Tom, Dick and Harry took lessons in indoor riding schools. A month's course guaranteed results. Many spills and broken wheels added to the costs.

Merry-go-round of eight wheels, with passengers pedaling their way around, indicates extremes of the cycling craze, touching both young and old.

apparently lapsed into disuse.

Michaux and his son Ernest continued to build their own velocipede business in the French capital. Everyone rode a wheel or aspired to own one—the prevailing price being about £8. The frame or backbone was made from a solid wrought-iron diamond-sectioned bar, formed into a fork at the rear end to accommodate the smaller diameter rear wheel. The machines weighed about 60 pounds. Pierre and Ernest Michaux continued to produce such velocipedes until 1869, when they sold their business.

In America, the riding fever spread across the nation, spawning dozens of academies of instruction, particularly in the larger cities. The *Velocipedist* stressed the economy of cycling, saying: "The two-wheeler is the animal which costs but little to keep. It does not eat carloads of hay. It is easy to handle —never 'rares up'—won't bite. It needs no check rein or halter, and will lean lovingly against the nearest support." So great was the interest, many journals conducted regular columns, giving advice, hints and instruction on all phases of cyclomania.

"Velocipede Mania—What it may come to!" A cartoonist's prediction of a nation awheel. Drawn by Thomas Worth for *Harper's Weekly*, 1869.

This straight-jacket of 1867 was known as "White's Improved Bicycle." Hand-cranks and stirrups absorbed the rider's attention.

Underslung model, the "velocipede carriage" of 1869, was designed for elders or invalids who wished to ride close to the ground.

DICYCLES AND TRICYCLES

For over eight decades, cycling mechanisms continued to vary. There were the two-wheeled vehicle, the three-wheeler or tricycle, the four-wheeler or quadricycle and, finally, a single-wheeler known appropriately as the monocycle. Not only in the number of their wheels, but in the method of propulsion, the placing of the saddle, the height of the handlebars . . . variety was expressed in ways both curious and amusing. The machines ridden in America at the time were importations chiefly from England, where the favor for multi-wheeled cycles was appreciably greater than in the United States.

The dicycle, built by E. C. F. Otto in 1881, was one of the unique offshoots of cycle development. It had two large parallel wheels of equal diameter at the rear; two smaller wheels at the front. The rider was perched between the large wheels and pedaled two cranks which transmitted his foot power by means of pulleys and steel-belts. Though 1,000 were built, "to supersede all bicycles and tricycles". . . the dicycle had only a short vogue.

Tricycles developed equal variety . . . in wheel arrangement and sizes, and the use of hand and foot power. Large makers like Columbia, Victor, and Pope produced tricycles and multi-wheeled types.

Premier tricycle of 1878, the conventional type that was later popularized as a three-wheeler for children.

Victor tricycle, made by the Overman Wheel Company, was declared "staunch and speedy—for health and pleasure . . . winner of all races in '83.

Butler's motor tricycle of 1885, known also as a "Petro-cycle," was operated by hand levers.

High-seated tricycle, 1887, was preferred by the president of the National Cyclists' Union.

Otto Dicycle of 1881, heavily laden with wheels, pulleys, belts and pedals.

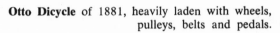

Tricycle of 1879, equipped with changing speed adjustments.

Columbia two-track tricycle, made in 1885 by the Pope Manufacturing Company. Its leading small wheel is at the right.

Chain-driven tricycle built for racing, 1878.

231

THREE WHEELING . . . BETTER BALANCE

During the period when the velocipede was being developed, both here and abroad, other multi-wheeled contraptions stemming back to primitive bone-shaker types were also used to a small extent. Their obvious advantage was the factor of safety for people who found difficulty in balancing—elderly gentlemen, ladies and invalids.

These tricycles, as they were later called, inspired some strange and involved bits of mechanism. Two Englishmen, Parker and Bramley, contrived the first tandem tricycle in 1831. One man steered by a rudderlike device, and at the same time operated hand-driven treadles (he really had his hands full)! The second rider, behind the steersman in a semi-prone and decidedly uncomfortable position, busied himself with another set of treadles. In the same year, Alexander Cochrane made a road machine employing a rowing type of motion. Subsequent inventors applied this basic principle to the bicycle, but without much success. The feet seemed better designed to supply motive-power—the hands for steering.

The first crank-driven tricycle appeared in 1840. It was constructed of wood, and the cranks were controlled by levers hung from the fore part of the frame, by the steering wheel. An extra hand lever was supposed to supply needed pushing power, when going uphill.

While many attempts had been made to popularize the tricycle, it was not until the mid-seventies that the three-wheeled movement got under way. The Dublin tricycle, originally built in Coventry, England, became fairly popular. A few were imported into the United States.

James Starley, later to become an important inventor of the modern bicycle, produced an unusual three-wheeled machine in 1876. It had a large, single driver wheel, fifty inches in diameter, at one side, accompanied by two smaller wheels set behind each other. A sprocket, pedal and chain arrangement propelled the big wheel while the two smaller wheels served for steering. It was known as Starley's Coventry and sold well.

"**Skiff Velocipede,**" so named by its inventor because "the mode of propelling is exactly like rowing a boat." Both hand and foot power were supposed to relieve the muscles in any one part of the body of over-exertion. 1869.

Treadle-driven tricycle imported from England, about 1850. A popular front-steerer, a contemporary authority called it "a very useful vehicle and admirably suited to meet the requirements of elderly gentlemen, ladies, and timid or nervous persons."

Hand crank velocipede, c. 1869, driving large front wheel manually, was designed to "eliminate danger of hernia and rupture by foot-pedaling." Steering by rear axle was controlled by feet in stirrups.

"American Lever Tricycle" made by H. B. Smith Machine Co., Smithville, N. J., about 1880. When pedals were depressed they actuated separate rear axles by way of spring-wound straps.

Dublin tricycle, built in 1876, had an old-fashioned wood seat mounted on coil springs.
Giant rear wheel was worked by foot treadles; the front wheels controlled the steering.

Tricycle-carriage equipped with overhead canopy, baggage rack and front lantern. Rider sat "in easy chair above forward axle and grasped the guiding handles." From *Scientific American,* 1881.

MOPPETS ON THE MOVE

Much as the child of today has his toy automobile, diesel-type locomotive, fire engine, and miniature airplane . . . moppets of the Nineties owned scaled-down versions of tricycles and velocipedes. These little conveyances were, in the earnest spirit of the age, invariably advertised as of benefit to the child's bodily development, as: "It is a gymnasium in miniature, since it calls most of the body into action"; or "This invention will be appreciated by the youngsters, and will make a pleasing change after using the velocipede propelled by the feet; with this machine the arms and chest will be developed"; or "This gives the rider a graceful and natural position, admits of the free use of the limbs in propelling the carriage, and affords perfect and easy control of its direction." Mr. S. P. Ruggles of Boston advised that his velocipede was "designed especially for the use of young girls and misses as a means of outdoor exercise and amusement, and for developing the muscles of the lower limbs, and in fact of the entire body."

Although children are great mimics and ardently wish to have for their play the articles they see the adults using—from cook stoves, ironing tables, cash registers, to automobiles—it is the wheeled toy which seems to hold the greatest fascination.

The rolling of hoops, by girls, is a pastime that flourishes after countless centuries. Carts — even when only crude boxes on wheels—are generally beloved of all small boys. In the days when many adults rode horseback, almost every child possessed a treas-

Horse-velocipede of 1880 used hand levers and foot pedals. Patented by Alfred Vick.

Pedal action on front axle of pony tricycle—patented in 1864.

Pony's legs are activated by rolling motion in this 1865 velocipede.

Saddled-pony tricycle, thrillingly had jointed animal legs to move with its speedy wheels.

ured hobby-horse, or coveted one madly. On rockers or small wheels, such toys were often of home construction—some being as beautifully carved from wood as a proud ship's figurehead; others however crude the poor man's attempt to give his children the toys which more fortunate children possessed.

From the early days of the steam engine, diminutive locomotives, freights, coal cars, and all the adjuncts of railroading have delighted—and continue to delight—small boys and their dads. So it is not surprising that, when seemingly the entire adult world rode bicycles, the manufacturers of children's toys were concentrating so largely on designing velocipedes, and cycles for youths old enough to be trusted with the precarious two-wheeled contraptions.

The pages of the *Scientific American* reported, in almost every issue during the Nineties, various versions of the velocipede or cyclepede. Some of the styles had a high front wheel and small rear wheels; others a small front wheel and high back wheels. Where certain of the styles for older children featured a bicycle seat, others were realistic-looking little horses or wooden chairs mounted on three wheels. Most were single seated but several styles boasted a front seat for the operator, and a rear seat for a companion. The little vehicles were variously propelled, with hand levers, foot pedals or a combination of both. Most were an excellent means of keeping children outdoors in fair weather and all served—as similar toys do today—to introduce the child gradually to the youth bicycle, more difficult to balance and more prone to accidents.

Driver, guest and doll, 1879; in the Ruggles velocipede with stirrups for the driver's feet.

Which way is front? Perkins velocipede, 1890, operated by two handles, one at each side.

Free-action velocipede, made by the Wilson Bros. Woodenware & Toy Co., New York, 1891.

Sober-looking children of the Nineties posed always wearing hats (or caps) and high shoes.

RAMBLING AT RANDOM

Social groups are brought together, and the size of the groups controlled, by the various forms of transportation. In carriage-travel, from gig to coach or tally-ho, the riders might be one, two, or a dozen. On railway and elevated trains hundreds of passengers are carried; on trolleys and buses the numbers may be around fifty.

Only the bicycle, dependent on an individual for its motive power, is limited to one who is both passenger and engineer. But the natural gregariousness of man soon led to the creation of the tandem or the "sociable"... designed for two or more riders. And, of course, the bicyclist was always free to organize his own group . . . whether it consisted of his family, a few friends, or a large number—such as members of one of the then popular cycling clubs.

The introduction of the "bicycle built for two" meant the dawn of a new day, an era when swain and sweetheart might enjoy unchaperoned hours of togetherness, in tandem or side by side. Outings were arranged into the nearby countryside or to New York's Central Park, often with picnic luncheons strapped to the cycle saddles. But the day of the chaperone was not yet past. Many groups of cycling girls and their escorts were accompanied by a chaperone, as a concession to the social amenities.

Courageous couples braved the tandem while the more timid souls took to the tricycle for safety. Riders seated between wheels were not subject to the accidental, headlong flights so common when riding on the ordinary. Many three-wheelers were hand-operated, and in many cases used both hand and foot-power, the two riders pedaling at the same time.

A contemporary magazine stated that "more happy unions were cemented on tandem bicycles because romantic lovers developed a rhythmic sense and thus became attached to each other."

Gay party of girls, from a lithograph by A. Morlon called "Nouveau Steeple-chase." Tricycles were popular with female cycling groups, in America, England and France. Scene in the Bois de Boulogne is watched by three dandies.

Tandem bicycle designed by H. P. Butler, of Cambridge, Mass., and first published in the *Scientific American*, April 10, 1869. The lady on the rear seat, side-saddle, seems more concerned with her parasol than with pedaling. The inventor made no provision for protection of voluminous skirts.

"Needham" Safety Tricycle, of British design and manufacture, was imported to the United States in limited numbers. Ease of operation and safe balances were maintained, as the rear rider used both hands and feet, with a system of levers and pedals. Engraving from *English Mechanic*, August 13, 1869.

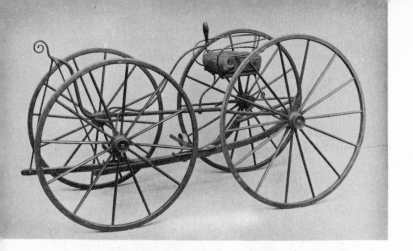

Ward treadle-driven quadricycle, with wooden wheels and framework, wrought iron hardware, was built in 1851.

Four-wheeled velocipede presented to H. R. H., The Prince of Wales, in 1858.

"The Day-Out Velocipede," four cornered and designed for a sociable outing, "to carry four persons—three gentlemen and a lady, the latter seated at her ease in rear." Built in 1869.

Machine to carry four persons, to be operated by one or two. Propelled by both hand and foot motion, it boasted a lantern in front. 1866.

"The Celeremane," recommended by its inventor as a "well contrived four-wheeler that affords one with just the right amount of healthful exercise." Actually this carriage was a

THEY ROLLED ON ALL FOURS

The Science Museum, of London, is authority for the statement that as early as 1819 "a pedal-propelled velocipede was built by the Reverend Edmund Cartwright, and other forms of 'pedomotive carriage' were built at later periods." From this it is apparent that, from the invention of the hobby-horse, two and four-wheeled vehicles had been simultaneously developed.

In a very real sense the quadricycle may be called a "horseless carriage" since its shape, form and construction reveal the conventional carriage chassis, with the addition of an elementary driving mechanism to replace Old Dobbin. Many different types were to be found on both sides of the Atlantic, but in England—where the four-wheeler met with more

The Sawyer quadricycle, built in 1852, with delicate spidery wheels of 30 spokes. The entire framework of wood was reinforced with iron.

"Ladies' Own Velocipede," built in 1867, had treadle action geared to front wheels. The raised seat was supported on iron springs.

Hand-propelled velocipede with driving mechanism of three spur wheels—"light running, easily propelled and not expensive." said A. C. Johnson, its inventor, in 1882.

rowing machine on wheels, requiring a four-man team, plus coxswain. Built and launched in 1869, it was typical of the extremes to which the cycling mania was carried.

popular favor—a greater ingenuity was displayed in its invention.

The principle of pedaling, as applied to the four-wheeled velocipede, resulted in a bewildering variety of rigs, difficult to place in separate categories. There were quadricycles for one rider, and others to accommodate two, three or more. Some were operated by foot-power—either by pedals or treadles—while others depended upon manual power, using rowing levers or revolving handles. Any combination of the various means might be observed.

The operational scope of these heavy and primitive machines limited them to the most ordinary travel needs. Very few incorporated any braking facilities and still fewer carried lamps or accessories for travel at night.

"Sociable Velocipede" designed for two or four persons. Driving levers were at the four corners of the spring-cushioned chassis. Built in 1869.

239

An early American High-wheeler, 1869. Soule's "simultaneous-movement velocipede" featured connecting rods between the cranks and walking beam, to be operated by "both hands and feet," advised the inventor.

THE EXTRAORDINARY "ORDINARY"

The name "bicycle" made its debut to the world of cycling in Great Britain, April 1869, in a patent granted to J. I. Stassen. It gradually replaced all other names, to become the generic word for two-wheeled vehicles propelled by man. But, in the early 1870's, what is conceded to have been the first real bicycle was affectionately called the "ordinary," because it was the standard, high-wheel ordinary bike for general use. This was the "Ariel," built in 1872 by Smith & Starley of Coventry, England. It had a large front wheel, metal frame, double wire spokes and steel rims. On the backbone frame, just above the small rear wheel, was an attachment controlling a brake by a cord connected to the front handle. Not long after James Starley produced the "Ariel," he made several improvements, including footrests for coasting, and became known as "Father of the Bicycle."

There were twenty firms producing bicycles in England in 1874 and, five years later, this number had increased to sixty making three hundred different

In 1874, wood was entirely superseded by metal, the best roadster weighing 40 to 50 pounds. This English "Paragon" was of the spider type.

The British "Ariel" was made by Haynes & Jeffries, of Coventry, in 1872 It had a lever (AA) rigidly fixed to its hub, which applied tension to the spokes. The felloes, V-shaped, held a narrow hoop or tire of rubber.

machines. The manufacturers now competed aggressively for the growing market and resorted to novel methods for bringing their wheels to the public's attention. Four riders traveled from London to John O'Groats, covering the distance of 861 miles in fifteen days. This performance not only established a record for distance and endurance—it demonstrated conclusively that the wheel was a practical means of individual locomotion—for touring, travel, racing or pleasure.

At this period, at least half of the bicycles used in America were being imported from England, so that whatever happened abroad was of immediate concern in this country. There developed a power race among foreign makers, with front wheels getting larger and larger. Obviously, the greater the diameter of the driving wheel, the farther a rider traveled with each revolution of the wheel, at the same time increasing the danger from instability. It was found that the safe and practical size for the ordinary was a sixty-inch front wheel, with a rear wheel of at least sixteen to eighteen inches, to avoid a "header."

First national meet of American bicyclists at Newport, Rhode Island, May 31, 1880. Various wheel clubs turned out for the event, and hundreds of riders participated, all on their high-wheeled ordinaries. Sketch by Charles Upham for *Leslie's Illustrated*.

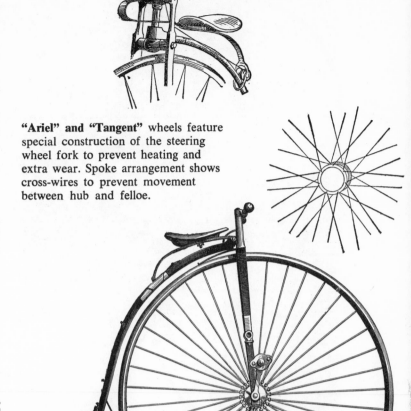

"Ariel" and "Tangent" wheels feature special construction of the steering wheel fork to prevent heating and extra wear. Spoke arrangement shows cross-wires to prevent movement between hub and felloe.

Columbia bicycle manufactured by Pope Mfg. Company, Boston, Mass. Backbones of steel are light, strong and rigid. Wheels are of spider pattern. Wheel bearings are conical, with tires of India rubber. Its makers called it "an ever-saddled horse that eats nothing and requires no care."

Ladies' bicycle manufactured by Ariel, contains special improvements including dress guard. Rider sits on left side of driving wheel, and rear wheel is off-center for better balance.

An American bicycle meet was always attended by throngs of spectators, both young and old. As the bugler sounded his note of assembly the air was charged with excitement and the purr of wheels, as groups fell into formation

Before the start, at Roxbury, cyclists get together to compare notes and wheels. Sociability ruled supreme when the wheelmen gathered in anticipation of a two-day outing—"For men only."

A WHEEL AROUND THE HUB

The city of Boston, known as "The Hub," played an important role in the history and development of the bicycle. It was the home of the first cycle periodical, *The American Bicycling Journal,* started in 1877. And the Boston Bicycle Club, the first of its kind, was founded on February 11, 1878.

Membership in a cycle club was a badge of acceptance and social standing in the sporting world, and there was hardly a city or town that did not boast a wheel club during the cycle's heyday, before the close of the nineteenth century. The club meets and runs were the occasion for fun and frolic, as well as wholesome outdoor living. High spirits and a holiday mood went hand in hand, on high-wheelers, when excursion parties set out for a day or week-end in the neighboring countryside. One of the best accounts of such a cycling party was published in *Scribner's Monthly* for February, 1880. Seven or eight bicycle clubs had been invited, and they sent more than 40 members to participate, starting from "the foot of a broad, winding avenue in ancient Roxbury. The town had seen many bicycles before, but never so many at once. There was something novel in the diversity of dress, in the equipments with knapsacks and compact *'multum-in-parvo'* bags; the odd uni-

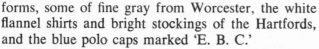

Picnic lunch at a shady spot in the woods, as the high-wheeled ordinaries rested against trees in the background. Afterwards, the men posed for the hard-working cameraman.

Below left: **On the rocks** at Cohasset— a welcome respite for wheels and wheelmen. Sea-breezes cooled hot tires and bearings.

Halt for stragglers. The advance guard made frequent stops to enable slow riders to rejoin the caravan.

forms, some of fine gray from Worcester, the white flannel shirts and bright stockings of the Hartfords, and the blue polo caps marked 'E. B. C.'

"Carriage people reined up to look, and teamsters to have a pleasant word. Ladies smiled from the windows, children thronged the walls and an irrepressible small boy shied his cap at the gleaming spokes and cried: 'Mister, your little wheel's loose!' "

Two light express wagons had been engaged to haul knapsacks and other baggage. A leader gave his signals, sounding calls on a small bugle. When all members of the party were assembled, the bugler sounded "boots and saddles" and the group was off. "Fluttering handkerchiefs of ladies receded fast, and fresh scenes opened to view as the rubber-tired steeds

charioteers." On the first day they rode west toward Massapoag Lake "up hill and down dale, through valley and over ridge, at eight miles an hour—in pursuit of pure pleasure, not of speed, and how exhilarating it was!" The leaders figured, at the end of the two days' meet, that they had covered a hundred miles. No doubt everyone had the time of his life and his quota of spills. This meet, at the height of the autumn season in September, 1879, was typical of the favorite weekend diversion of thousands of ardent bicyclists all over the land.

sped noiselessly along the winding avenue, across and beyond the busy streets, past fine new mansions and quaint old houses," continued the chronicler in his lengthy description. After a while, the bugler sounded the call to dismount near Jamaica Pond, "a charming sheet of water, where a photographer—an accomplished knight of the camera—was on hand and all set up to take a group picture of the pleasure-bound

"En silhouette"—an artistic study against the early evening sun, as riders near the end of the first day's run.

BIG WHEELS OF WHEELING

The League of American Wheelmen was founded in 1880 and soon became a very powerful influence in directing attention to the wretched condition of roads throughout the country. The first convention of the League, held a year after its organization, attracted more than a thousand cyclists from all over the nation. Its parades were spectacles not to be missed: the conglomeration of large wheels whirling and riders precariously perched provided such excitement and thrills as were not soon forgotten.

The L. A. W. lobbied for lower hotel rates for its members, free transporting of wheels on railroad and steamboat lines, equal rights and privileges such as

On Belmont Avenue, Philadelphia, over a hundred "big wheels" gathered for their annual frolic. Many thousands of spectators lined the streets to watch the excitement and

Sketches by Joseph Pennell, for *Harper's Weekly,* December 20, 1879. Upper left: "Easy enough—when you know how"; left: "Coasting"; below: "Taking a header."

244

were granted carriages on the open road. By 1890, the League's 15,000 members became a vociferous force, with a far-reaching platform touching upon political issues. In every town of any consequence a "League counsel" could be found to give accurate touring information, and to provide a warm welcome and reservations for the night's lodgings. The League had self-governing state divisions which assured national coverage for information, and programs to be pushed. High state officials often held key positions in state League counsels, furthering their political careers considerably. The League, interested in building strong bodies and developing racing prowess, awarded many medals, one of which, the "Century," required a 100 mile trip in ten hours.

wave to members of the local wheeling clubs. A bugler headed the procession—this one several blocks long.

Upper right: "A little fancy;" right: "The rear-guard;" below: "At rest."

HIGH-WHEELERS ON PARADE

In the early 1880's, concurrent with the spread of wheel clubs throughout the country, the bicycle craze developed steam-roller proportions. Groups gathered and took to the cycle paths in increasing numbers. Before anyone knew how it happened, a sizeable parade had been organized and, once established, it became a feature in most metropolitan cities.

New York, Brooklyn, Philadelphia, Washington and Boston were the scenes of regular gatherings of cyclists, not only from within the city limits but from all their suburban areas. The League's first annual parade was staged in Boston on Decoration Day, 1881, and saw "nearly a thousand wheelmen from all parts of the country being reviewed upon the Common by the Mayor." The long park drives, the spacious boulevards with fine gravel, the smooth streets, made cycling in the cities both a sport and a pleasure. But before long, as free-wheeling gathered momentum, cycling became a tire-to-tire affair comparable to the bumper-to-bumper crop of present-day Sunday motorists.

Riverside Drive in New York, Prospect Park and

Third Annual Meet of the L. A. W. took place in New York in May, 1883. The procession numbered many hundreds and rolled along on spacious Riverside Drive, heading north to about the Manhattanville vicinity before disbanding.

the twin cycle paths running from the park down to Coney Island, Brooklyn, were favorite thoroughfares for high-wheelers. The Brooklyn fans were a very special breed in admiration of their wheelmen and never failed to make a good turn-out. Coney Island offered a rare opportunity with its fine boulevard running the entire length of over five miles, swept by ocean breezes at all times. When the Coney Island Cycle Paths opened officially, the parade drew contingents from as far away as Boston. Reviewing stands were gaily decked with flowers and colorful bunting. As the riders rolled by, three and four abreast, the stream of whirling steel and the hum of wheels were thrills that rated long columns of rave reviews in the press. Riverside Drive, in New York, was also the setting for long processions of cyclists, who started generally at Seventy-second Street, proceeding north past Grant's Tomb and the Claremont. The course was wide and smooth, and the tree-lined paths paralleled the beautiful Hudson River—an idyllic setting. Parade formations called for special agility and prowess, if they were to be maintained without mishap over the entire route.

The League of American Wheelmen held its first parade on Decoration Day, 1881, in Boston, Mass. Here a group is reviewed by the Commander as he passes along on Commonwealth Avenue. The bugler is second in line, followed by high officials.

PLEASURE BENT...LOW GEAR

Every cycling journey into the open countryside was a junket fraught with danger and despair, with seldom any guarantee that the excursion, planned as a pleasurable sport and sociable outing, might not put the rider on the casualty list. The "open road" was quite aptly named — its chuck holes and deep grooves, ruts and soft shoulders a constant challenge to the bicyclist to keep his eyes wide open. If he missed seeing the rock in the road, he went flying into space. After a few such spills, a rider soon developed an awareness, if he wished to keep up with his group and be counted in at the finish line.

But notwithstanding roadside terrors, the bicycle craze continued to grow until, in the final decades of the Nineteenth century, the wheel had become an accepted way of life; a national institution. A writer during the Eighties said: "If the bicycle were only adapted to the racing path or public exhibitions, if it had only its record in competitive and ornamental athletics, its use might be characterized as a fashion sport—a healthful, humane, manly, and attractive fashion, to be encouraged like that of cricket or archery, to be sure, but not of practical moment to the majority of busy, utilitarian Americans. But since it is a vehicle ready to the hand and foot, conserving time and energy while it reduces distance; since it is more economical, more effective and more attainable than a horse and buggy, suiting the needs of the messenger, the agent, the doctor, the lawyer, the merchant, the botanist, the surveyor, in their journeyings to and fro, it takes on the dignity of a modern improvement and is entitled to rank with the hundred other things which go to make or keep our crowded life worthwhile."

The narrator, describing a cycling group on a New England tour says: "The lead was down a winding hill toward Brook Farm. Two long notes from the captain's whistle—'slow up'—repeated along the line, were understood to mean 'take the hill with care,' and were obeyed by all but Freddie. His saddle had been well set up to the head of his roadster, so that he was nicely poised over the center of his wheel which, getting the better of brake and back-pedaling, took on a speed of fifteen miles an hour, till suddenly meeting a stone, it stopped,—Freddie yielded to the force of circumstances and took a 'header', left his bike with its rear wheel aloft, reached out his hands to Mother Earth, and kissed her frantically while his high-tempered steed lay at his side."

To **"Take a header,"** aptly illustrated, as this wheelman cast an ominous shadow on the road ahead.

"Bicycle vs. Buck-board, or a Chance Brush," drawn by A. S. Daggy. *Harpe[r]* related: "The charm of the buck-board consists in being bounced without jerk[ing]. The bicycle gives a smooth ride provided there are no stones in the way[.]

Roadside sketches drawn by A. W. Taber, for *Scribner's Monthly*, February, 1880. The ambulant artist in any cycling entourage could fill his note book with delightful sketches made en route.

MUSCLES MAKE THE DIFFERENCE

While bike-racing as a sport is virtually extinct today, in the heyday of the cycling craze it drew huge crowds comparable to present-day baseball. Professionals covered a regular circuit which embraced most of the big cities and many smaller ones as well. Public interest finally waned to the point where, one by one, tracks were forced to close, ending a colorful era. Racing had its amusing and thrilling aspects, and offered extremes and novelties to whip up excitement. The so-called paced race was highly favored in the '80's and '90's. This form of racing originated with pacers on tandems, tricycles and so on up to septuplets. The racer would trail the pacemaker as closely as he could, with several riders warming up behind the pacing machine for a mile or so. When the starter thought the racers were fairly even, his gun would bark out the signal and they would be off. Races might cover from five to a hundred miles, with twenty-five miles the favorite distance.

Who has not heard of "Mile-a-minute Murphy?" Charlie Murphy, an amateur bicycle rider, boasted he could keep up with any locomotive if only the wind resistance could be eliminated. While people scoffed, an enterprising Long Island Railroad official saw a great chance for publicity. He laid out a

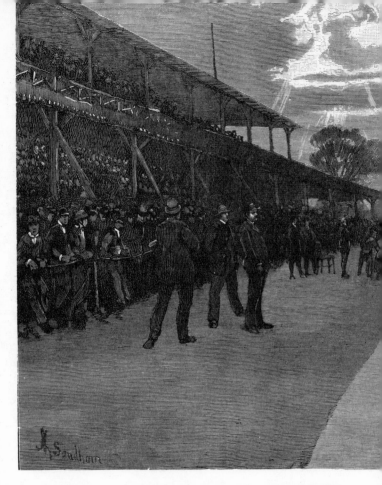

Promateurs and professionals, the newly created division of racers as designated by the League of American Wheelmen, first appeared at the Cycling Tournament, Springfield,

Gruelling twenty-five mile race at the American Institute, indoor track in New York, January, 1880. Tracks were ice-cold in mid-winter but racers got up their own steam in the long grind.

Mass., September, 1886. The promateurs were called "makers'-amateurs" in England, where they rode to display the merits of a maker's machine.

smooth board track three miles long, between existing rails. Then he built a projecting hood or vestibule at the end of a passenger car to accommodate the speeding bike-racer and shield him from outside winds. On June 30, 1899, Murphy made his test run, behind this specially-constructed car filled with newspaper men and photographers. After a mile for warming up, the engineer opened the throttle and, at the end of the measured mile, Murphy and the locomotive had negotiated the distance in exactly 57⅘ seconds. The first human to speed the mile in under a minute, Murphy had made good his boast, and his incredible record withstood the onslaughts of many famed racers for forty-two years.

On May 17, 1941, Alfred (Alf) Letourner, the great six-day racing star, rode behind a protected windshield of a racing car, on a highway near Bakersfield, Calif. He officially covered the mile in 33.05 seconds, at the rate of 108.92 miles per hour. Letourner rode a bicycle having a gear ratio of 252, the front sprocket of 57 teeth driving a rear sprocket of only 6 teeth.

But in the early days of racing on ordinaries, no such speed records could be made. In 1886, at the Springfield, Mass., Tournament, the winning mile was run in 2 minutes, 38 seconds, "remarkably good" for the time.

Bicycle tournament at Hartford, Conn., September, 1880. This mile race for amateurs included a variety of high-wheelers, some with leading small wheel.

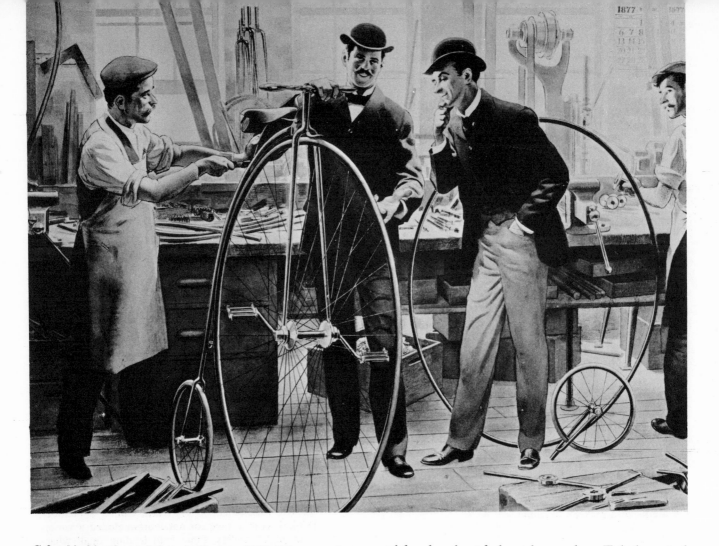

Columbia bicycle workshop, in Boston, 1877. When proud Col. Pope met with his designers, the talk was of spokes, rims, rubber tires and handle-bars.

WHERE "WHEELS" WERE MADE

The growing interest in cycling needed only the impetus of the Centennial Exposition at Philadelphia, in 1876, to send it on to greater activity. Several English manufacturers displayed their "ordinaries" and the demand was so instantaneous that orders were booked for the importation of many thousands. Col. Albert Pope, a former Civil War officer and maker of pistols, sensed a strong potential market in the United States, made a trip abroad to acquire rights and, promptly on his return, started work on his first run of high-wheelers. Pope negotiated a contract with the Weed Sewing Machine Company, of Hartford, Conn. to produce bicycles under the trade name "Columbia Bicycles".

Pope and the Weed company did not attempt, at first, to construct an entirely new machine, or yield to the almost universal Yankee temptation to invent something better than the English had made. They adopted the more prudent course of taking a good model, already tried and popular. Tubular steel perches had not been made in this country, nor semi-tubular rims for the wheels. Round rubber tires and the proper cement for holding them to a metallic rim were also unknown here. In a bicycle of the period, there were some three hundred parts and these had to be constructed so that their total weight did not exceed forty to fifty pounds. The company started with a view to making all parts and making them interchangeable, in the best production technique. This involved designing machinery, adapted to do the jobs, and training skilled mechanics.

A decade after the Centennial every magazine and newspaper in the country was devoting columns of space to the cycling craze. *Frank Leslie's* in a report accompanying the engraving shown here—said: "There are few who appreciate the magnitude that the manufacture of these graceful vehicles has attained these past ten years. It is estimated there are now seventy-five thousand riders, and about one hundred clubs, and half the machines ridden are of American make. The process of manufacture is exceedingly interesting, using the most modern and intricate machinery. The amount of capital invested in the industry runs into the millions."

Gormully & Jeffery Manufacturing Company, of Chicago, was the largest producer of bicycles in the West. In 1902 it branched out into a newer field—the automobile—and built the Rambler.

FINISHING THE LEATHER WORK

NICKEL PLATING ROOM

BUFFING A BACKBONE

PART OF THE REPAIR SHOP

SCREWING IN THE SPOKES

A PORTION OF THE POLISHING ROOM

THE ASSEMBLY ROOM

A CORNER OF THE MACHINE SHOP

253

J. K. Starley, of England, developed his Rover safety bicycle in 1884, the prototype for types to follow. Main features included a braced single backbone type of frame, saddle, and sprocket and chain between wheels.

Shergold safety bicycle built in 1878 in England. Note long link chain drive, a forerunner of present type.
Steering handle, located at center, connected with rods.

Lawson's Bicyclette of 1879, the inventor's third safety type after six years of development. Significant as the first sprocket and rear-wheel chain drive.

"Psycho" bicycle, built by Starley Brothers, c. 1887, had an improved cross-frame, safety type. Metal frame of tubing, handle bar grips of wood. Metal mudguards for both wheels in original, now at Smithsonian.

"SAFETY FIRST" ON A SAFETY

The era of the high-wheeled "ordinary," its riders "perched on high like oversized monkeys"—prone to accidental upsets that a mere pebble in the road could cause—was destined to come to a close. Its demise was not sudden but it was certain, following on the heels of an excited interest—a feverish activity that sparked the effort of a thousand inventors both here and abroad. The "safety" was a long time in coming; its advantages were obvious to all who were willing to give it a fair trial, but its arrival did not exactly relegate all high wheels to the attic or museum—the diehards continued to ride and race them for a decade.

Curiously, the safety with its two equal-sized wheels was a reversion to the elemental form of the hobby-horse that Baron Drais had first used over sixty years earlier. The intervening years had seen the wheels rise to enormous proportions, with both front and rear wheels alternating for dominant position.

In the late Seventies, H. Bates of Croyden, England, built the first bicycle using a rear wheel chain drive, naming it the "Flying Dutchman." Its drive was by pulleys and cord instead of the modern sprocket and chain. This machine never made much headway, though its mechanism represented a decided advance in propulsion.

In 1885, there appeared the form of bicycle which

"Whippet" spring-frame safety bicycle by Lindley and Biggs, 1885. A popular intermediate type on which many records were made.

New Rapid Bicycle, built by St. George's Engineering Co., Birmingham, England. Frame of metal tubing, tangential wire spokes, thin rubber tires. Tool bag suspended from steering-head stay. Oil lamp.

Ladies' Victoria model, built by Overman Wheel Co., of Boston, Mass., 1889. This type with drop frame was invented for women to ride astride without catching the skirt.

set the pace and pattern for the cycling world. J. K. Starley's design was the outgrowth of several forerunners he had built, starting with his Rover tricycle. This was a great favorite in England, with its two medium-sized front wheels, a low frame and a trailing third wheel called a steerer. The third model of Starley's may be regarded as the production prototype of the present safety bicycle demonstrating, in a practical and convincing way, the superiority of the safety arrangement of frame design. The steering was direct, the head was raked, but the forks had no set to align steering-head line with the point of tire contact with the road, and the frame was in no sense triangulated. The machine weighed 37 pounds.

During the next few years many improvements appeared in rapid succession, resulting in the diamond frame that was to become standard. The "Whippet" spring-frame machine was introduced in 1885, its chief feature being a frame of triangular design that determined the set positions for saddle, pedals and handlebar, isolated from the main frame. This spring-frame cycle, supposed to absorb the shocks, was in demand until J. B. Dunlop introduced the pneumatic tired wheel in 1889. By 1892 Dunlop's notable contribution to smoother riding was in general use by the burgeoning bicycle millions on both continents. In inventing the cushioned tire, so that his delicate son might enjoy more comfortable riding, the Irish veterinary surgeon unwittingly willed a great legacy to the as-yet-unborn motoring millions.

Ladies' Victoria, improved model, 1894. Rigid drop frame, covered mudguard and chain drive. Compare with earlier model above.

Columbia ladies' safety, 1892. Many improvements included full chain guard, front spring fork, twin forward frames and hand brake.

Columbia light roadster safety, ridden by Robert D. Garden, champion, in 1889.

Young bloods of the Mid-West, c. 1891. Start of the Columbia Bicycle Club's Sunday outing.

BICYCLISTS AND BICYCLE CLUBS

By 1880, the bicycle—whether the high-wheeled "ordinary," or the "safety" with two wheels of equal size—had become the favorite of American sportsmen. The same year, the League of American Wheelmen had been founded at Newport. Within a decade, the League was the world's largest athletic association. Every large city had its bicycle clubhouse; some cities boasted several, appealing to different social groups. Topics of keen interest to wheelmen were solemnly discussed in the clubs, not only in cities but in towns and villages. The art of balancing, correct weight ratios of bicycles, the best way to grasp handle-bars when racing—all were subjects for serious study. The pneumatic tire is said to have created a sensation, club members hailing it as "the most salutary invention of the day."

In the four years, from 1878 to 1882, bicycle makers invested about $70,000 to promote the clubs and add to the popularity of the wheel. The club membership lists read like a "Who's Who" of each community, and society women "captained" lady cyclers.

Bicycle schools sprang up everywhere. Pupils were often taken out to what was described as "a piece of unfrequented road, generally about dusk, as the pupil cuts a more or less awkward figure, and is naturally averse to furnishing the public with a free spectacle." Learners were earnestly assured that "anyone can ride in safety; it is as easy as walking."

One of the greatest achievements of the League of American Wheelmen was its road-improvement program which prompted state legislatures and local townships to devote more adequate funds to the building of better roads, to the gain of country property owners, farmers, rural postmen, as well as the ever-growing numbers of touring cyclists.

Pennsylvania Bicycle Clubhouse, impressive residence on Girard Avenue, Philadelphia.

Long Island Wheelmen enjoyed this handsome clubhouse located on Bedford Avenue, Brooklyn.

Manhattan Bicycle Club was housed in this substantial building on West 70th Street, New York City.

New York Bicycle Club offered hospitality at West End Avenue and 72nd Street.

Touring, it was pointed out, was the most pleasurable feature of cycling. "Long-distance journeys no longer command astonishment," it was editorially observed, "as any decent rider can tour any distance if he has the time." Constantly men of national or local importance were making record rides: Francis Thayer of Hartford, George Nellis of Herkimer, N. Y., Theodore van Mehrbekse of New York City and F. E. Weaver of New Haven, had all toured across the United States, while others had ridden from Boston to Chicago, or from Chicago to New York. Thomas Stevens, previous to 1890, had made the most spectacular tour, entirely around the world. The roads in Canada, England, and France were said to be superb, and Thomas Stevens reported that "the finest road in the world is in India."

In a supplement on cycling, in 1890, *Harper's Weekly* said: "English servant-girls market on tricycles; royalty cycles in its private enclosures; and the Prince and Princess of Wales and Lord Randolph Churchill recently graced a race-meet promoted for the honor and edification of His Royal Highness.

"In the United States the wheelmen are becoming more numerous and more powerful. Those who go abroad on wheels are of many types: the reporter who collects news a-wheel; the clergyman who makes his rounds; the multitudinous army of clerks who fight off dyspepsia, melancholia, and general incapacity by a ride in the park or on the roads after business hours. Then, there is the large army who take up the sport not as a life-preserver, or appetizer, or muscle-maker, but for the merits of the thing itself, for the opportunity it gives one to wander far afield in search of beauty and recreation. There are two other classes, those who tour, and those who race."

Winners of road records were idolized by the public. W. F. Murphy, shown here, held the Irvington-Milburn road record.

AGOG OVER WHEELS

The United States has embraced many fads with lusty enthusiasm but none with the mad devotion that was lavished on the bicycle. "Cycling," an enthusiast wrote in the Nineties, "has now so great an impetus that nothing can stop it. . . . Everyone may ride, from the small boy to the bishop. . . . New factories have been built; new styles of wheels introduced. The number of meets has multiplied; the men ride more; new clubs are being organized every week."

The League of American Wheelmen called itself "the greatest athletic organization in the world," and boasted over 15,000 members. In most of the large cities there were hotels designated as "Official League" hotels, where one's L. A. W. membership card assured the holder a good room and preferential treatment. Social historians say that it is impossible to understand how marvelous the bicycle seemed to people of the 1890's. Though ministers deplored it . . . to their shrinking congregations; though elderly people were shocked that men and girls rode out

The farmer of the Nineties had as little admiration for speed maniacs a-wheel as his descendants of today feel toward racing motorists.

A Century Run . . . on the homestretch. The cyclist's proudest achievement, the Century Road Club's gold badge, awarded for "riding a century," 100 miles in ten hours.

together, unchaperoned; though a New York theatrical producer bemoaned that patronage had fallen off —he no longer went in Summer to Boston, Baltimore, and Washington because, as soon as the roads were good, everybody was out bicycling . . . the vogue gained in momentum.

Business men predicted that the country was on the verge of an economic collapse, due to the bicycle. . . ."In 1896 the watch and jewelry business was all but defunct; piano business was off 50 percent; young women were spending their 'parlor-set' money on bicycles; saddle, harness and carriage firms were closing; cigar sales were fewer by a million a day; and a book-seller in New York said his sales were off very drastically. Most pathetic were the barbers: after a day's work a man no longer had a shave and dressed up . . . he went out cycling! And, as the barbers pointed out, "When a man skips a shave today, we can't sell him two tomorrow; that sale is lost forever." The Reverend Asa A. Blackburn told his congregation in the Church of the Strangers, "You cannot serve God and skylark on a bicycle."

But no warnings could cool the fever. Though 312 factories in the United States were making bicycles in 1899, the demand outran the supply. Between 1890 and 1896, Americans spent over $100,000,000 on "wheels." Men and women deprived themselves of necessities to own and ride a bicycle. Yet, as soon as cyclists left a city, they encountered impassable rutted roads, some as bad as those which had plagued travelers in the early 1800's. Of the great cities, New York, Brooklyn—then an independent city, Boston, and Chicago offered the best roads for the cyclists. Through New York's Central Park, over to Riverside Drive and along the Hudson River to Grant's Tomb and the Claremont Inn; or in Brooklyn from Prospect Park on fine roads out to Coney Island; or in Chicago along Michigan Avenue . . . the gay processions of ardent pedalers passed. On sunny Sundays, the more daring or the more expert cycled up beyond the Harlem River, on into Van Cortlandt and Bronx Parks. While the first bicycles sold for $300—even in 1895 their price was $100, when eggs were fourteen cents a dozen.

Country folk were affronted by the influx of cyclists, especially by the tandem, with half its motive power of the feminine gender. Demure as these damsels appear in our eyes, they were jeered as jezebels in the Nineties.

THEY RODE THE ROAD TO ROMANCE

Girls of the late Eighties and early Nineties would pedal forth alone, hopeful of meeting a dashing bachelor a-wheel, or girls and men cycled forth together. In any case, the open road, the freedom from stuffy late-Victorian parlors, the absence of fluttering mothers or odious brothers . . . all created a happy atmosphere that fostered romantic attachments. Just as the craze for "wheels" helped in the building of better roads, it also led to many marriages and new homes. Cycling—whether on a single bicycle, on a tandem, or a cosy two-seated three-wheeler—brought to women a keen, new interest in an active sport where, previously, they had been limited largely to croquet or badminton, played in hobbling skirts worn over tight corsets.

In England, the high-wheeled bicycles were called "penny-farthings," a name derived from the difference in size of their two wheels—the front one being four or five feet in diameter, while the back wheel was usually only 10 or 12 inches in diameter. The tires were solid rubber. Riding the high front-wheelers was often very precarious, for they could be upset by even a small pebble in the road. As has been mentioned, the same high-wheeled bicycles in America were referred to as "ordinary" bicycles, to distinguish them from the "safety" type with two wheels of equal size.

So many accidents occurred, often with fatal results, that the large front-wheeler bicycle was modified—with the small wheel being used in front and the high wheel in the rear. This arrangement placed the rider's weight somewhat in front of the hub of the rear wheel and the pedals—instead of being rotated—were pumped up and down, pulling on leather strips attached to the hub. This style, called the "Star," offering increased safety, enjoyed only a brief vogue.

Tricycle built for two . . . first evolved in England, the twin-seated Columbia three-wheeler cost $250.

Moonlight on the Hudson . . . bicycle lamplight on the Riverside Drive, New York City, a setting rich with romantic possibilities.

An article published in *Choice Literature,* in England in 1884—written by an anonymous physician—emphasized that, devoted as he was to horse riding and also to walking, he found that those exercises left him tired, with weary muscles, and unfitted for mental work for several hours afterwards. Cycling, however, left him "with no sense of fatigue, but agreeably refreshed and ready for study or other mental occupation." If his professional ethics demanded anonymity of authorship, his endorsement of bicycling was unqualified. He assured readers earnestly that he would prefer to ride 40 miles on a cycle than 25 miles on a horse. An American physician, Dr. Henry Smith Williams, wrote—in *Harper's Weekly,* April 11, 1896: "The bicycle has come among us with such volcanic suddenness as a new social force that it is not to be expected that we should fully adapt ourselves to the novel conditions it imposes, in a day or a decade. . . . But this much is already plain: the bicycle is inducing millions of people to take regular exercise who have long been in need of such exercise, but who could never be induced to take it by any means hitherto devised." With medical authorities and romantic couples alike endorsing it, the bicycle vogue attracted ever more devotees.

Idyllic tricycling in England . . . Joseph
Pennell's drawing of Maytime riders
on the Ripley Road.

Shared tastes . . . literature, joined
to outdoor exercise, doubled the
allure of the open road.

GIBSON BELLES...IN BLOOMERS

The feminine ideal of beauty, from the early Nineties, was the Gibson Girl. Her sailor hat, shirtwaist with mannish collar and leg-of-mutton sleeves, and trim skirt had been sufficiently shocking to an older and gentler generation but, when the skirts were shortened or bloomers substituted, the bicycle which inspired these fashions was exposed to new abuse. Well-bred girls however were undeterred by ridicule. Wearing such costumes, they modestly encased their calves in close-buttoned gaiters. Like the billowing bloomers, the voluminous-sleeved jackets must have set up a high degree of wind-resistance, a handicap to speed for the fair enthusiast, but fashion in that day seldom yielded to the practical. It was Mrs. Amelia Bloomer of New York who, about 1850, daringly donned the bifurcated garment—trousers buttoned around the ankle—which afterwards came to be known by her name.

Some girls slashed their street skirts, weighted the hems with tailors' leads, and created the divided skirts which later were modified and made for the sportswoman's wear. By 1895, the Gibson Girl costume was practically a uniform for women of all ages.

Lillian Russell rode in a leg-of-mutton sleeved cycling costume of white serge, circling twice around the Central Park reservoir on her gold-plated bicycle that made national gossip . . . its handbars of mother-of-pearl emblazoned with her monogram in emeralds and diamonds. "Propaganda of a bicycle maker!" scoffed some, but others hinted it was the gift of 'Diamond Jim' Brady who, himself, rode a bicycle sparkling with gold plate and silver spokes.

Of the feminine members of the exclusive Michaux Cycle Club, it was reported that, "As a rule there is no display of short skirts, and no bloomers or knickerbockers are to be seen. The men usually wear knee-breeches or knickerbockers and sack coats, though those who went directly to the club from their offices of Winter afternoons, bicycled in their business suits."

Chaperones were not totally dispensed with. When young people organized a "supper-ride," as horse-riders still do frequently today, the young men and women rode with their chaperone . . . generally along the Central Park paths and Riverside Drive for dinner at the Claremont Inn where, in pleasant weather, gay Japanese lanterns lit the outdoor tables. The ride home through the late evening was lighted by the glow of bicycle lamps.

Bloomers, gaiters, leg-of-mutton sleeves, plus a pert bird-winged hat . . . the cycling costume of this owner of a **Columbia,** 1895.

All the cycle types of 1890—the safety, followed by a high-wheel ordinary, two-wheel tandem, tandem tricycle, and single tricycle.

264 **Festival of Cyclists** in the Albert Hall of the Crystal Palace, London. Every stunt known to the circus acrobat was performed by strong men on wheels. Tires alone, or spokes only, wheels misshapen, entertained 1890 spectators.

The Humours of the Wheel was the title of this page from *The Sketch*, London, November 4, 1896. Gibson Girl leg-of-mutton sleeves and bloomers; silhouettes of many shapes, and various styles of pedaling, attracted the artist.

Copeland's steam-driven tricycle, of which about 200 were manufactured, in gala form with fringed canopy, photographed before the Smithsonian Institution, Washington, about 1888.

MOTORIZATION COMPLETES THE CYCLE

Long before the peak of the bicycle's popularity, the climax of its mechanical perfection, men in America, France, Germany, and England had begun to experiment with its motorization. Few probably foresaw that these efforts would eventually destroy the happy halcyon days of bicycling . . . or that the sport which had so enormous a following would be abandoned and almost obsolete— at least in the United States— in a relatively few years.

De Dion in France had made a successful petrol-powered tricycle about 1860; Michaux had produced a steam-powered bicycle in 1867. S. H. Roper of Roxbury, Massachusetts, had exhibited his steam-driven velocipedes at country fairs and race tracks in this country by 1865, racing them against the fastest horses. Carl Benz in Germany had produced a benzine-powered tricycle in 1885, and Gottlieb Daimler was riding his gasoline-powered tricycle in the same year. L. D. Copeland of Philadelphia had experimented, in 1885, with attaching a steam-driven motor to a Star bicycle and later, to a tricycle, of which about 200 were manufactured by the Moto-Cycle Manufacturing Company. A version of Copeland's tricycle, fringe-canopied, was photographed—with the Smithsonian Institution as background— about 1888.

By 1897, the De Dion and Bouton gasoline tricycle had been entered in the Paris-Marseilles-Paris race for automobile vehicles, and revealed "very remarkable features of speed, power, and endurance . . . one of these light vehicles, despite its apparent frailty, was the third to arrive, beating a good number of large and powerful competitors." It had made the run of 1073 miles in 71 hours, at an average speed of 14 miles an hour. In England, as early as 1870, Sir T. Parkyns and A. E. Bateman had attached a steam engine to a front-drive tricycle. In a history of the automobile, most of these velocipedes, tricycles and bicycles—with their small motors, variously powered and frankly appended to the regular cycle chassis—are considered among the earliest forms of motor cars.

Within a few years, after 1900, the Thomas, the Indian, and the Harley-Davidson were conspicuous as the first true motor-cycles. To the bicycle, the motorcycle, automobile, and even the airplane are indebted for such inventions as pneumatic tires, wire wheels, ball-bearings, chain and shaft drives, and countless improvements in engineering techniques, mass production, as well as in machine tools and metals. Some of the pioneers in bicycle design were

Electric motor cycle built by Andrew Riker, of Brooklyn, N. Y. Box near rear axle carries batteries.

Gasoline-driven bicycle—one of the earliest built, c. 1886. A continuous leather belt drives the large rear wheel.

Upper right: **Clark gasoline tricycle** built experimentally, in 1897, by the Pittsburgh Motor Vehicle Co., headed by Louis S. Clarke, the inventor. The Co. name was changed, in 1899, to the Autocar Co., still in business

also those who made the first automobiles: Elwood Haynes, the Apperson brothers, Charles E. Duryea, Colonel Albert A. Pope, George N. Pierce, F. C. Stearns, Thomas B. Jeffrey, H. A. Lozier, among others. The Wright brothers—in their Dayton, Ohio, bicycle shop—not only repaired cycles but built their own designs which, doubtless, eventually led to development of certain parts for the airplane.

The League of American Wheelmen, with its pioneering for better roads, had also paved the way for the motorist—so soon to sound the knell of the cycle.

In other lands, with citizens not so affluent as the American, the bicycle still remains an indispensable means of transportation for the worker, and a popular leisure-hour delight.

Below: **De Dion & Bouton's tricycle,** side and rear views. It raced from Paris-Marseilles-Paris, against heavy automobiles in 1897, and placed third.

The Perreaux steam velocipede, shown at an Industrial Exhibition in Paris, 1880. Its speed was 15 to 18 miles an hour.

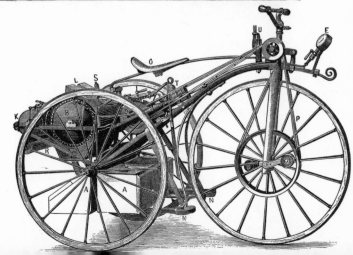

FILL'ER UP

POUR IN THE MAGIC POTION . . . mix pleasure and power with reason. To each golden drop add dream-stuff . . . man's dominion over distance.

HAIL THE HORSELESS CARRIAGE . . . born in Europe, bred in America . . . the product of backyard tinkerers and basement mechanics . . . an instrument of democracy for the enjoyment of millions, the benefit of mankind.

SERVANT OF MAN, conserver of time and energy . . . blazer of trails and builder of roads . . . the motorcar transforms horse-and-buggy ruts into satin-sleek highways. It lifts the burden from the back of man, brings happy reunions with families and friends, extra hours for leisure and recreation.

STEP ON THE GAS! The motor purrs, the road unrolls . . . a concrete ribbon flung across a continent. The merry old 'mobile speeds motorist from stifling cities of steel and stone to restful meadow and tranquil stream, exhilarating seacoast and wind-swept mountain.

ROAD CLOSED . . . DETOUR. Sunday motorists, bumper-to-bumper . . . trials of temper and patience . . . traffic tickets . . . death on the highway.

SAFETY FIRST!

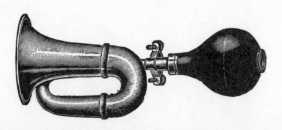

Rambler Runabout, 1902

Stanley Steamer, 1908

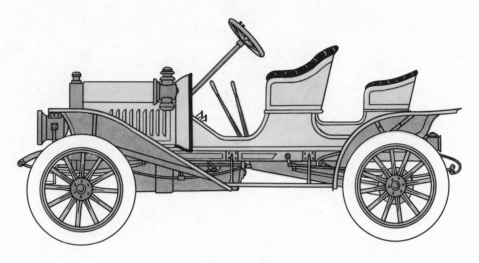

Buick, 1908

First Chevrolet, 1913

Nathan Read's working model of a steam car, built in 1790. Read, of Warren, Mass., had applied for a patent for a steam engine operating both on land and water. It was said to be light, strong, and safe but there is no record that it was ever manufactured in quantity.

Hand Bill for a steam buggy . . . "the most wonderful invention of modern times. It can be driven, with two persons in it, 150 miles a day, upon common roads . . .
Will match it against any trotting horse anywhere in the world."

The Mechanic.

JULY, 1834.

[For the Mechanic.]
STEAM-CARRIAGES.

[Evans' Steam-Engines. See page 176.]

HAVING traced the steam-engine from its first invention to the successful application of its power for the purpose of navigation, by Fulton, it now remains for us to continue the subject, by a brief history of its application to land-carriages on common roads, and its superior advantages on railways. Two individuals, in particular, are claimants for the honor of this invention, both of whom also claim the invention of steam-boats; but as all claims to the invention

Dudgeon's steam carriage, built in 1853, carried 12 persons; hourly speed 14 miles. Exhibited at the Crystal Palace, N. Y., 1858, also shown at first Auto Show in 1900.

PIONEERS IN PROPULSION

The idea of a steam engine, applied to propel carriages on the common roads, attracted the thoughts and efforts of a number of men on both sides of the Atlantic. Even before the horseless rail-coaches had been perfected, inventors — self-taught or college-trained—were making various attempts to supplant Dobbin with a motor.

James Rumsey demonstrated before President George Washington a steam engine he had started working on in 1774. The demonstration, with the engine powering a boat, took place in 1786. In the same year, John Fitch—the first to organize a company to build motors—had constructed a scale-model of a self-propelled road vehicle. He and his Dutch watchmaker partner, Henry Voight, had a combined capital of $300. Fitch built four steam-boats in five years, then turned his attention again to the steam carriage. Both Rumsey and Fitch, knowing the preference for water-borne transport due to the poor conditions of the roads, had demonstrated their engines in boats. Then, there was Nathan Read. Blessed, like John Stevens, with wealth, Read had studied and taught at Harvard University. In 1783 he was experimenting with steam engines, seeking a way to reduce the size and weight, to make them more adaptable for use on road vehicles. He obtained a patent in 1790 but evidently preferred to serve in Congress. His working-model was exhibited, but there is no record that it was ever put into production. Many other engines were built, some only to explode on their trial runs. Each was placed in a conventional carriage, or wagon body. No man built a special vehicle to house his motor.

Evans' Orukter Amphibolos. When the first wheels and axle-trees broke under its weight, Evans' workmen "voluntarily offered to make without wages other wheels and axle-trees." Exhibited in Central Square, Philadelphia, for 25 cents; advertised July 13, 1805.

INVENTOR, PERSUADER...OLIVER EVANS

The first American to build a road vehicle that moved under its own power was Oliver Evans. He filed specifications for a patent in 1792, the first motor car patent to be issued in the United States. When Evans first read the descriptions of the bulky engines built by James Watt and Thomas Newcomen in England, to pump water from mines, he realized that these were suited only for stationary installation, and he said that the principles were wrong. Evans was confident that he could build a small engine, a fifth or a tenth the size of the English ones, which would have equal power, and be applicable to a road vehicle. His many-sided genius evolved so many inventions that no mention can here be made of most of them. He was an ardent persuader as well as an inspired inventor. His communications to the press, his appearances before state legislatures—as early as 1775—in behalf of a "steam engine . . . an entire new plan . . . propelling land carriages to travel with heavie burdens up and down hills without the aid of animal fource with such velocity as may be convenient, and be guided by a person sitting therein" kept young America aware of the possibilities of land carriages. Richard Trevithick in England is said to have seen Evans' sketches of his high-pressure steam engine and to have been influenced by them in his own inventions. Thomas Blanchard in 1825, Richard Dudgeon in 1853, Sylvester H. Roper in 1863, are a few of the other inventors who kept alive the idea of steam carriages through the Civil War period. Samuel Morey, in 1826, obtained a patent for a gas or vapor engine.

THE GREATEST
MECHANICAL
EXHIBITION
IN THE WORLD.
THE
STEAM
BUGGY!

Pronounced by scientific men to be the most wonderful invention of modern times. It can be driven, with two persons in it, 150 miles a day, upon common roads. It is light and strong, and can be managed better than any horse, and can be driven faster than any person dare to ride. Will match it against any trotting horse in the world.

THE ONLY
Steam Velocipede
IN THE WORLD.

Pronounced a perfect triumph in mechanism. It can be driven up any hill, and will out speed any horse in the world.

TO BE SEEN AT
600 BROADWAY.
ADMISSION . . . . 25 Cents.

The Mechanic, published in July, 1834, its "First Special Automobile Number." Evans' steam engine was on the cover. This was the first magazine to devote an entire issue to news and views of motorized "land carriages."

Dickson's improved steam carriage of 1865, could be "instantly converted into a stationary engine without disconnecting any part."

273

William Symington's atmospheric steam coach, shown in Edinburgh, 1784. It was never developed for practical use.

Britain had two major assets, when the ferment about steam carriages was stirring in men's minds. The country possessed a number of inventors—who had been building steam engines for stationary installation—and good roads maintained for the smooth progress of stage coaches. As early as 1784, William Symington had built an atmospheric steam engine which was shown as a model in Edinburgh. It was not developed, and Symington finally specialized in steamships.

Richard Trevithick's name is first in every account of steam engine development. Credited as the "father of the locomotive," Captain Dick of Cornwall built a tramway engine in 1803 which was tried out in Wales on February 24, 1804. It conveyed ten tons of bar iron and seventy passengers from Penydarren to Marther Tydvil, a distance of nine miles. The locomotive worked satisfactorily from a mechanical point of view but was not a success commercially, being found more costly than horse traction. Goldsworthy Gurney built a six-wheeled steam coach in 1827 which, two years later, he drove from London to Bath and back—a distance of 212 miles, at between 12 and 15 miles an hour. He later became "Sir" Goldsworthy Gurney, an automotive giant. Thomas Hood wrote that *"instead of journeys, people may now go upon a Gurney."* Gurney and steam carriage had become synonymous. Another English inventor, Walter Hancock of Marlborough, built nine successful types of steam carriages between 1827 and 1838,

Richard Trevithick's high-wheeled road carriage, 1802, the first steam car to use variable speed transmission.

Walter Hancock, a competitor of Gurney, built the "Enterprise," the fifth of his nine successful motorized coaches.

Goldsworthy Gurney's successful steam stage coach, 1827. Two years later, Gurney drove it from London to Bath.

operating them between London and Paddington, also between Finsbury Square and Pentenville. Francis Maceroni a former associate of Gurney—patented in 1833, with a partner named Squire, a "simpler and safer" steam coach which was operated between Paddington and Edgeware. Dr. William Church built a steam carriage that could carry forty passengers. He formed a steam coach company in 1835, for a route between London and Birmingham, but the company failed. In 1858, Thomas Rickett manufactured a remarkable three-wheeled vehicle for the Marquess of Stratford, who drove it from Buckingham to Wolverton. Many other men developed practical steam carriages.

But there were two strongly opposing interests: the companies operating the horse-drawn stage coaches, and the proprietors of the toll roads, who resorted to amazing measures to block the progress of steam. Where a horse-propelled coach paid a toll of 4s., a steam carriage was charged £2, 8s. If the stiff tolls did not bankrupt the steam coach operators, their drivers were likely to find stone barriers at the turns of sharp corners in the roads, certain to break axle-trees or cause devastating wrecks. In addition, the horse-breeders joined the opposition and, despite the eloquence of the steam coach interests, magistrates invariably ruled for the horse partisans. Finally, in 1877, Parliament passed the "Red Flag Act," requiring that a horseman with red flag precede all steam coaches—prohibiting travel faster than four miles an hour. The steam carriage operators temporarily relinquished their struggle, while other nations swiftly took the lead in building steam-powered vehicles.

Francis Maceroni and his associate, Squire, patented this steam coach in 1833. It covered 1700 miles without repairs.

Dr. William Church's imposing steam coach carried forty. Built in 1835 for his steam carriage company which failed.

Hancock's "Autopsy," a closed steam bus. Built 1834, it ran between Finsbury Square and Pentenville, carrying six.

Thomas Rickett built this three-wheeled car for the Marquess of Stratford, 1858, who drove it with his titled friends.

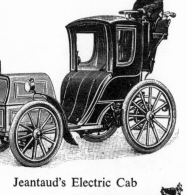

Jeantaud's Electric Cab

Kriéger's Vis-a-vis

Jeantaud's Electric Coupé

FAMOUS FIRSTS IN FRANCE

The first horseless carriage in France is generally credited to Nicholas Joseph Cugnot. An artillery officer, he is reputed to have completed his first experiment in 1760, and to have built a car for four passengers five years later. Commissioned to build a motorized wagon that might drag cannon into place, Cugnot constructed a cumbersome three-wheeled vehicle which, on its second trial, went out of control and was wrecked. The next steam vehicles were built by Charles Dallery, who had them running in Paris by 1790.

De Rivaz, Renard, and Louis Pecquer—from about 1807 to 1825—each had built "self-moving" carriages before Charles Dietz invented his steam road vehicles. In 1834 Dietz had several road tractors hauling omnibuses in Paris. Lotz in 1866 built a three-wheeled steam car; Michaux in 1867 designed a steam-propelled bicycle, and Ravel launched a light, oil-fired steam car, 1868.

Then, in 1872, Amadée Bollée (pére) built a steam car he named L'Obéissante which, fitted with a new type of steering, apparently proved as dutiful and obedient as its name implied. Bollée next constructed a 28-ton traction engine with six wheels,

Jeantaud's Electric Drojki

Amedée Bollée's Steam Carriage

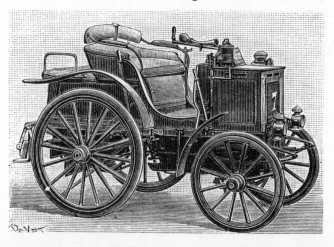

M. Serpollet's steam phaeton, Paris, 1890. The road carriages illustrated represent entries in the Paris-to-Amsterdam race of The Automobile Club of France, 1898. Included were eight electrics made by Jeantaur, four by Kriéger.

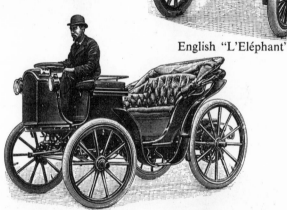

English "L'Eléphant"

Jeantaud's Electric "Mylord"

and then several Victorias. It was said that the entire Bollée family on a Sunday outing in one of Papa Bollée's steam carriages was one of the pleasantest sights in the earlier age of motoring. His son Amadée carried on the work of building steam cars, at the time when De Dion and Serpollet were constructing notable steam and road vehicles. But the day of petrol was approaching. Though water was cheaper than fuel, it also was much heavier. De Rivaz had pioneered in 1807 with internal combustion. Lenoir had applied an internal combustion engine to a four-wheeled brake in 1860. The Comte de Dion, who considered steam better for heavy vehicles, now built with his associate Bouton a petrol-powered tricycle which was an immediate success.

Peugeot, Lepape, Delahaye are other Frenchmen who made notable contributions to the history of "self-propelled" vehicles. Panhard & Levassor had purchased Daimler's patents and were building Daimlers in France.

The 1895 French automobile race proved a triumph for petrol. There were 15 petrol-powered entries, and 8 steamers. Eight of the petrol-driven cars finished, but only one steam-powered carriage. This was Amadée Bollée's *La Nouvelle* of 1880, driven by Amadée *(fils)*.

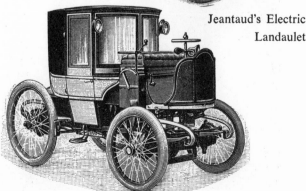

Jeantaud's Electric Landaulet

Jeantaud's Electric Coupe

Panhard & Levassor's
Petrol Phaeton

277

Carl Benz's three-wheeled vehicle with horizontal cylinder and vertical crankshaft. Mannheim, 1885.

Benzine-propelled carriage exhibited in Munic 1888, built by the Rhine Gas Motor Works, Benz & C

278

MADE IN GERMANY

In Germany, too, inventive men were working on "self-propelled" land carriages. There also were various claims of "firsts." In 1873 an Austrian, Sigfried Marcus, built a gas-powered vehicle which was successfully operated. Seven years later, the atmospheric engine produced by Nikolaus Otto and Eugen Langen had appeared. It adopted the spark system developed by Lenoir in France, but with a greater economy in fuel. In 1874, inspired by another Frenchman, Beau de Rochas, Dr. Otto perfected an engine on the four-cycle principle, smoother and more silent than his earlier engine.

Then, in 1885, the most famous of the German auto inventors—Carl Benz and Gottlieb Daimler—each working separately, demonstrated small gas-powered vehicles. Daimler, who had been associated with Dr. Otto in a gas motor plant at Deutz, and had severed this connection in 1882, began to apply his motors to road locomotion. He devoted three years to perfecting his petrol engine, by which time Carl Benz brought out his motorized, benzine-powered, wire-wheeled tricycle. Carl Benz, whose father and grandfather had been blacksmiths and burgomasters in a Black Forest village, had been left an

orphan at two. As a boy he showed an interest in mechanics, graduated in engineering from the Polytechnic Institute and, after marriage, invested in a stationary gas engine shop in Mannheim. But his secret interest was in an engine that would drive a carriage. His first road test was a failure; his second vehicle went out of control and was wrecked; but his third attempt—after twelve years of experimentation—proved successful. The vehicle traveled about 100 yards! He obtained a patent in January, 1886. The Benz was the only gasoline-powered car displayed in Paris, in 1889.

"Probably the first petrol car brought into England," the Science Museum, London, says of this 1888 Carl Benz motor vehicle.

THE NOBLE EXPERIMENTERS

Elwood Haynes, as superintendent of a natural gas company, did a great deal of traveling over the rough and gutted roads of his native Kokomo, Indiana. Being jounced about continually by horse and buggy transport inspired him with a burning desire to build a motor-driven vehicle. Not being a mechanic, Haynes found it necessary to take his plans and sketches to the machine shop of the Apperson Brothers, Elmer and Edgar . . . a pair with a great flair for mechanical ingenuity. After about a year of slow progress the machine was ready for its first public demonstration. On July 4, 1894, it attained a speed of six miles an hour before cheering crowds.

Ransom E. Olds, a hard worker employed in his father's machine shop, continually dreamed of perfecting a gasoline-driven carriage. As early as 1887 he had produced and built a three-wheeled steam vehicle which he drove through the streets of Lansing, Mich. To avoid stampeding horses, Olds had to arise at 4 A.M. and guide his carriage about the empty streets, which prompted angry protests from the citizens. Over the years he built several other steam-driven types, but in 1895 he tinkered furiously at his gasoline-powered vehicle, hoping to compete for the prize money in the Chicago race. In 1897 he produced a four-passenger auto now reposing in the Smithsonian.

Top: **Haynes' first run** in his motor-drawn
   vehicle at Kokomo Ind., July 4, 1894.

Left: **First Oldsmobile** was this 4-passenger
   carriage with wagon wheels, 1897.

Below: **George Selden's** driver poses proudly beside
   the Selden wagon, built to prove patent claims.

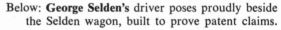

George Selden was a patent lawyer in Rochester, N. Y. Having visited the Centennial Exposition in 1876, he saw a two-cycle gasoline engine, talked to its inventor, George Brayton, and became convinced that by the use of such an engine a successful, self-propelled vehicle could be developed. He drew up plans and applied for patents covering the use of gasoline for propulsion. He managed to keep his application open while the growing automobile industry caught up with his fondest hopes. Finally, when granted in 1895, Selden's patent became the basis for wide claims, handsome royalties and the formation of the Association of Licensed Automobile Manufacturers. The Selden name, however, did not appear on a manufactured car until later, being produced from 1907 until 1912.

Henry Ford, the farm boy, deserted the farm for the lure of the machine. The mysteries of the engine and the workings of all things mechanical intrigued him. Before he was 24, he had tinkered with agricultural machines, repaired clocks and watches and developed an obsession that drew him to the city. He obtained a job as machinist and engineer, though he had little formal education, and built a machine shop in back of his house on Bagley Avenue, Detroit. This was the birthplace of Ford's first motorized wagon, the one he wheeled out in the morning air, 1896. Ford's first step up the ladder of success, this gave him a secure place in the history of the motorcar. The Ford Motor Company was formed seven years later, in 1903.

James Ward Packard and his brother William Dowd were the sons of a well-to-do Ohio pioneer living in Warren, O. A mechanical aptitude and experience in the electrical business had kindled in the Packard boys a desire to build an automobile as early as 1893, but the depression period forced them to lay aside their blueprints. Years later, when James bought a Winton and was dissatisfied with its performance he decided, on a dare from its maker, to build a better car himself. This first model was completed in November, 1899. It is preserved at Lehigh University, donated by Packard in gratitude to his alma mater.

Top: **Pioneer motor-builder,** Henry Ford, sits at tiller of prototype he built in 1896.

Right: **The sole survivor** from the first Auto Show exhibitors in this 1900 Packard.

Below: **Winton and five** friends in his car that did 33 mph at a Cleveland track, 1897.

Alexander Winton, born in Scotland, came to this country at the age of 20. In 1884, he settled in Cleveland and opened a bicycle shop. Nine years later he built himself a motorcycle and in 1896 a four-wheeled vehicle, incorporating a two-cylinder engine with friction clutch and pneumatic bicycle tires. By 1898 Winton had built and sold a phaeton model, the first of 25 scheduled for production that year. But mechanical difficulties led Winton to decide upon a drastic measure to publicize the fine qualities of his product . . . an 800 mile trip from Cleveland to New York, which he personally made in about ten days. An expert on publicity stunts, Winton scored heavily in track and road racing, hill climbing and reliability runs of all types.

A RACE WAS WON...AN ERA BEGUN

" 'Ready!' shouted Judge Kimball, as he stood, watch in hand at the side of the Duryea wagon. J. F. Duryea leaped into the wagon, followed by Arthur W. White, the passenger-umpire. At 8:55 o'clock the word 'Go' was shouted and the motorcycle passed swiftly through the crowd, which opened and closed in as it rushed on. A minute later the Benz wagon, of the De la Vergne Refrigerating Machine Company was started, amid cheers of the massed spectators. Frederick C. Haas, the inventor of the steering gear operated the Benz, with James F. Bate as umpire alongside. The Benz motor in this case proved unequal to the task of getting over the bad piece of road from the starting point to Fifty-fifth Street. The wheels slipped around in the snow, but failed to go forward. Then Mr. Haas decided he would not attempt to race, and the wagon was shoved over to the deep snow to a better part of the road."

This was a contemporary description of the start of an epochal "speed" contest, as reported in the second issue of *Motocycle*. The date of the race: Thanksgiving Day, 1895. The course: from Jackson Park, Chicago northward to Evanston and back, a distance of 54 miles. The prize: $2000 first prize plus consolation prizes totaling another $3000. The sponsors: Chicago's *Times Herald* owned by H. H. Kohlsaat.

Frederick Adams, an enthusiastic engineer and journalist who worked for the *Times-Herald* was the real sparkplug who actually conceived the race, shortly after the very important French race from Paris to Rouen had convinced him of the future possibilities of the "horseless carriage." A whole year lay ahead for making preparations for the event, and Adams did much barnstorming around the country, encouraging American inventors and tinkerers to speed up-on unborn projects a-building in workshops and basements. He even conducted a contest in his paper for a suitable name for this new marvel of the machine age. Among those submitted were "quadricycle", "autocycle", "automotor", "petrocar", "motorcar" and several hundred others. After much deliberation the judges divided the prize money of $500 among three contestants who suggested "motocycle". This name never met with favor except with the sponsoring newspaper while other journalists considered it poison and refused to use the term. The French who have given us so many other automotive designations finally settled the matter by inventing the word "automobile".

On the evening before the race eleven competitors declared they would start, but what with mechanical failures of one kind and another and the newly fallen snow, the starters dwindled down to six. The Duryea wagon crossed the finish line at 7:18 P.M. having covered the distance in 10 hours, 23 minutes at an average speed of 5:05 miles per hour. The Benz car did not arrive till after midnight, with Mr. King alone at the tiller. The owner, Oscar Mueller, had dropped out en route, overcome by exhaustion!

The next day the *Times Herald* proudly announced the race as a tremendous success with the future of the "motocycle" assured, while its angry competitor, the *Chicago Tribune,* called the whole affair a ridiculous failure. Nevertheless, the dramatic contest focused attention on the future of the motor-driven wagon.

Through snow and mud car No. 5, driven by J. F. Duryea, its builder, finished first after 10½ grueling hours.

Prototype of the famous Duryea line, this car proudly rests in the Smithsonian Institution. It was built in 1893 at Springfield, Mass., by the Duryea brothers.

The Curious Crowd in Jackson Park, Chicago, saw only 6 actual starters of a field of 80 entrants.

Charles E. Duryea and prize-winning runabout, the very carriage Barnum & Bailey used to head its daily circus parades. It was the show-stopper in 1896.

Duryea Phaeton, 1904, with sleek, curvaceous lines, sold for $1500. From Ford Museum, Dearborn.

Passengers posing in 3-wheel phaeton. This Duryea model boasted triple-cylinder motor, central control and lubrication system.

Waverley Electric, 1901. Ideal for a lady . . . "so easy to manage, so comfortable to ride in."

Columbia electric phaeton, built about 1904.

OUT FOR A SPIN...IN AN ELECTRIC

There was just one electric carriage in the 1895 Paris-to-Bordeaux race, a Jeantaud. By 1898, a large number of the French entries were electric-powered. Meanwhile, at the Chicago World's Fair in 1895, a Keller-Degenhard electric perambulator appeared. Columbia made an electric carriage by 1895. In 1899, the *Scientific American* in its issues of August 12, September 30, and October 14, respectively described and illustrated three new electrics: a Riker electric brougham, a Chapman electro-mobile, and a Riker electric demi-coach. It was observed that "the chief objection to electrical automobiles is their great weight and limited radius of action. The advantages are their ease of operation, safety, and freedom from vibration." Pope was making its Waverly electrics in 1905 and, at the same time, Baker was showing early models. While the Chapman, on a bicycle carriage, weighed only 380 pounds, most electrics were 4,000 pounds or more. They had a range of 25 miles before re-charging, and could travel 10 to 25 mph on a level macadam road. Argo built an electric in 1913; Rausch and Lang an electric coupe in 1915.

Apparently ostentation was not an attribute of the motorist at the turn of the century. The Woods motor company stressed, in its catalog of 1901, the general conformity of its carriages to established horse-drawn types, thus *"relieving the occupants of any sense of embarrassment or conspicuousness."* It was emphasized that, though "America *leads* Europe in *inventions,* she *follows* it in *fashions."* Now that Queen Alexandra, Madame Melba, and other ladies had their electrics, well-to-do Americans were eager to enjoy this "rapid, noiseless gliding on rubber and easy springs."

Wood's spider (below), 1901. Very high fashion.

Victoria built by Woods, 1901. Typical of the elegance which distinguished electric cars.

Hansom-cab . . . "So easy, so luxurious, so refined." It had an electric light in the roof.

Brougham had its plate glass windows set high to give the cherished exclusivity. Woods-built, 1901.

Road-wagon. Woods said "a child can drive it."

Victoria, with seat for chauffeur and footman.

Electric Stanhope (below), built by Woods, 1901.

Park Trap, also by Woods, encouraged conversation.

Pre-1900—electric delivery wagon.

Charles E. Duryea tested his first car in 1892. He continued to experiment with it.

BEFORE THE TURN OF THE CENTURY

The Civil War and Reconstruction years halted development in self-propelled vehicles. Yet Sylvester H. Roper of Massachusetts—who was associated with a skillful promoter, W. W. Austin—had been exhibiting his steam carriages since 1863 at county fairs and race tracks, and George Brayton—an engineer of Boston—had his petroleum engine on exhibit at the Centennial in Philadelphia, 1876.

George Selden, attorney and inventor of Rochester, New York, saw the Brayton and Dr. Otto engines at the Centennial, and preferred Brayton's. Selden went home and drew plans for a gasoline-

George Selden's earliest car. His patent stated that the engine could be run by hydrocarbon.

powered vehicle, applying for a patent May 8, 1879. By constant modifications, Selden kept his application pending for 16 years. When the patent was granted on November 5, 1895, Selden arranged to license other automobile makers and collect royalties. He sued the Winton Motor Carriage Company for infringement of patent and won. Later, Selden sued Ford, who had firmly resisted paying royalties. The first ruling, 1909, was in Selden's favor but Ford appealed the case and the court held, 1911, that Ford had not infringed on Selden's patent. Selden had adapted the Brayton engine; Ford's engine was of the Otto type.

1899—private electric hansom cab.

Electric dog-cart on steel tracks.

By 1890, electric-powered vehicles were proving their practicability.

A study in nerves at a grade crossing.

Gasoline-powered
runabout, 1899.

Stanley Steamer, the first built by the Stanley
brothers in 1896. By 1899, 200 were sold.

Elwood Haynes, of Kokomo, Indiana, made the
first road trial of his little gasoline-powered car in
1894. Though the Smithsonian Institution designated
this the "first gasoline motor car built in America,"
the claim was challenged by Charles E. Duryea who,
with his brother Frank, had built their first gasoline-
powered motor carriage in the Fall of 1892. Duryea
cars were continually re-designed until, in 1895, a
Duryea car won the *Times-Herald* contest. Other
men—Nadig, Schloemer, Black, and Pennington—
had built gas-powered cars before 1895.

Elwood G. Haynes, in his air-cooled single
cylinder automobile which he had built in 1893

Stanley Steamer of 1902-03. Light, easy to drive, instantly responsive, ideal for city use.

THE STANLEYS GET UP STEAM

As in the gasoline-powered vehicle field, a number of inventors had built steam-driven automobiles, before the more famous Stanleys. Almost countless men, earlier, made attractive, silent steam carriages. Roper of Massachusetts, and Dudgeon of New York had produced practical steamers during the 1860's; Carhart of Racine, Wisconsin, perfected a steam vehicle in 1871. But these names were overshadowed by the emergence of the cars made during the '90's, more appealing in design, which appeared when the public was more ready to accept the idea of self-propelled locomotion.

F. E. and F. O. Stanley—identical twins who dressed alike, trimmed their beards alike, and wore derbies of the same shape—had a profitable photographic supply business which they sold, in 1896, to begin the manufacture of steam carriages. Though they scorned to advertise, they drove their cars to various races and other gatherings, and effectively impressed people with the quiet, dependable qualities of steam.

By 1899, the Stanleys sold their rights to the Locomobile Company of America, for a quarter-million

Stanley of 1910. Wood wheels had been substituted for wire. It was still lightweight and sold for $850.

The Stanley twins dramatically dressed alike. They built this, their first steamer, in 1897.

288

dollars. Later, when they planned again to build steam carriages, Locomobile—unable to stop them —sold back the manufacturing rights for a fraction of what it had paid, and turned to making gasoline cars.

The Locomobile Company called its first car a 'mobile steamer. It was a Stanhope in body, with a two cylinder engine, and light in weight—about 800 pounds. The price was just $750.

During the years — 1902 to 1912 — when the White steam touring car was manufactured, it participated in long distance tours for which steam cars were not generally considered suitable. Nine White steamers were entered in the A. A. A. tour of 1904, from New York to St. Louis, and all nine cars completed the run. The White of 1905 had a wooden frame, a 15 hp compound steam motor. In contrast to the other steam cars, light in weight, it was heavy: 2,433 pounds. Where a Stanley price started at $850, the White cost $2,500.

Of the first New York Automobile Show, in Madison Square Garden, 1900, *Motor* of February 1916 reported retrospectively: "The steam car, light, attractive, moving rapidly and noiselessly . . . under the most absolute control . . . was undoubtedly the favorite."

Locomobile of 1900 carried the firebox under the seat and rear deck. The price was $750.

First Automobile Show held at Madison Square Garden, New York, on Nov. 3 to 10, 1900. Sponsored by the Automobile Club of America, it exhibited 31 makes of cars including 8 electrics, 8 steam-driven and 15 gasoline motors.

THE SHOW OF SHOWS

The National Automobile Show, timed to coincide with the introduction of the latest models, has become a tradition in America. But in 1900, when the first auto show was opened in Madison Square Garden, attendance there ran a poor second to that at the Annual Horse Show. An enthusiastic crowd turned out to see the early motor carriages but, the records show, that a great many more people preferred the flesh and blood thoroughbreds.

In the first years of the motor age, opposition to the "noisy, terrorizing" vehicles was common. Letters to newspapers pointed out the danger of runaway horses, frightened by the sputtering automobile, and objected to the "completely unnecessary" speed of eight miles an hour. Pioneering automobilists hoped to overcome such hostility by bringing the public into direct contact with the new vehicles. So, the 1900 show, first to feature the automobile exclusively, was sponsored by the newly formed Automobile Club of America.

About 70 manufacturers were represented, displaying a variety of now-obsolete cars. One publication said: "No matter whether you wanted a light runabout for quick work, a phaeton, a smart spider or Stanhope, a brougham, Victoria or racing machine, everything was at hand for your inspection. The exhibit of accessories was equally comprehensive. One company demonstrated the hill-climbing ability of its car by constructing a ramp on the roof of the gar-

Hotel Astor Ballroom exhibits a variety of expensive types of foreign cars, circa 1912.

The New York Armory was the scene of annual auto shows for many years. Its spacious floor afforded an unobstructed view of exhibits . . . in 1915.

290

Pergolas and numberless floral wreaths, plus striped bunting overhead, made a striking décor at this Automobile Show, in 1916.

den. Up and down this incline a driver guided his "Mobile" and stopped several times on the way down to impress the crowd with the safety of the brakes.

When the demonstration track was not being used for contests, it was turned over to exhibitors who gave free rides to any show visitors who cared to take a chance. A news account said: "Many people took their first trip on an automobile in the ring at the Garden, and by the pleased expression on their faces as they swiftly glided about the circle, one is led to believe that motoring made many converts by this feature alone."

Officials reported that none of the vehicles broke down or behaved badly, and that manufacturers received enough orders to keep them busy for months.

Over three hundred models were exhibited at Armory auto show, arranged along five main aisles, with commercial vehicles shown at extreme ends.

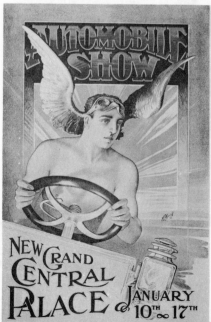

Early Automobile Show posters use allegorical as well as "pin-up" themes, c. 1905-11.

THE PERILS OF THE OPEN ROAD

The perils of early motoring years extended beyond the chances of finding oneself miles from a trained mechanic, when something went wrong with the motor. If you didn't encounter broken glass or discarded farm implements planted in the mud—to puncture the tires—you might drive straight into a fine wire rigged across the road, stretched from tree trunk to tree trunk, at face level. Small boys delighted in inflicting this particular form of torture, setting the wires at dusk when the driver seldom noticed them in time. The pictures on these pages—from that where all the farm fowl assault the approaching motorists, perils of the open car added to those of the open road, to that where the farmer and his horse turn more than reproachful glances at the passing runabout—are typical of incidents of the 1905 era.

The tools spread over the road, while the rain lashes the unfortunate tourists, and lightning flashes its danger, are reminders of but a few of the extensive array of implements which every pioneer motorist considered essential to any excursion into the

Joseph Boggs Beale, illustrator, of Germantown, Pa., painted the scenes shown above and on the upper right hand page. For thirty-five years prior to his death, in 1926, he recorded his keen observations of the American scene. . . . making 1676 black and white drawings intended for lantern slide use. From a set of 8 drawings, entitled "The First Auto," now in the Edison Institute, Dearborn, Mich.

country. An auto tool kit, suggested by Hammacher, Schlemmer & Co., New York City, in 1906, weighed 18 pounds. As late as 1916 a list of chisels, punches, pliers, hammers, nuts, bolts, and screws which were recommended as necessary numbered 32 different articles, plus spare parts which totalled 30 more, including blowout patches, vulcanizing cement, extra spark plugs, extra bulbs for headlights and tail lights, extra tire casings and inner tubes, an 18-inch length of radiator steam hose, a tire pump, a towing cable, a leather tire sleeve, and countless other objects. To these, many motorists added picnic and camping

equipment. Yet, with all his other tribulations, the motorist was considered legitimate prey for the cartoonists of the day. *The London Graphic* of October 18, 1902, captioned the illustration shown below, " 'The Dust Fiend': A Motor-car in a Country Road," while *Life,* the now-defunct humor magazine, of July 4, 1912, devoted a double spread to the scene at the top of the opposite page, with the helpless motorists in the equally-helpless hands of the blacksmith . . . to the amusement of the town constable and others.

Oldsmobile famous Curved Dash runabout, first built in 1900, with single-cylinder motor. It was priced at $650, and an immediate success.

FORERUNNERS OF A GIANT INDUSTRY

Four outstanding motor car companies—all now divisions of the great General Motors Corporation —were already making automobiles in the first 12 years of this century. The cars were differentiated by price then, as now, but Chevrolet's earliest (1912) car sold for over $2,000 while the first Cadillac (1903) was only $750.

The famous Curved Dash Oldsmobile runabout of 1900 was an immediate sensation, 425 cars being sold in 1901; 5,000 during 1904. Ransom E. Olds, its builder, sold his interest in the company in 1904, which was bought in 1908 by General Motors.

Buick traces its present lusty position to a successful maker of bathtubs, David D. Buick who, in Detroit in 1902, designed the first water-cooled, valve-in-head engine. During 1908, almost 9,000 Buicks were sold.

A perfectionist, Henry M. Leland, established Cadillac quality. He started work on his car in 1902, naming it for the French explorer. Leland merged with General Motors in 1910.

The Chevrolet Motor Company, formed in 1911, had its first six-cylinder touring car on the market in 1912, designed by Louis Chevrolet, a former racing driver. By 1914, Chevrolet's *490* sold at $490.

Buick runabout of 1908—a great favorite, rugged and dependable, with four-cylinder engine. $900.

Cadillac two-seater, a beautiful little car,
first produced in 1903. It had a water-cooled
single-cylinder engine. Its price: just $750.

Chevrolet touring car, the *Classic Six*, appeared
in 1912, and retailed at $2,150. Its appeal was
instantaneous; 3,000 were sold the first year.

Henry Ford—farm boy with a passion for machinery— built a fabulous motor empire and put a nation on wheels. His first gasoline-powered car appeared, 1896.

MOTORING FOR THE MILLIONS

In November 1895, when the Chicago *Times-Herald* contest was stirring much interest among makers of motor cars, an article appeared in the *American Machinist* of November 7 describing the Pennington internal combustion engine. The article came to the attention of Henry Ford. He said later, in his autobiography, that the information was of help to him in designing a small engine. Working in his little brick-walled shed on Bagley Avenue, in Detroit, Ford produced a light two-passenger machine which he called a "motor-wagon." The year was 1896. The car, with steering tiller, had a two-cylinder engine and four rubber-tired bicycle wheels. Its invention eventually brought motoring within financial reach of almost every American. The Ford Motor Company was formed in 1903. From 1896 to 1908, Henry Ford experimented with a variety of vehicles. To focus attention on his cars, he concentrated for a time on racing cars and drove one of these, an 80 horsepower racer at 94 mph. In 1902, he engaged Barney Oldfield, then a famous bicycle racer, to drive the "999," which Ford equipped with a two-handed steering device.

Ford's second "motor-wagon," a two-seater like his first, gained in charm by the addition of flared fenders. The Ford early Model A came out in 1903

At left:

The Ford of 1901, a buggy type steered by a tiller, had a speed of more than 10 miles an hour. Made by the Detroit Automobile Company, organized by Ford and others, 1899.

The Ford Model N of 1906, with brass-trimmed radiator, had a four-cylinder motor. It is considered the immediate forerunner of the famous Ford Model T, introduced in 1908.

Henry Ford at the wheel of a *Lenoir*. This car was built in 1907 from the French patent of the 1860's. The time is during the Selden patent suit against the Ford Motor Company.

and, in 1906, the Ford Motor Company produced a six-cylinder, to sell for $2,500, and a four-cylinder Model N, forerunner of the fabulous Ford Model T. The idea of a mass-produced, low-priced automobile was now uppermost in Ford's mind. In 1909, he declared that "the automobile of the future must be superior to the present car to beget confidence in the man of limited means, and sufficiently lower in price to insure sales for an enormously increased output. The car of the future must be a car for the people . . . the market for a low-priced car is unlimited."

The Model T Ford was introduced to the public by an advertisement in *Motor* of October, 1908. The

car was almost unchanged 18 years later. By December, 1927, over 15 million Model T's had been produced. In the last decade of its glory, half of all the cars made in America were Ford Model T's. It had sold for $850 in 1908; $360 in 1917. By December, 1924, the price of a Ford roadster was just $290.

Other light cars, more attractively styled, were giving the Model T heavy competition. But the much-joked-about "tin Lizzie," also affectionately called a "flivver," or a "jalopy," had done marvels to abolish the isolation of the farmer, and to introduce the joys of country motoring to the city-dweller.

As early as 1903, Ford offered a choice of two-passenger or four-passenger cars. His Model A sold for $800 with two seats; with four seats, it cost a hundred dollars more.

The Ford of 1914, one of a long line of Model T's, introduced in 1908, which remained practically unchanged for 18 years. Over 15 million Model T's were produced.

Interior of the brick-walled shed on Bagley Street in Detroit, where Henry Ford built his first little *motor-wagon*. This is preserved in the Ford Museum at Dearborn.

Packard in 1903 had a single-cylinder 12 hp engine, capable of 40 mph. The famous "Old Pacific," in a production version, sold for $2,500.

Studebaker Electric runabout of 1912. Purchased in that year for Thomas A. Edison's own use, it served Mr. Edison (below, left) until 1925.

GREAT OAKS FROM LITTLE ACORNS

When James W. Packard bought a Winton automobile and had much trouble driving it home, he protested to Winton who asked: "Why don't you build a car yourself?" That started Packard, mechanical engineering graduate of Lehigh University, on his successful way. In 1899, the first Packard car was made. Of all the American manufacturers exhibiting at the New York Automobile Show in 1900, Packard is the last of the line to disappear from the market.

Studebaker's long history goes back to February, 1852, when five Studebaker brothers opened a blacksmith and wagon-building shop. Only one brother was living when Studebaker's first gasoline-powered car appeared, 1904. In between, they had built 100 wagons for the Government in 1856 for troops' use in Utah . . . filled huge orders for carts and harness for the Union Armies . . . won many awards for their vehicles in Paris. Studebaker built electrics from 1902 through 1912.

The Nash of today started as the Rambler, which had its beginning in an English bicycle of that name, introduced by Thomas Jeffery in 1879. He and his

Rambler, forerunner of *Nash,* in 1904 had a twin-cylinder, 20 hp engine, and sold for $1,350. Its top, windshield, and picnic baskets were extra.

Hudson Model 20 roadster, 1909, had a racy-look, and a "four-cylinder water-cooled motor of the Renault type." Price, including top, $1,000.

son then decided to build automobiles. They exhibited two cars at the Chicago Coliseum, 1902, priced at $750 and $825. The Jefferys later changed Rambler's name to their own. Then, in 1916, Charles W. Nash—formerly of GM—bought the Jeffery company, and launched the Nash in 1918.

The Hudson automobile appeared later than many other makes, but was well ahead of its day—July 1909. The founders—J. L. Hudson, Roy D. Chapin and others—advertised in the *Saturday Evening Post,* June 19, 1909, and sold over 4,000 cars by the year's end. Hudson is credited with over 60 "firsts," and the greatest number of victories of any stock car over America's speedways.

Franklin "D" Runabout 1908

Autocar "XV" Roadster

Royal Tourist "G-3"

Cadillac "T" Touring

Peerless "18" Touring

Pierce Great Arrow Touring

Pierce Great Arrow Suburban

Packard "30" Landaulet

Oldsmobile Flying Roadster

Pope-Toledo "XVIII" Touring Runabout

Franklin "D" Touring

Stevens-Duryea "S-Big Six"

Cadillac "T" Coupe

Thomas "4-20" Town Car Landaulet

Locomobile "I" Limousine

Winton "16-6" Limousine

Women were warned against complexion wrinkles, but Gibson girls enjoyed the rumble vis-a-vis.

Daring exposure of cotton-clad legs, as these beauties pose on an air-cooled Franklin, c. 1905.

SOCIABILITY...ON WHEELS

Actress Anna Held—she of the milk baths—piloted her Panhard on Paris boulevards before her arrival in New York in 1900, to appear in a Ziegfeld show. Popular, charming, she issued a challenge to American women to race with her from New York to Philadelphia. The challenge had no takers. But wealthy Newport society women were already driving their own cars.

In its October 1899 issue, *Automobile Magazine* told of the latest craze, a floral parade. "The automobile festival, long-expected parade of Newport's 'upper ten' in their much cherished rigs, finished the Summer season of America's 'four hundred' in a blaze of glory." Held on Mrs. O. H. P. Belmont's estate, it had attracted greater throngs than the Newport regatta and the horse show. There was a motorcade of twelve cars, "smothered with flowers, doves, stuffed eagles and banners," with an obstacle course laid out on the grounds, and prizes awarded for the most beautiful floats.

What Newport started, other cities followed.

The well-beloved Maude Adams won an electric car in a popularity contest, staged by the Electrical Show in Madison Square Garden, 1899. Five years later, *Theatre Magazine,* in its June 1904 issue, showed photographs of Lillian Russell, Mrs. Leslie Carter, Maxine Elliott, Julia Marlowe and a number of other famous actresses, each at the wheel of her car, with the comment: "Real motoring is to manage one's own machine. To manage a car, a woman must be self-reliant . . . have firm nerves, and complete self-possession."

Meanwhile, President Theodore Roosevelt's daughter, Alice, several foreign ambassadors' daughters resident in Washington, and wealthy women across the nation were piloting their own electrics and, later gasoline-powered cars—provided that they had strength sufficient to crank the motors, away from the home garage or chauffeur. "The automobile's part in the emancipation of women," says Anderson, in *The Story of the American Automobile,* "began with the installation of the electric self-starters in 1912."

With respected feminine personalities in society and the theatre obviously enamored of the freedom-bringing motor car, the sport soon attracted a number of women enthusiasts. With them came sociability . . . attendance at races, participation in motor tours, even entry in—and winning of—several races open to women, as early as 1900. Women accompanied their husbands on un-marked trails over wretched roads as far as the Pacific coast. Automobile clubs staged tours—from a morning's run to a week's jaunt.

A problem for ladies in long skirts . . . the steep step into this 1904 rear entrance Cadillac.

Lucky monkey visits three genial girls in a Studebaker Electric Stanhope of 1903.

Showcase supreme at race meet or polo game, the electric coupe, perfect way to see and be seen.

Envied by the porch-bound, the family free to go for Sunday motor drive, or Summer holiday.

Sportsmen's delight, the swift horseless conveyance to riding stable or hunting lodge.

Pity the tourist, lost by night! No route marks, few decent roads, often a pencil-drawn road map.

Nocturnal jollity en route, typical of the 1904 organized tours, run for endurance . . . not speed.

THEY TOOK TO THE ROAD...AND FOUND MUD

For centuries the leading countries of the Old World boasted highway systems that put to shame America's horse-and-buggy and cowpath network. France's fine roads proved a great incentive to the spread of automobilism, while in Britain, with the lifting of the archaic Red Flag Act, motor travel soon spread over the excellent highways. Hard-surfaced roads in Europe were the legacy of efficient road-builders dating back to the days of Caesar's legions. What an anachronism that the United States, forging ahead in all directions, should have struggled along through mud, sand, dust and deep ruts—even past the dawn of the Twentieth century.

To the rapidly growing numbers of motorists, eager to explore the roads stretching beyond town limits, mud and mire were formidable barriers that checked long trips and ruined the enjoyment of short runs. The land between cities and hamlets was crisscrossed with a network of roads going everywhere, but these were the old roads that had served the simpler needs of cart and carriage, stagecoach and Conestoga wagon. Even the cyclists of the Eighties and Nineties had found such roads impassable and, with the protests of the wheel makers, had become a powerful force in focusing attention to America's need for improved highways, surfaced for motor travel.

Certain states had built and maintained turnpikes and were not interested in helping to pay for a broad, national network of roads. The farmers preferred to make their own local road repairs rather than cash payments by way of increased taxes. The railways knew that improved highways would make inroads on their revenues. But the familiar old ruts and potholes began slowly to give way to macadam and asphalt.

Marooned in mud, a flivver could go so far and no farther. Muck and mire reached to the hub-caps.

"**My kingdom** for a horse!" doubtless came to the mind of this motorist, mired in wheel-high mud.

A fork in the road offered little choice between mud and more mud.

Winter's hazards were always the worst as snow and deep mud made wheels spin . . . and get nowhere.

Road transport and commercial vehicles suffered along with pleasure cars, as this Arkansas road indicates, in 1918.

A "mudlark's" journey of 20 days, in 1915, could test the mettle of any man, before the Federal Road Act.

Endurance runs in the early days were more a test of man's endurance than that of the machine he drove.

The cars pile up as the roads get softer and the ruts deeper, on this Glidden Tour

"What now . . . brown car?" It was often better to walk the rest of the way than go deeper into trouble.

"Get a horse!" was no empty jeer when real horse-power was the only way out of the ruts of the road.

Chains and towlines were standard equipment for the open road. Note 4 extra tires on running board and chains on most wheels.

Farmers laughed, when early automobilists called for help, but were always willing to lend a hand and make an extra dollar.

Mule power and mules' pace were eagerly welcomed by the tourists in a car immobilized by a stalled motor.

Bogged down on roads that made little trouble for high-wheeled carts and carriages, was just one of the early motorist's troubles.

"GET A HORSE!"

Most people were tolerant, in the early days of horseless carriages, of the noisy experimental vehicles. Many a man tinkered at building one for himself, and little resentment was shown towards those who drove, especially as courtesy still was a rule of the road. It was not an infrequent custom to stop a car at sight of a horse. Only after the animal and its driver or rider had passed in safety, did the motorist proceed on his careful way. But, as cars became larger and more costly, as drivers became more certain of their engine-power, such courtesies were often ignored. The new cars came to be looked upon as playthings attainable only by the wealthy, and scornful epithets such as "Get a horse!" became the least odious evidence of mass envy. Woodrow Wilson observed, in 1906, that "nothing has spread socialistic feeling more than the use of the automobile . . . a picture of the arrogance of wealth." Often the car owner felt himself the victim not only of his car's idiosyncrasies, but of every garage man, farmer, blacksmith, gasoline vendor, and teamster. Muddy roads, swampy ground, a dozen unforeseeable incidents, made a horse or team the stalled motorist's most pressing need. The best roads were inadequately marked and often deteriorated into impassable areas on which only a high-wheeled cart could travel. Yet the motorists still kept coming, and farmers tried to discourage them with broken glass and tacks scattered in the roads. Residents of some country communities buried old rakes, teeth up and—on one of the early Glidden Tours—it was reported that the blade of a crosscut-saw was set at a narrow stretch in a road so that every driver racing over it had all four tires punctured and flattened. After four cars had traveled over the saw, it was discovered and dragged away. A watch was posted, but the culprit was never found.

In 1905, two curved dash Olds, *Old Scout* and *Old Steady,* raced cross-country from New York to Portland, Ore. They covered 4400 miles in 48 days—a tribute to light car performance.

The Rapid Truck was the predecessor of today's GMC truck. This Rapid of early vintage is proud of having climbed Pike's Peak and covering the Glidden Tours of 1907, 1908 and 1909.

After six months of the most grueling travel
the famous Thomas Flyer driven by Montague
Roberts and George Schuster got ovation in New York.

ENDURANCE RUNS SELL MOTOR CARS

In order to publicize their products, the early automobile manufacturers engaged in many freak demonstrations, hill climbs and reliability runs that seem
ridiculous today. But, at the time, these frenzied efforts did much to support the makers' claims and the
public responded with greater purchases of the prize-
winning cars. Nothing can quite compare with the
sensational "Around-the-World" race staged by *Le
Matin,* the Paris newspaper, and the *New York
Times,* in 1908. Here was an endurance contest of
gargantuan proportions, over rugged, mountainous
terrain, arid deserts and wide stretches of rivers and
waterways where no bridges existed. On February
12, the small band of brave adventurers lined up at
the start in Times Square, before a crowd of 50,000.
There were six cars as starters including 3 French,
1 German, 1 Italian and the sole American car, a
Thomas Flyer. The arduous route took them westward to San Francisco, by boat to Alaska, across the
Bering Strait to Vladivostok and thence on the long
and perilous journey across the Asian and European
continents. Of the three cars that crossed the finish
line in Paris, the Thomas was the winner in the
elapsed time of 170 days. A more fantastically grueling expedition was never conceived! The Thomas
company ran behind in deliveries for over a year.

This French team in Round-the-World race drive
a De Dion Bouton. They weathered the winter
in U. S. A. but withdrew from race in Siberia.

Cross-country races proved the nation needed
roads desperately. Best way to manage the
Western plains was to ride the railroad ties.

Convoy of cars awaiting the signal to start rolling on this Glidden Tour of 1911.

Starting line at the Plaza, New York, shows Cadillac, Maxwell, Pope-Hartford and others raring to go.

"MEET ME AT THE MEET"

Before the twentieth century America was virtually a land without highways. All of the hard-surfaced roads, before 1900, would scarcely have reached from New York to Boston. A few carriage routes went beyond town lines, and these, in wet weather, turned into winding rivers of mud. In dry, hot weather they were deeply rutted and unbearably dusty. Under best conditions, they offered little encouragement to the pioneers of the dawning motor age.

These roads often ended abruptly, leaving the frustrated motorist with the choice of blazing a trail across uncharted terrain, or retracing his ruts. The motoring enthusiasts of that early day were a hardy and adventuresome lot and by 1902, one had even managed to drive an automobile from coast to coast, across a thousand miles of roadless wasteland. Against great odds, the potentialities of motor travel were demonstrated.

Adequate highways designed to facilitate overland transportation were years away. The meager, muddy trails at the turn of the century soon became a major source of irritation to the motor industry. Before the general public would support heavy investment in road building it needed proof that the horseless carriage could run for more than short distances, could climb hills and give reliable service.

Car owners, still in the minority, took it upon themselves to prove to a doubting world that the

Sociability and gayety were the keynotes at the Meet where good fellows got together.

Officials in car were always in evidence to check contestants for rules observance.

Road watchers en route checked on cars, occupants, speed, etc., under a complicated scoring system.

automobile was worthy of trust. "Reliability tours" became one of the day's popular sports. Convincing performances had been registered by test cars and racers, but now the tours were meant for the ordinary stock car and its performance.

The St. Louis World's Fair of 1904 provided a convenient publicity tie-in on "reliability"— the distance to be covered being a third of the way across the continent from New York to the fairgrounds. It was a tremendous trip for those days. The contestants, appropriately named "The Mudlarks," who managed to cross the finish line, made a big hit.

The following year, a wealthy auto enthusiast, Charles J. Glidden, offered a trophy to the winner of a reliability tour, and this became an annual affair bearing his name. The Glidden Tours were widely publicized. Mud-covered cars, in small groups, entered towns that had rarely seen autos, and with their pennants flying and the gala spirit of their riders many victories were won for the cause of motoring. Rules for the competition were complex and final scores were tallied only after close inspection of each car in the race.

By 1915, after ten years of the tours, the novelty wore off and interest waned, especially under the wartime restrictions. But the motoring enthusiasts had won their point and demonstrated very convincingly that the automobile was here to stay. It was more than thirty years before the tours were again revived, this time by the interest of antique car fans.

St. Louis Tour of the A. A. A. was a real test of stamina and endurance. Spare tire was carried on the radiator.

Around Long Island, tourists in a Reo show the usual flag waving and contented faces.

Congestion ruled on busy city streets as cars and crowd gathered for the big event.

Sturdy Olds with both male and female passengers correctly dressed for the occasion.

Goggles and dusters were standard equipment as many early meets traversed dry and dusty terrain.

Indianapolis Raceway, 1909, attracted famous racers from here and abroad. Car 32—De Witt; 33—Louis Strang; 34—Louis Chevrolet, all racing Buicks.

Courage, stamina and fearless daring were requirements of early racing teams.

"GOING LIKE SIXTY"

Many of today's superhighways throughout the nation permit a driving speed of sixty miles per hour, some even more. But in the early 1900's "going like sixty" was a phrase that suggested the devil-may-care attitude of a speed demon or a racing driver . . . surely not a person in his right mind driving on the existing roads of the day. A mile-a-minute speed was the dream of wildly enthusiastic automotive pioneers, not the down-to-earth realist.

To begin with, that memorable Thanksgiving Day race won by Duryea in Chicago, attained an average speed of 5.05 mph. In 1899, Jenatzy, ace speed king of France, managed to achieve a speed of 40 mph. With each succeeding race, whether in Europe or America, previous records were toppled, though many of the available accounts of racing in the opening years of the century are difficult to substantiate (at least, before the formation of the A.A.A.). But it is quite clear that the great dream of a "mile a minute" was realized sometime in 1903. F. E. Stanley, driving his Stanley Steamer especially designed for racing, hit about 59 mph., a mark soon to be surpassed. In July, 1903, Barney Oldfield drove Henry Ford's racer 999 one mile in 55.8 seconds. This took place at the Empire City Track, Yonkers, New York.

The year 1904 saw speed records tumble precipitously. In January, Henry Ford, at the wheel of his revamped racer, covered a mile in just 39.4 seconds. Barney Oldfield, driving the Winton Bullet No.

Auto racetracks were wide cinder paths with crude stands lining the track.

Scores of mechanics worked on the racing cars. Each entry had its own tent and special crew.

Thousands of spectators crowded the track. Admission was free except in the grandstands.

Racetracks sprang up in many parts of the country. The best known were in Long Island, Savannah, Milwaukee, San Francisco and Santa Monica, Cal.

Quick change-overs and repairs took place in the pit where seconds counted like gold.

As the gun sounds at Indianapolis, they're off in a cloud of dust. The winner: Harry Grant driving his famous Alco.

Barney Oldfield, one of the greatest racers of all time, raced for Ford at an early date. He appeared on tracks and fairs everywhere, winning hundreds of trophies.

2, made a record at 83.7 mph at Daytona Beach. And so it went, with new records at every race, and the public being hard put to remember each new mark as the companies eagerly sought to proclaim the advantages of their superior speed and reliability attainments.

Competition was keen among the growing number of automobile manufacturers and it was necessary for each company to dramatize its product in order to capture the imagination of the public. The young industry was highly sensitive to every promotional stunt that American ingenuity could devise. These included the Glidden Tours, the reliability runs and the many racing events that were established in the period. The outstanding races included the Vanderbilt Cup Races, Elgin Road Races and the American Grand Prix.

Since so much depended upon the results of these races and their tremendous publicity value, the larger companies maintained special crews of mechanics and drivers, and thus were assured of capturing most of the prizes. These companies included Winton, Pierce, Lozier, Knox and Marmon, and in later years National and Stutz. The auto makers exploited every possible advantage from these victories, but it is not to be assumed that the only results were the bombastic claims of the winners. Many valuable engineering improvements were derived from data accumulated in these contests as the auto emerged . . . a full-fledged machine of locomotion, shedding its humble origins.

Families flocked to the races for a grand outing, excitement, thrills and spills.

THE THRILL OF A LIFETIME

A thrill unmatched in the experience of children of the present generation, born to motor transportation . . . this first unforgettable ride of New York orphans.

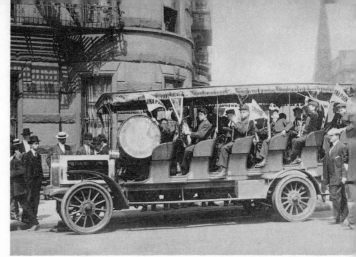

There was the tumultuous excitement of crowding into the touring cars lined up in sedate 87th Street, as the grocer's horse looked on, and upstairs maids gazed discreetly from windows of the brownstone residences. The occasion: a grand tour to Coney Island in 1906.

Men in bowlers and straw-sailors lined up at the curb, to see the uniformed boys' band, whose faces wore a nonchalance becoming to high-school years. Their bus is a forerunner of present-day sightseeing buses, made more gala by its canopy with the fringe on top.

There were *Reos,* and *Franklins, Hayneses* and *Oldsmobiles* among the gasoline-powered cars, 18 *White* steamers, and some electrics in the procession of over 100. A few had New Jersey license plates. Many of the cars were owner-driven; some had liveried chauffeurs.

This driver was in the groove with his cap and goggles and that handsome velvet-collared Melton topcoat was doubtless more flattering than the shapeless dusters of the day. Girl orphans had been provided with large straw hats, soon doffed as the procession moved off.

Every child waved a flag, and it is to be hoped that there were no eye casualties in the close-packed tonneaus. Drivers wore the conventional neck-to-ankle-covering dust coats, though some women were seen in dressy velvet suits at the wheels of their own cars. It was the era when little girls wore high-buttoned shoes and to be dressed in white symbolized a party.

"See Creation, a Lifetime Memory," the sign on one post urged, but the boys and girls were collecting a lifetime memory, as they held tightly to the pennants from *"Dreamland,"* under the somewhat austere eyes of the leg-o'-mutton sleeved dowager in the back seat.

The ubiquitous chiffon veil on a hat riding slightly askew, and the eagerness of every child passenger to have his face plainly seen in the photograph, are to be noted in this seven-passenger car carrying ten, as it sweeps by an electric trolley on Brooklyn Bridge.

The Electric Scenic Railway and a Skating Rink might hold allurements for others, but on this memorable day of the orphans' outing nothing could match the rare adventure of riding in an automobile, in a long cavalcade of horseless vehicles; a day to dream of, forever.

Balconies, terraces, and steps were thronged, as the flag-decked cars, the flag-waving youngsters sped by. Drivers stood to salute dignitaries in the reviewing groups. There never had been such a day in the lives of the children, and the thrills of "Coney" lay ahead.

Visored-cap, chiffon-veiled, and leather gauntlets . . . worn with a dressy bolero.

Ostrich-plumed picture hat, chosen for fair weather, by a trim driver of an early Franklin.

GOGGLES, VEILS AND DUSTERS

Since runabouts, touring cars, and other early automobiles were exposed to all weathers—without benefit of windshields and roofs—dressing to ride or drive in a motor car was a matter of much concern. Photographs of society women and favorite actresses, driving or riding in their own automobiles, accelerated the public interest in motoring. Parisian modistes were designing automobile gowns of silk jersey, costing $500, and the fashion columns reported that wealthy women were finding such gowns "simply indispensable."

Newport dressmakers, under direction of their clients, were making such gowns and the details were meticulously given: "The skirt is somewhat longer than that of the golfing costume, but 2 or 3 inches shorter than an ordinary walking skirt. This is so that the foot, which plays such an important part in managing the automobile, can be readily used. The waist, unlike the ordinary shirt waist, should fit very tight . . . so that there are no folds or frills to prevent the rapid action of the arms and hands on the lever and the steering tiller."

But, primarily, protection for the face and head—against dust, wind, and rain—was essential. Cravenetted visored-caps, dust hoods, voluminous veils, hats draped with dust curtains, driving masks, rain hoods, caps with attached goggles all were being designed. Materials were of the choicest, for early motorists could afford the best. There were ankle-length coats —for men and women—made of linen, leather, rubber, and fur. Those for men not only included raccoon, but Australian opossum and Somali leopard;

Cut to cover, not to flatter, these dust coats, vintage 1906.

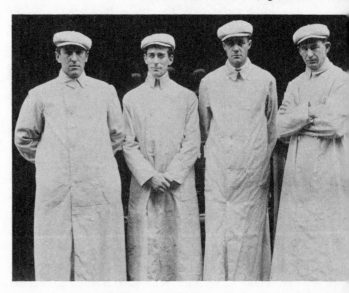

Motor millinery of 1905, the most conservative of many varied styles.

To enjoy the Fall foliage, fur coats, fur lap-robe, chiffon-veiled heavy hats.

while the women wore, in addition, coats of muskrat, hair-seal, squirrel, Russian pony, and civet cat. Fur foot-muffs, fur-lined gloves, and fur lap-robes were other luxuries bought avidly by hardy motorists who did not put their cars in storage for the winter.

The *American Automobile,* September 1899, reported that the French had a "passionate enthusiasm" for red, such a red as is used in the bodies of horse-less carriages driven in Paris. The modistes were driven almost to insanity for this gay red in gowns and bonnets.

Millinery fashions probably imposed the heaviest handicaps on feminine motorists, many of whom drove their own cars while wearing the elaborate hats of the era. These, laden with ostrich plumes or birds' wings combined with ribbons or flowers, were perched precariously on complicated coiffures to which they were tied by yards of veiling. Obviously unsuited to open cars, such headwear appears in many *fin de siècle* photographs.

Cane-patterned coachwork; visored chauffeur; riding-booted footman.

Epitome of elegance, crest on the door-panel; proud pooch; languid lady.

THE PASSING OF THE HORSE

There were about 30 million horses and mules in the United States in 1917, and three acres of land were needed to raise food for each animal. It was estimated that the animals were consuming the equivalent of food that could sustain 36 million more people. "The horse is the poorest motor ever made," Thomas Edison said. "He consumes ten pounds of fuel for every hour that he works, and yet his thermal efficiency is only two percent."

Despite all the centuries through which the horse had served man, and all the *rapport* an appreciative driver or rider might feel between himself and a high-bred, mettlesome beast, there was much to be said in favor of horseless transportation. The early makers of electric carriages were quick to point out the advantages: "The care of these vehicles is very simple. Instead of the continual grooming, feeding, and stable-cleaning, there is but the instantaneous connection of the supply current with the storage batteries. . . . There is, obviously, a saving in the renting of a stall, rooms for provender, harness, and the like. . . . And absolute control . . . the *owner ties it up,* when he puts into his pocket the little reverse lever." *Puck* of February 22, 1899 said: "The horseless state will be accepted as a matter of course, just as we accept all the other miracles of this amazing age."

Juxtaposition of hansom cab and motor car, from an ad of 1902, *Tires for all vehicles.*

Etiquette of the highway. The rule for passing horse-drawn vehicles: 1) stop the car; 2) cut off the motor, if the driver requests it.

Everyone to his own taste, published in an illustrated London paper, August 3, 1907.

"Off with the Old Love: on with the New." Apples and carrots cannot restore horse spirits as the chauffeur-driven *Fiat* takes the lady away.

Harbinger of change, horses of the American Express Company look over the horseless vehicle.

Horse Show, 1901. *Judge* of November 16, that year, devoted its center spread to this illustration in color. The motor car in many shapes was Fashion's love.

Picnicking was fun in the early days of motoring. Here in this charming setting, as painted by Leslie Saalburg especially for the 75th Anniversary Issue of *The Lamp*, of the Standard Oil Company of New Jersey, we see the clothes and accouterments once considered essential to a fashionable motor-outing. People came from far and

320

near, chugging along rutted roads to reach this restful woodland retreat. The early arrivals, lined up on the left, include a 1904 Franklin with air-cooled motor and rear entrance tonneau, in the foreground. Immediately behind, a 1904 Northern, with opposed-cylinder motor. Next, a 1910 Buick, four-cylinder, two-speed transmission

touring car, alongside a 1906 Compound, with one of the three cylinders operating at low pressure on exhaust gases from the other two. In the rear of the right-hand group is the famous 1906 Cadillac with curvilinear clam-shell body. Behind the lady, in motor veil and duster, focus-sing her Brownie box camera, is a tiller-steered 1904 Knox

surrey. Then, a 1905 Pierce Great Arrow tourer with King-of-the-Belgians body. In the foreground, a 1911 Stanley Steamer, running on high-pressure steam generated by a gasoline or kerosene burner. Late arrivals about to ford the stream are a 1911 Maxwell roadster, leading, and a 1907 Reo. The date: about 1912.

Outside trunk compartment replaced the open rack and preceded the built-in spacious luggage area. Always there was excitement at a trip's beginning.

In 1920 only 128,000 cars visited our national parks but by 1940 this number had grown to 4 million. The automobile brought such natural wonders as Old Faithful, Grand Canyon and Niagara Falls within the reach of all who rolled on rubber tires. Instead of the short week-end junket of a hundred miles or so, people ventured to spend their entire vacation of two weeks just moving from place to place, the more miles the merrier. California, Florida, even distant Mexico, became the goals of the Daniel Boones of the highway.

SEE AMERICA FIRST!

Long before our transcontinental roads were in passable shape, the lure of the National Parks and the Rockies began to reach out and beckon the more adventurous motorists of the nation. Long-distance motor trips before World War I involved arduous planning, mapping, and extra tins of gas and spare tires strapped to the running board. Highway signs were few and the Blue Book was the brave and hardy nomad's bible. "Follow car tracks on Main Street, go 4.6 miles to blacksmith shop on left, then 2.3 miles to Baptist Church, cross over wooden bridge and continue for 3.2 miles till you arrive at grain elevator." Such were the detailed instructions most of us followed.

Roads were bad and an average of 25 miles an hour was good time if one was fortunate enough not to run into special motor troubles. For the overland journey the recommended standard equipment called for chains, a tow rope and a pick and shovel, just in case! To brave a long trip, in addition to the usual baggage and personal effects, the traveler needed tent and camping supplies, bedding roll and a portable stove, plus food staples, if he wished to insure himself against hunger. Overnight cabins, swank motels, and roadside restaurants still were years in the future.

Many tourists, for mutual help and service, joined national organizations like the Tin Can Tourists, whose hallmark was the tin can carried on radiator cap for easy recognition . . . a welcome sign for the exchange of travel information and likely camp sites ahead.

As these motoring pioneers multiplied in numbers the older established hotels suffered, at first, while the vogue for camping out became a national cult. Instead of the customary two weeks' sojourn, vacationers merely stopped overnight and moved on to fresher, greener pastures "just around the bend." Certain railroads serving vacation spots lost 80% of their former business due to motor travel and the newly acquired transient habits.

Loaded to the gunwales, or running board, with a dozen or more valises held in position with rope and wire rack.

Washington's Headquarters at Valley Forge, Pa., a favorite mecca for easterners bent on a historic pilgrimage.

Along the Cody Road in Shoshone Canyon, typical of the grandeur of the West that many Americans saw for the first time, by motor.

Pillars of Hercules in Colorado, part of the national forests preserve that attracted many early motoring parties.

The rugged mountains and deserts of the Rockies . . . a magnet for millions of motorists with an urge to cover ground.

Oriental temple or Shinto shrine? Just a bit of the East transplanted on American soil for eager sightseers.

The blacksmith fits an odd-shaped shoe.

The early tank car was drawn by horses.

Portable hand carts retail gas at curbside.

THE START OF "SERVICE WITH A SMILE"

After a few competitions in France and the *Chicago Times-Herald* race in the United States, it became apparent that gasoline engines were more desirable than those powered by steam or electricity, for the rough roads of the period. Gasoline could deliver more power than electricity and, in a few years, it could be bought at almost any roadside grocery, livery stable, or garage. Even the blacksmith branched out as a supplier. Ever since the exciting Pennsylvania oil rush of 1859, the great refineries had been producing kerosene—"the heart of every home was the kerosene lamp." One of the other products was gasoline which, in the early days, was thrown away. It scummed over creeks and lakes . . . a chance to give it away would have been welcomed.

A County Agency serves as garage. Gas 10¢, c. 1912.

Night and day service . . . cargo trucking starts.

A passing farmer gives directions to the early
motorists. The curbside gas pump appears.

Insurance companies warned against the storage of
gasoline as a fire hazard, but daring men continued
to try to adapt gasoline to make engines run. Just as
kerosene had been peddled to housewives by the oil
huckster, for lighting and heating uses, gasoline was
first wheeled in hand carts to the car of the motorist.
"The specialized service station became possible,"
says *The Lamp,* in its 75th Anniversary Issue, "with
the development of curbside pumps, which would
deliver measured quantities of fuel from storage
tanks. One early station was opened in Memphis in
1912 . . . it had 13 pumps (located in a rear yard,
not on the street), with a ladies' rest room . . . fore-
shadowing the development of a distinctly American
roadside institution, the service station designed for
the convenience of a public forever on the move."

Service station of the new era, Detroit, 1924.

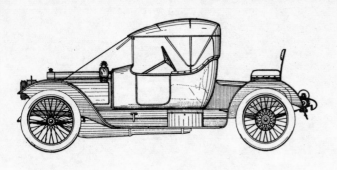

Princeton Runabout

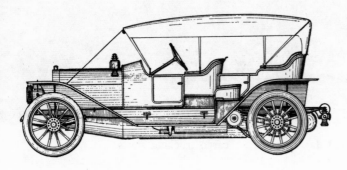

Fore Door Toy Tonneau

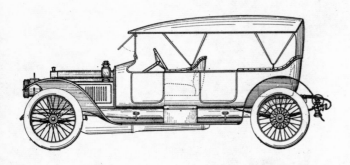

5 Passenger Touring

4 Passenger Victoria Touring

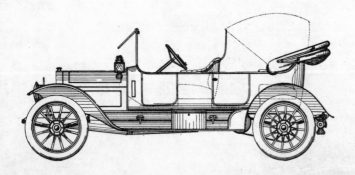

7 Passenger Touring

Special Brougham

Colonial Limousine

7 Passenger Limousine

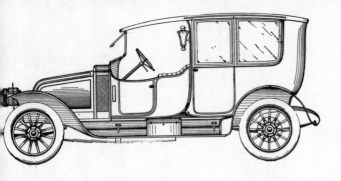

7 Passenger Royal Limousine

Fore Door Landaulet

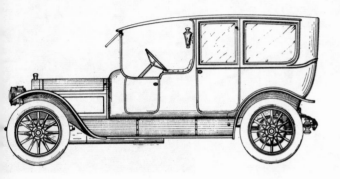

7 Passenger Limousine

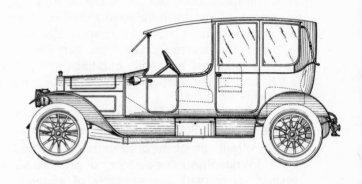

Princeton Landaulet

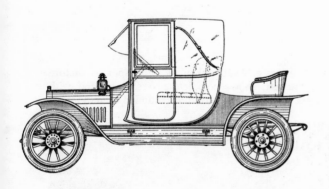

Interior Driven Landaulet

Coupe Landaulet

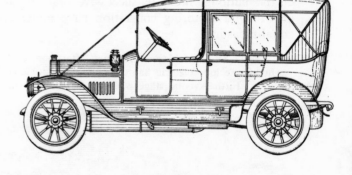

Quarter Glass Touring Landaulet

Club Runabout

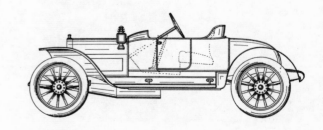

IN THE CITY...TRAFFIC JAMS

City congestion, crowded steets and traffic jams have been more or less synonymous for ages, but contrary to popular belief the automobile did not cause all this, it merely aggravated it. Our founding fathers, in planning narrow lanes to accommodate carriage and stagecoach, created the basic ills from which many of our cities have never been able to recover.

The larger metropolitan centers, principally New York, Boston and Philadelphia have long suffered from the same centuries-old disease that had plagued leading cities of the Old World. In ancient Rome the town trumpeter cried out: "Citizens of Rome! Be it decreed that henceforth the streets shall be closed to all vehicles during the first 10 hours of the day. Exception to this decree shall be made only for wagons carrying materials for public buildings . . . for carriages used by the Vestal Virgins . . . and for official chariots."

New York City, with its teeming millions and countless autos choking the long, cavernous streets, presents traffic problems of an extremely acute form. Fifth Avenue illustrates the story of progressive congestion, along with the spectacle of glamour and flamboyance. "Destiny and democracy," says Simeon Strunsky, "have combined to make Fifth Avenue the longest and straightest of the world's great boulevards. In its entire length it is not one thing but everything . . . a symbol, a compendium, a cross-section of the national life." In successive eras its steady growth and motoring congestion have increased in equal measure.

Easter Parade on Fifth Avenue has always been a gala display of fashion and finery. In 1913, the turnout of electrics and limousines already outnumbered horse-drawn carriages and hansoms.

St. Patrick's on a Sunday afternoon, c. 1904, shows one lone electric hansom cab. The double-decker Fifth Avenue stage is drawn by 3 white horses.

Fifth Avenue, c. 1920, taken at same spot as picture on the left, shows complete reversal of trend with only a single, horse-drawn hansom surrounded by motorcars.

328

On the outside looking in. The horse and coachman are hoping for a break in the line-up of motorcars.

Manhattan Bridge Plaza shows a typical traffic snarl as commercial and passenger vehicles honk horns impatiently.

329

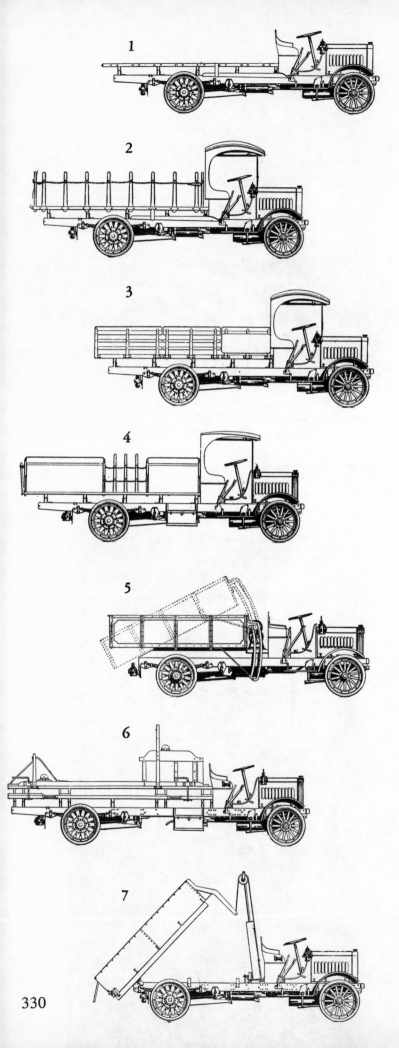

HORSES TO HORSEPOWER

The role of trucking and the contribution made since its development from the first crude commercial vehicles is so much taken for granted that few of us grasp its import in the creation of wealth in this country. Without transportation our farms could not move their produce to the city markets. Our factories, with their low-cost mass production techniques, need millions of consumers who can be reached only if transportation facilities are adequate, at prices kept within reason.

This nation has grown swiftly out of the home workshop era since the advent of the automobile, only because transport has kept pace with industrial development. In the early nineteenth century, there were the canals and river steamboats to deliver manufactured goods to the Ohio country and to bring back agricultural products. Then came the railroads, year by year extending their network of ribbons of steel to make ours the largest free-market region in the world. But magnificent though the railroad achievement was, it could not reach the tiny hamlets and out-of-the-way places and thus large areas of the country were neglected. Furthermore, railroads had to operate on rigid schedules, which could hardly be changed to meet the growing needs of an ever-industrious people.

1. Platform body
2. Freight or transfer body
3. Combination platform body
4. Transfer body
5. Hand dump body
6. Lumber trade body
7. Dump body with Hydraulic hoist
8. Grocery body
9. Panelled express body

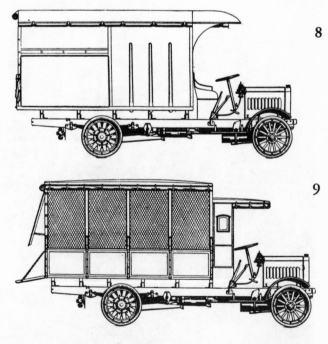

Coupled with improvement in the truck's power-plant, came the miracle of the century . . . the highway age, with roads fanning out to supply the missing link in our transportation chain. Over three million miles of improved roads mean that a truck can go anywhere, bringing life and its bounties to communities far from the nearest railway connection.

Trucks have become America's sturdy workhorse, supplanting Old Dobbin and taking on a variety of shapes and forms from light delivery vehicles to bring you pills or parcels . . . to tremendous earth-moving equipment capable, literally, of moving mountains. Trucks help drag our raw materials from earth to forest. They help the farmer grow his crops and deliver them to market. They aid the manufacturer by tying him to other plants with night-and-day deliveries. They carry stuff from jobber to wholesaler to retailer and back again to the customer's doorstep. Because of the truck and its capabilities Americans have become the greatest eaters of perishable foods on earth, since only on truck schedules can foodstuffs reach the stores while still fresh, and this may include anything from California artichokes to lobsters from Maine. The magic and efficiency of deliveries by truck are truly a vital part of America's economic growth. It is not surprising to learn that the trucking industry has adopted a slogan: "If you have it, a truck brought it."

10. Steel tank body
11. Wood tank body
12. Metal body for dairy use.
13. Standard body
14. Brewery body
15. Steel dumping coal body
16. Ice dealer's body
17. Self-dumping coal body
18. Van body
All body styles, c. 1920

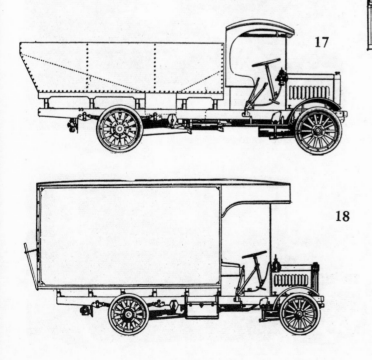

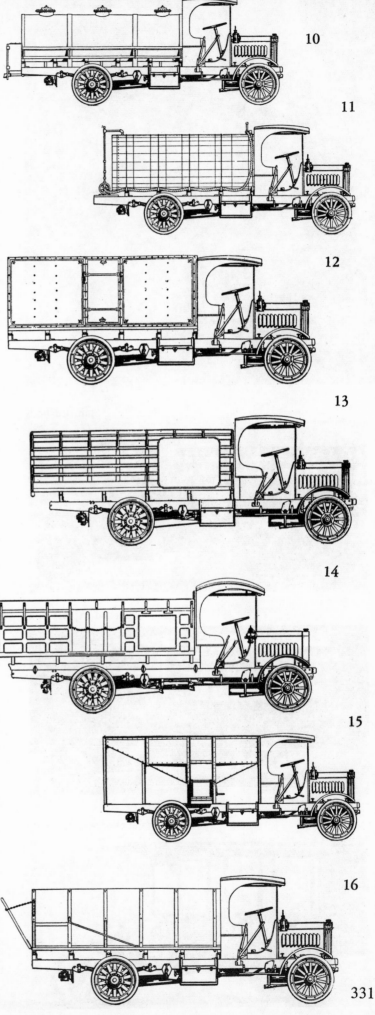

"The Spirit of Transportation" by R. F. Heinrich contrasts the modern heavy-duty truck with the mountaineer's ox team.

THEY DELIVER THE GOODS

Trucks designed especially for light delivery service were originally built in two distinct weight classifications, with carrying capacities of three-quarters and of one-and-one-half tons. In each of these two broad classes could be found vehicles for most common delivery needs including express, foodstuffs and light cargo as well as service trucks, ambulance and mail cars. The American truck manufacturers developed such a wide variety of body types, with proven performance records and economy of fuel consumption, that they shipped their products to all parts of the civilized world. In World War I, American trucks and ambulances played a major role in winning the war.

Open body with passenger seats

Standard body

Panelled express body

Closed body police wagon

Panelled express body

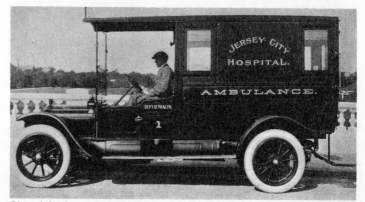

Closed body ambulance

Closed body delivery

Open body with passenger seats

Closed body delivery

Closed body delivery

Fleet of express bodies

Combination platform body

Van body

Combination platform body

Closed body delivery

Hearse

333

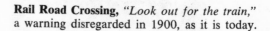
Rail Road Crossing, *"Look out for the train,"* a warning disregarded in 1900, as it is today.

REQUIEM FOR ROADSIDE WRECKS

When the first inventors of "steam carriages for common roads" tried out their experimental creations, many a vehicle promptly exploded, or went out of control and was smashed. Most of the time, the unhappy inventors lived to try again. But, well before the start of the Twentieth century, automobiles were being built that were dependable in performance. All they required were drivers who would use skill, common sense, and care. That these qualities were not inherent in every person with money enough to purchase an automobile was as apparent over fifty years ago as it is today.

True, tires might skid on a rain-soaked road, headlights might fail in a dark lane, an unpredictable obstruction might break an axle but, then as now, there were motorists who gambled on outdistancing a train, or on passing another driver, or who took some other ill-advised chance which often led to the car's destruction and the death or injury of its occupants.

Since most motor cars of the early 1900's could not travel faster than 15 miles an hour, it would seem—contrasting this with the speeds of today—that serious accidents could not then have occurred. But photographs from half-a-century past reveal mangled and twisted wrecks which appear very similar to those which happen on present-day highways.

The automobile, of itself—as many people have pointed out—has never injured anybody. It is the

End of the tour for two early "speed demons" and their cars.

An early Cunningham skids to land topside down in a muddy stream; spectators reflected in water.

careless, thoughtless, incompetent, inebriated, or sleepy driver who creates the havoc, endangering his own life, the lives of those who ride with him, and the safety of other motorists, as well as pedestrians.

Meantime, the auto graveyards multiply . . . hideous blights on landscapes that otherwise could be charming. The toll in dead and disabled human bodies which these twisted wrecks of metal have taken, since the introduction of the automobile, amounts to millions.

Humor and horror mix, as the car breaks away to smash a porch pillar, and its repairer "rests on his laurels."

Rust in Peace: the tragic and ugly reminders of lives lost and bodies maimed. The auto-graveyards of the United States are hideous blots on landscapes all over the country.

PICTURE CREDITS

The following abbreviations have been used to indicate key positions of illustrations on the page:

(T) top; (TL) top left; (TR) top right;
(C) centre; (CL) centre left; (CR) centre right;
(B) bottom; (BL) bottom left; (BR) bottom right;

All pictures shown in this volume, unless otherwise accredited as to source, are from the author's collection.

2,3 Drawings by the author

4 Hornung, Clarence P., *Handbook of Early American Advertising Art*

5 Hornung, Clarence P., *Handbook of Early American Advertising Art*

7 (T) *Scien. American*, Jan. 31, 1880
(CL, CR) *Illustrated catalogue*, International Exhibition of 1862, London.

8 (B) *Scien. American*, Dec. 13, 1882

9 (T) Hornung, Clarence P., *Handbook of Early American Advertising Art*

10 (B) Hornung, Clarence P., *Handbook of Early American Advertising Art*

11 (T) *Scien. American*, Jan. 22, 1876

12 (C) *Scien. American*, March 6, 1869

14 (T) *Scientific American*, Jan. 1, 1881

Part One: WHOA . . . GIDDAP!

16 (TL) *Scien. American*, Mar. 16, 1867
(CL) *Scien. American*, Oct. 27, 1866
(BL) *The Hub*, June 1887
(BR) *Scien. American*, Mar. 7, 1868

17 (TR, CR) *The Hub*, June 1887, advertisement of English & Mersick
(CL) *The Hub*, March 1887, advertisement of C. R. & J. C. Wilson
(BR) *Scien. American*, July 3, 1869

18 (Both) G. & D. Cook & Co.'s *Illustrated Catalogue & Advertiser*, New Haven, Conn., 1860

19 (Both) G. & D. Cook & Co.'s *Illustrated Catalogue & Advertiser*, New Haven, Conn., 1860

20 (TL, TR) Smithsonian Institution, *Harper's Monthly*, 1885

21 (T, B) Bureau of Public Roads

22 (TL) Weld, Isaac, Jr., *Travel Through the States of North America*
(TR) Bureau of Public Roads

23 (C, BL) Bureau of Public Roads
(R) Bryant, William C., *Picturesque America*, 1872

24 (T) *Harper's Weekly*, May 4, 1889
(B) *Harper's Weekly*, Mar. 16, 1872

25 (all) Continental Distilling Corporation, Philadelphia, Pa.

26 (BL) Maryland Historical Society, Baltimore, Md.

27 *Harper's Weekly*, March 6, 1886, drawn by T. de Thulstrup

28 (T) *Harper's Weekly*, March 12, 1881, drawn by Howard Pyle
(BL) Baltimore & Ohio Railroad

29 (TR) *Harper's Weekly*, June 6, 1891, drawn by Howard Pyle
(CR) *Harper's Weekly*, May 20, 1882, from a painting by A. Wordsworth Thompson
(BR) *Ballou's Pictorial Drawing-room Companion*, Oct. 13, 1855

30 (TR) Bureau of Public Roads
(B) Drawn by Stanley M. Arthurs

31 (T) Library of Congress
(CR, B) Bureau of Public Roads

32 (B) Continental Distilling Corporation, Philadelphia, Pa.

33 (T) Chicago Historical Society
(CR, BR) Bureau of Public Roads

34 (TL, TR) Stratton, Ezra M., *The World on Wheels*, 1878
(B) *Harper's Weekly*, Dec. 5, 1885, reprinted from *Valentine's Manual*

35 (TR) Hornung, Clarence P., *Handbook of Early American Advertising Art*, 1947
(B) *Gleason's Pictorial, Drawing-room Companion*, March, 12, 1853

36 (T) "Emigrants Crossing the Plains," painted by F. O. C. Darley, from Wm. C. Bryant's *Picturesque America*, 1872

37 (T) *Harper's Weekly*, April 24, 1858
(CL) Thayer, William M., *Marvels of the New West*, 1887
(BL) *Frank Leslie's Illustrated Newspaper*, May 1, 1880, drawn by H. A. Ogden
(BR) Bureau of Public Roads, "Old Oregon Trail" painted by Robert Wesley Amielt

38 (T) *Ballou's Pictorial Drawing-room Companion*, Aug. 15, 1857

39 (T) *Harper's Weekly*, June 12, 1869, drawn by Theo. R. Davis
(BL) *Harper's Weekly*, Jan. 15, 1887, drawn by R. F. Zogbaum
(BR) "The Emigrants," painted by Fred Remington

40 (TL) Hornung, Clarence P., *Handbook of Early American Advertising Art*. Engraving by Alexander Anderson
(B) New York Public Library. Drawing by Edward Penfield

41 (T) *Harper's Weekly*, Aug. 20, 1870, drawn by W. C. Cary
(BL) Chicago Historical Society
(BR) Carriage House, the Suffolk Museum at Stony Brook, N. Y.

42 (T) *Harper's Weekly*, Jan. 27, 1866
(BR) Carriage House, the Suffolk Museum at Stony Brook, N. Y.

43 (T) *Harper's Weekly*, Dec. 11, 1858
(B) *Harper's Weekly*, Jan. 27, 1866

44 (T) Library of Congress
(CL, BL, BR) National Archives

45 (T, CR, BR) Studebaker Corporation, South Bend, Ind.
(BL) Library of Congress

46 (TL) Smithsonian Institution
(CL) Studebaker Corporation, South Bend, Ind.
(B) *Gleason's Pictorial Drawing-room Companion*, May 3, 1851

47 (T) *Harper's Weekly*, Mar. 17, 1877
(B) *Gleason's Pictorial Drawing-room Companion*, May 10, 1851

48 (T) *Gleason's Pictorial Drawing-Room Companion*, Dec. 25, 1852
(B) *Harper's Weekly*, June 8, 1867

49 (TL) *Harper's Weekly*, Aug. 23, 1890
(TR, CR) *Scientific American*, Feb. 8, 1890
(BR) *Scien. American*, April 20, 1872

50 (T) *Harper's Weekly*, Oct. 25, 1873, drawn by W. M. Cary

51 (T) Pennsylvania Railroad
(B) *Harper's Weekly*, June 3, 1876, drawn by Schell and Hogan

52 (T, CL, CR) *Scientific American*, Feb. 8, 1879
(B) Catalog advertisement, G. & D. Cook & Co., New Haven, Conn., 1859

53 (B) Catalog advertisement, G. & D. Cook & Co., New Haven, Conn.

54 (B) Catalog advertisement, G. & D. Cook & Co., New Haven, Conn.

55 (all) Carriage House of the Suffolk Museum, Stony Brook, N. Y.

56 (all) Carriage House of the Suffolk Museum, Stony Brook, N. Y.

57 (all) Carriage House of the Suffolk Museum, Stony Brook, N. Y.

58 (all) Carriage House of the Suffolk Museum, Stony Brook, N. Y.

59 (all) Carriage House of the Suffolk Museum, Stony Brook, N. Y.

60 (BL) *Harper's Weekly*, Sept. 20, 1890. Painting by Frederic Remington
(BR) *Harper's Weekly*, May 1, 1875, drawn by Frenzeny and Tavernier

61 (TR) *Harper's Weekly*, Sept. 14, 1878, drawn by Henry R. Poore
(BR) *Harper's Weekly*, Oct. 25, 1890, drawn by W. A. Rogers

62 (all) Bureau of Public Roads

63 (TR) Bureau of Public Roads
(B) Timken-Detroit Axle Company, Detroit, Mich. Illustration by Leslie Saalburg

64 (TL) Drawing by A. B. Frost, Bureau of Public Roads
(CL) Bureau of Public Roads
(B) *Harper's Magazine*, Nov. 1895, drawn by Frederic Remington

65 (all) Bureau of Public Roads

66 (T) Shaler, N. S., *The American Highways*, 1896

122 (T) *Frank Leslie's Illustrated Newspaper*, April 30, 1859
(CL) *Scien. American*, Sept. 7, 1861
(B) Dredge, James, *Transportation Exhibits at the Columbian Exposition*, New York, 1894

123 (TL) Pullman Company
(TR) *Harper's Magazine*, May 1872
(CR) *Scien. American*, Oct. 13, 1877
(BL) *The American Railway*, 1889
(BR) New York Central Railroad

124 (B) *The American Railway*, 1889

125 (TR) *The American Railway*, 1889
(BL) Canadian National Railways
(BR) Association of American Railways

126 (T) Baltimore & Ohio Railroad
(B) U. S. Patent Office

127 (BL) *The Railroad Gazette*, June 4, 1886
(all others) *The Railroad Gazette*, Aug. 26, 1887 and Sept. 14, 1888

128 (TL) *The American Railway*, 1889
(all others) *Harper's Weekly*, Aug. 25, 1888

129 *The Railroad Gazette*, Oct. 21, 1887

130 (T) *Harper's Weekly*, May 29, 1869, drawn by A. R. Waud
(B) Lithograph, Association of American Railroads

131 (TL) Chesapeake & Ohio Railway
(TR) *The American Railway*, 1889
(B) Canadian National Railways

132 *Harper's Weekly*, April 25, 1891

133 (B) *Harper's Weekly*, Mar. 11, 1882

134 (TL, TR) *Harper's Weekly*, Oct. 9, 1875
(B) Lithograph, New York Central Railroad

135 (both) *Harper's Weekly*, Oct. 9, 1875

136 (both) Leslie, Frank, *Historical Register of the Centennial Exposition*, 1876

137 (all) Leslie, Frank, *Historical Register of the Centennial Exposition*, 1876

138 (TL) *The American Railway*, 1889
(CL, BL) *Harper's Magazine*, Aug. 1885

139 (all) *Harper's Weekly*, Sept. 20, 1873

140 (T) *Harper's Weekly*, Nov. 13, 1886

141 (all) *Harper's Weekly*, Feb. 10, 1883

142 (all) *Harper's*, Aug. 21, 1869

143 (TL, TR) *Harper's*, Aug. 21, 1869
(BL, BR) *The American Railway*

144 (T) *Railroad Gazette*, Feb. 11, 1887
(BL) *Scien. American*, Aug. 25, 1881

145 (TL, TR) *Catalogue*, Manning, Maxwell & Moore
(B) *Scien. American*, April 20, 1878

146 (TL) *Harper's Weekly*, Jan. 23, 1864
(CL) *The American Railway*, 1889
(B) *Harper's Weekly*, Jan. 27, 1883, drawn by Charles Graham

147 (T) Association of American Railroads. Currier & Ives lithograph
(all others) *Scientific American*, May 5, 1888

148 (TL, CL) Sipes, William B., *The Pennsylvania Railroad*, 1875
(BL) *Harper's Weekly*, Nov. 10, 1866
(BR) *The American Railway*, 1889

149 (TR) *The Railroad Gazette*, Feb. 14, 1890
(CR) *Scien. American*, June 8, 1889
(B) *Scien. American*, Mar. 11, 1876

150 (TR) *Harper's Weekly*, Feb. 10, 1872
(all others) *The American Railway*

151 (TL) *Harper's Weekly*, May 10, 1873
(all others) *The American Railway*

154 (TL) *Harper's*, April 17, 1886
(BL) *The American Railway*, 1889
(BR) *Frank Leslie's Illustrated Newspaper*, March 26, 1887

155 (TR) *Harper's*, Aug. 29, 1885
(BR) *The American Railway*, 1889

156 (all) *The American Railway*, 1889

157 (TL, TR) *The American Railway*
(B) *Harper's Weekly*, April 3, 1886, drawn by Joseph Pennell

158 (all) *The American Railway*, 1889

159 (all) *The American Railway*, 1889

160 (T) *Scientific American Supplement*, June 5, 1880
(C) *Scien. American*, Oct. 8, 1881
(B) *Railroad Gazette*, July 7, 1882

161 (T) *Railroad Gazette*, Sept. 8, 1882
(B) *Railroad Gazette*, Sept. 17, 1886

162 (T) *Railroad Gazette*, Oct. 20, 1882
(C) *Railroad Gazette*, May 1, 1885
(B) *Railroad Gazette*, June 10, 1887

163 (all) Dredge, James, *Transportation Exhibits at the Columbian Exposition*, New York, 1894

164 (TL, BL) *The American Railway*

165 (T, BR) *The American Railway*
(CL upper) *Frank Leslie's Illustrated Newspaper*, Dec. 31, 1887
(CL lower) *The Railroad Gazette*, July 29, 1887
(BL) *The Railroad Gazette*, March 22, 1889

166 (T) New York Central Railroad
(B) *The American Railway*, 1889

167 (T) New York Central Railroad
(B) *The American Railway*, 1889

Part Three: FARES PLEASE!

168 (all) Fairchild, C. B., *Street Railways*, New York, 1892

169 (all) Fairchild, C. B., *Street Railways*, New York, 1892

170 (Both) Fairchild, C. B., *Street Railways*, New York, 1892

171 (Both) Fairchild, C. B., *Street Railways*, New York, 1892

172 (TL) Hornung, Clarence P., *Handbook of Early American Advertising Art*
(TR) *Gleason's Pictorial Drawing-room Companion*, Jan. 1, 1853
(B) *Ballou's Pictorial Drawing-room Companion*, Oct. 17, 1857

173 (BL) *Frank Leslie's Illustrated Newspaper*, March 12, 1859
(BR) *Scien. American*, Jan. 5, 1867

174 (TL, BL) Easton, Alexander, *Horse-power Railways*, 1959
(TR) *Ballou's Pictorial Drawing-room Companion*, Sept. 8, 1855
(BR) *Ballou's Pictorial Drawing-room Companion*, April 25, 1857

175 (TL) *Ballou's Pictorial Drawing-room Companion*, Dec. 13, 1856
(TR) *Ballou's Pictorial Drawing-room Companion*, June 7, 1856
(BL) *Frank Leslie's Illustrated Newspaper*, Oct. 1, 1859
(BR) *Ballou's Pictorial Drawing-room Companion*, June 6, 1857

176 (TL) Leslie, Frank, *Historical Register of the United States Centennial Exposition*, 1876
(BL) *Harper's Weekly*, Feb. 24, 1872, drawn by Paul Frenzeny
(BR) *Harper's Weekly*, July 19, 1890, drawn by Max F. Klepper

177 (TR) *Harper's Weekly*, Sept. 21, 1872, drawn by Sol Eytinge, Jr.
(CR, BR) Roy D. Graves, San Francisco, Cal.

178 (T) *Scien. American*, Jan. 25, 1868
(BR) *Harper's Weekly*, Jan. 20, 1877, drawn by I. P. Pranishnikoff

179 (T) *Ballou's Pictorial Drawing-room Companion*, Feb. 21, 1857
(BR) *Harper's Weekly*, Jan. 12, 1884, drawn by George Inness, Jr.

180 (T) *Harper's Weekly*, Mar. 23, 1867
(all others) *Scientific American Supplement*, April 2, 1892

181 (TR, CR) *Harper's Weekly*, March 23, 1867
(all others) *Scientific American Supplement*, April 2, 1892

182 (all) Museum of the City of New York

183 (all) Museum of the City of New York

184 (TL, TR) Roy D. Graves, San Francisco, Cal.
(CL upper) Bureau of Public Roads
(CL lower, BL, BR) Museum of the City of New York

185 *Harper's Weekly*, Oct. 27, 1888

186 (T) Drawing by the author, based upon an old print
(BL) Drawn by the author

187 (TR, B) *Scien. American*, May 24, 1884

188 (both) Collection of Roy D. Graves, San Francisco

189 (all) Collection of Roy D. Graves, San Francisco

190 (T) *The Graphic*, Jan. 13, 1883
(BR) Roy D. Graves, San Francisco, Cal.

191 (TL, TR) Roy D. Graves, San Francisco, Cal.
(B) Chicago Historical Society

192 (TR) *Harper's*, Sept. 14, 1889
(B) *Scien. American*, June 5, 1880

193 *Harper's Weekly*, July 15, 1882

194 (TL) *The Electrical World*, April 20, 1889
(TR) *Electrical World*, Nov. 19, 1887
(CR) *Electrical World*, May 25, 1889
(BR) *Electrical World*, Aug. 7, 1886

195 (TL) *Electrical World*, Dec. 18, 1886
(CL) *Electrical World*, Oct. 2, 1886
(BL) *Electrical World*, Aug. 14, 1886
(BR) *Electrical World*, Dec. 25, 1886

196 (all) Fairchild, C. B., *Street Railways*, 1892

197 (all) *Electrical World*, Sept. 25, 1886

198 (T) *Gleason's Pictorial Drawing-room Companion*, April 1, 1854

199 (TR) *Scien. American*, Oct. 15, 1853
(BL) *Scien. American*, Nov. 26, 1853
(BR) *Scien. American*, Sept. 9, 1865

200 Double-page spread:

201 *Frank Leslie's Illustrated Newspaper*, March 3, 1866

202 (TL) *Scien. American*, May 10, 1890
(all others) *Scientific American*, April 1, 1876

203 (T) *Scien. American*, April 13, 1872
(BL) *Frank Leslie's Illustrated Newspaper*, March 3, 1866
(BR) *Scientific American Supplement*, Feb. 5, 1887

204 (B) *Harper's Weekly*, July 25, 1868

205 (T) *Scien. American*, April 1, 1876
(CR, BR) *Scientific American*, Oct. 25, 1879